T0367190

Luminos is the Open Access monograph publishing program
from UC Press. Luminos provides a framework for preserving and
reinvigorating monograph publishing for the future and increases
the reach and visibility of important scholarly work. Titles published
in the UC Press Luminos model are published with the same high
standards for selection, peer review, production, and marketing as
those in our traditional program. www.luminosoa.org

The publisher and the University of California Press Foundation gratefully acknowledge the generous support of the Sue Tsao Endowment Fund in Chinese Studies.

The Funeral of Mr. Wang

The Funeral of Mr. Wang

Life, Death, and Ghosts in Urbanizing China

———

Andrew B. Kipnis

UNIVERSITY OF CALIFORNIA PRESS

University of California Press
Oakland, California

© 2021 by Andrew Kipnis

Suggested citation: Kipnis, A. B. *The Funeral of Mr. Wang: Life, Death, and Ghosts in Urbanizing China*. Oakland: University of California Press, 2021.
DOI: https://doi.org/10.1525/luminos.105

Library of Congress Cataloging-in-Publication Data
Names: Kipnis, Andrew B., author.
Title: The funeral of Mr. Wang : life, death, and ghosts in urbanizing China / Andrew B. Kipnis.
Description: [Oakland, California] : University of California Press, [2021] | Includes bibliographical references and index.
Identifiers: LCCN 2021001644 (print) | LCCN 2021001645 (ebook) | ISBN 9780520381971 (paperback) | ISBN 9780520381995 (ebook)
Subjects: LCSH: Funeral rites and ceremonies—China—21st century. | Death—Social aspects—China. | Social change—China.
Classification: LCC GT3283.A2 .K57 2021 (print) | LCC GT3283.A2 (ebook) | DDC 393/.9309510905—dc23
LC record available at https://lccn.loc.gov/2021001644
LC ebook record available at https://lccn.loc.gov/2021001645

28   27   26   25   24   23   22   21   20   19
10   9   8   7   6   5   4   3   2   1

CONTENTS

LIST OF ILLUSTRATIONS

MAPS

FIGURES

ACKNOWLEDGMENTS

Like all projects this one could not have succeeded without help. Many institutions have given support, including the Australian National University, the Chinese University of Hong Kong, Nanjing University, Beijing University, and Yangtze University. Individuals at these and other institutions showed an interest in my work, provided introductions and research assistance, and listened to my presentations.

As I completed my research on this project between 2013 and 2019, I could sense the academic environment at many Chinese universities deteriorate. Talks that I was scheduled to give were canceled or moved to venues where few could attend. Already completed, already under-contract translations of my previous books were blocked from publication. More and more people began to self-censor what they said and wrote. As I finish this book while living in Hong Kong, the Communist Party has imposed its "National Security Legislation" that criminalizes "collaboration" with foreigners who advocate the division of the Chinese nation. As supporting Taiwanese or Hong Kong independence, or even less repressive policies in Xinjiang or Tibet, could constitute dividing the nation, many Hong Kong academics fear that any remaining semblance of academic freedom in Hong Kong will vanish. What will happen is anyone's guess, but these circumstances make me hesitate to name any of the scores of Chinese academics and graduate students who have helped me with this project, regardless of whether they are currently located inside or outside of China. Those who allowed me to interview them, or simply put up with my presence and questions, likewise deserve to be named, but I am not willing to do so.

Purely academic debts are easier to acknowledge. When I first started this project, two bright young scholars, Lucia Liu and Ruth Toulson, welcomed me into their circle of anthropologists interested in funerary ritual. Much of this book has been worked out in conference panels that they helped organize, and their feedback at various forums has proven invaluable. Adam Chau, Tom Cliff, Deborah Davis, Judith Farquhar, Zoe Hatten, Ian Johnson, Reed Malcolm, David Palmer, Robert Weller, and Angela Zito have provided feedback, encouragement and support. Colleagues at the Chinese University of Hong Kong, including Gordon Matthews, Sealing Cheng, Teresa Kuan, Leilah Vevaina, Sharon Wong, Ju-chen Chen, Hsuan-Ying Huang, Sidney Cheung, Venera Khalikova, Wyman Tang, and Weng Cheong Lam endured several presentations from this book and asked stimulating questions at the right moments.

Grants awarded by the Australian Research Council (DP140101294 and DP140101289) and the Hong Kong Research Grants Council General Research Fund (Project Number 14604318) helped fund research undertaken for this book. Parts of chapter 3 appeared in *Review of Religion and Chinese Society* (Kipnis 2019), parts of chapter 5 in *Modern Asian Studies* (Kipnis and Cliff 2020) and *PoLAR* (Kipnis 2018), and parts of chapter 7 in *HAU: Journal of Ethnographic Theory* (Kipnis 2017).

Thanks always to Kejia, Jonathan, and Elliot. Love to my parents, whom I mourn, and my cousin Peter, whose death led me to experience grief for the first time.

MAP 1. Chinese cities mentioned in this book.

The Funeral of Mr. Wang

Mr. Wang died of cancer at the Nanjing Municipal Hospital of Chinese Medicine during the wee hours of the morning on December 14, 2014. He was eighty-four years old and had been at the hospital for almost two weeks. Before coming to the hospital, he saw a series of doctors about pain in his legs and hips, but checked into the hospital when the pain increased. About five days before his death, a doctor at the hospital told his younger daughter that a prostate cancer had spread to his bones and become incurable. The news was a bit of a shock to his family, who had imagined that his pain stemmed from some sort of arthritis. The family did not tell Mr. Wang of the prognosis, but he guessed from their demeanor and asked them to contact his middle child, who lived abroad. His treatment consisted primarily of pain relief, though no opiates were used and Mr. Wang often complained of discomfort.

Mr. Wang had two daughters and one son, all of whom were in their fifties at the time of his death. His son (the eldest child) and the younger daughter lived in Nanjing, while the older daughter had emigrated to England. As in many Chinese hospitals, the hospital administered his medicine and checked his vital signs regularly, but did not provide much physical care. It was up to the family to cook his meals, feed him, help him to go to the toilet, wash his body and change his clothes. Mr. Wang needed someone to be in the hospital room twenty-four hours a day, as the pain from the bone cancer prevented him from getting out of bed without help. A cot was set up so whoever was with him could sleep. His wife was too old and frail to provide this help (she rarely ventured outside of their apartment), and much of the burden fell on the younger daughter, with some help coming from the son. It was too much for the second daughter to handle. She had to return to her home to cook meals for her father, and also could not get time off from work every day. So she hired a helper from the countryside, at a cost of 120 yuan per eighteen-hour shift. (During the period of research, 1 USD was worth approximately

6.5 yuan.) The elder daughter flew back to Nanjing in time to see her father before he died, but not in time to be of much practical assistance.

The father died the night after the elder daughter returned. She had stayed with him the previous afternoon and evening, but arrangements had already been made for the helper to spend the night in the room, so Mr. Wang urged his daughter to return to his apartment and spend the night with her mother. "We have already had a good talk; you have been a good daughter to me too; we can have another talk tomorrow morning."

At 5:30 in the morning, the younger daughter received a phone call from the helper. Mr. Wang had passed away sometime that night. He was alive when she checked him at about 1:00 a.m., but when she woke after 5:00 a.m., she discovered that he had stopped breathing. She called in the duty nurse from the hospital, who brought in a doctor. The doctor declared him dead and his body was moved to the hospital morgue (太平间). The helper told the younger daughter that she knew someone who could arrange the funeral (known in Nanjing as a "one-stop dragon" (一条龙) because they arrange the convoluted process from start to finish). The helper said that she could take the daughter to the one-stop dragon shopfront, which was right outside the hospital's rear gate, and the younger daughter agreed to meet her at the hospital. The younger daughter called her husband, her brother, and her mother, who told the middle daughter. The three siblings agreed to meet at the shopfront of the one-stop dragon entrepreneur; the younger daughter texted them the address.

The helper called the one-stop dragon entrepreneur, a Mr. Chen, who, since people die at all hours, took calls twenty-four hours a day and slept in his shop. By 7:00 a.m., all of the siblings were at the shop. Mr. Chen explained that it was traditional to arrange the cremation, farewell meeting, and burial of the cinerary casket on the third day after death, with the day of death counting as the first day. If they needed more time they could do it on the fifth day or the seventh day, but it would be inauspicious to arrange the funeral on the second, fourth, or any even-numbered day after the death. The siblings agreed that they would arrange the funeral for the third day—December 16. Mr. Chen then explained the prices for his services. His base price was 900 yuan, which would include accompanying and directing the family through all of the government procedures necessary after death; setting up a home altar in Mr. Wang's apartment and helping with ritual procedures there; accompanying the family to the state-run crematorium and funeral home and making arrangements there; accompanying the family after the cremation while they took the cinerary casket to the cemetery; directing an interment ritual at the cemetery and arranging a banquet for those who attended the interment ritual. He would advise the family on the proper way of acting for the entire procedure and could also arrange many optional extras, such as musicians to play dirges at appropriate points in the process, religious specialists to perform parts of the ritual if the family were religious, and the purchase of a cemetery plot if the family didn't already have one.

Because this price was heavily discounted, the family would also need to purchase a cinerary casket (骨灰盒) from Mr. Chen's shop, a set of "longevity clothes" (寿衣, the clothes in which Mr. Wang would be dressed for display in an open casket at his funeral and then cremated), and the "return gifts" which the family would give to those who gave a cash gift to the family during the ritual period. Mr. Chen finally explained that the family would need to prepare about 500 yuan of additional money to give to various people who would assist in the process along the way, and should also be prepared to spend between 5,000 and 10,000 yuan for a basic funeral at the state-run crematorium/funeral home (殡仪馆). The purchase of a graveyard plot could range from 15,000 yuan to well over 200,000 yuan, depending on the cemetery and the size of the plot. The cost of the banquet would depend on the level of food that they offered, the restaurant they chose, and the number of people who were to attend. If they anticipated an extremely large or grandiose funeral, the price would, of course, be much more. After a bit of negotiation, the siblings and Mr. Chen came to the following agreement: they would pay 900 yuan for the basic service, purchase a 2,500-yuan cinerary casket from Mr. Chen's shop (his shop displayed cinerary caskets running from 1,500 yuan to over 10,000 yuan), and buy between twenty and thirty return gifts at a price of 35 yuan per gift. Since their father had already prepared a set of clothes to be dressed in for his funeral (the middle daughter had brought these with her from her parents' apartment), they did not need a set of longevity clothes. In addition, the family had already purchased a cemetery plot. Finally, the family was not particularly religious and did not want any musicians or other ritual specialists. Since they did not anticipate too many people attending the funeral, they would arrange a relatively simple and inexpensive ceremony at the state-run funeral home. They paid Mr. Chen the 3,400 yuan for the cinerary casket and the three days of service in cash, and said that they would pay the money for the return gifts as soon as they determined how many they needed.

Mr. Chen, one of his assistants, the helper, and the three siblings then walked across the street to the hospital morgue, leaving Mr. Chen's shop in the care of another of his assistants. Mr. Chen called the funeral home to arrange for a car to come to pick up the body and transport it to the funeral home, where it would rest in cold storage until the funeral. Mr. Chen also asked the siblings if they wanted to wash the body of their father one last time and then change him into his funerary clothes, or whether they would like to pay one of the attendants at the hospital 200 yuan to do this for them. The middle daughter was quite overcome with grief (she told me that she felt guilty for not having been able to spend more time with her father, and because her father seemed to have waited to see her one last time before dying). She sobbed and insisted on bathing her father's body herself, so Mr. Chen got his assistant to fetch a bucket, a sponge, and a towel so that she could give her father a sponge bath. With the help of her younger sister, the middle sister undressed her father, rolled him from side to side as she sponged him off and dried his body, and then dressed him in his funeral clothes.

Mr. Wang had been a low level cadre, so he did not want to be remembered in the "Tang dynasty" style of longevity clothes (many of which were for sale in Mr. Chen's shop). Such outfits were decorated with dragons and other symbols of good fortune and reeked of "superstition" in the view of secular communists. So his final outfit, specified in a discussion with his wife before he entered the hospital, was a western suit. But, in accordance with the Nanjing tradition of "five collars and three waistbands" (五领三腰), the outfit had five layers on top and three on the bottom: an undershirt, a long-sleeved thermal shirt, a blue dress shirt, a sweater, and a tweed jacket on top, and underpants, thermal pants, and dark dress trousers on the bottom. As with the number of days to wait after death before conducting a funeral, an "odd" number of layers is specified because an even number suggests "doubling," and it would be inauspicious to suggest a doubling of something like a death. The layering was also important because it prevented the soul from becoming cold in the afterlife. While the daughters were washing and dressing the body, Mr. Chen took the helper aside and paid her a 250-yuan referral fee. The helper then said goodbye to the siblings and left.

The car from the funeral home arrived at the hospital twenty minutes later and four attendants from the hospital carried the body to the hearse. Mr. Chen told the siblings to form a procession to the car, led by the son and in birth order, and asked them to pay the four attendants 50 yuan each for their service. After the hearse left, Mr. Chen asked if they had any photos of the father that could be used for a portrait on the home altar. The younger sister had a photo on her mobile phone that the siblings decided was appropriate. Mr. Chen then suggested that they break into two groups. One would drive to the police station and then the funeral home to do the necessary paperwork. The other would go to the photo shop to have the portrait made from the digital photo and assemble the other materials needed for the home altar. He also told the siblings to think of which friends and relatives they needed to notify of the death. Since the brother had driven there, they decided that the brother and Mr. Chen would drive to the police station, the younger sister and the assistant would go to the photo shop, and the middle sister would return home to accompany their mother.

Mr. Chen and the older brother first walked to an office in the hospital where they settled accounts and obtained the death certificate. Then they drove to the apartment to pick up Mr. Wang's household registration booklet, his identity card (身份证), and the receipts showing that he had purchased a plot in a cemetery. Next they drove to the neighborhood police station, and showed the papers to one of the officers. The police officer removed Mr. Wang from the official (computerized) household register, crossed his name off of the brother's paper version, destroyed Mr. Wang's identity card, and issued the older brother a "certificate of household registration erasure" (户口消灭证). Next, they drove to the Nanjing Crematorium and Funeral Home, which is located at the southern fringes of the urban area, roughly a thirty-five-minute drive from downtown Nanjing. At the funeral home, they used the death certificate, the receipts from the cemetery, and the certificate of household registration erasure to obtain two more certificates: a certificate of permission to cremate a body and a certificate of permission to dispose of the ashes of a cremated body (to be used at the cemetery).

After obtaining these certificates, they went to the business counter of the funeral home to arrange the "farewell meeting" (告别会). As the siblings had agreed, the brother selected the most basic (but relatively standard) form of service available. The farewell meeting would be in a small room (large enough for about forty people, and rented for one hour), and the room would be decorated with flowers at the basic level. They would not use a separate room for people to visit the body before the funeral itself (守灵厅). Mr. Wang's body would be lightly preserved (a slight injection of formaldehyde rather than a full embalming; it was winter and the body only needed to last another forty-eight hours), and a low level of make-up would be applied to his face. At the farewell meeting he would be displayed in a basic coffin, in which his body would then be burned. He would be cremated in the standard rather than the upgraded crematory oven (which is "greener," takes a bit less time to cremate the body, more fully turns the bones to ashes, and completely separates the ashes of each body cremated). The fees for the rental of a small room and its decoration, the transport of his body to the funeral home and its storage for two days, the preparation of the body, the master of ceremonies at the farewell meeting, the cremation, and the coffin would come to 6,200 yuan.

The elder brother also gave some basic information about Mr. Wang's career and family to the funeral home workers to use when giving the eulogy at the farewell ceremony. Many of the time slots for farewell meetings on December 16 had already been taken (because Nanjing people like to hold funerals in the morning, funerals start at 6:00 a.m. and go until 10:00 a.m. to allow the funeral and cremation to be finished before noon), but they secured an 8:00 a.m. slot for the small room, followed by a 9:30 a.m. cremation. The brother then paid the 6,200 yuan in full, and obtained a receipt and the name of the room that they had reserved. Mr. Chen and the brother next went to the cemetery where Mr. Wang had purchased a plot, which was another ten minutes' drive away from the city center, south of the funeral home.

There are thirteen public cemeteries and a number of private ones (reserved for people of particular villages) near Nanjing. Six of the cemeteries are located fairly close to the funeral home. All except for the most prestigious (the Garden of Merit, Gong De Yuan 功德园) are located far from the city center. In 2006, Mr. Wang had purchased a plot in one of the less expensive cemeteries. Prices had been rising rapidly, so Mr. Wang secured a plot for himself and his wife (most plots are for couples, with places for two cinerary caskets, though single and family plots are available). After 2012, to prevent "real-estate speculation," greater restrictions were placed on the advanced purchase of cemetery plots. Since 2012, purchasers have had to present a death certificate, a certificate from a doctor declaring the person for whom the plot is being purchased is terminally ill, or an identity card showing that the person is over eighty. When Mr. Wang purchased the plot, he tried to pick one with the best geomancy (风水) possible, though he did not pay the graveyard extra money to get advice from a master of geomancy. He selected a site that would get the morning sun and that was as far as possible towards the left hand side (as you faced it) of the section of the cemetery in which it was located. He also selected and paid in advance for the style of tombstone that he wanted.

At the cemetery office, Mr. Chen showed the certificate of permission to dispose of ashes to the registration desk, and announced their intention to bury a cinerary casket on the sixteenth. The manager there suggested that they pay an extra 800 yuan for cemetery staff to conduct a burial ritual at the cemetery, but Mr. Chen told them that he would direct the ritual himself. However, they would still need some workers to seal the grave, and he said that they would conduct their ceremony at about 11:30 a.m. on the sixteenth. Mr. Chen then asked to review the tombstone style and the names and information to be carved on it. The tombstone would have the names of the father and mother, their birthdates, the names of all the children and grandchildren and children-in-law. There were also spaces for the death dates of the mother and father, and they could now give the death date for the latter. It would take a week to do the carving of the tombstone, so it would not have all of the names at the time of the burial, but that didn't matter, Mr. Chen said. They should revisit the grave once a week for forty-nine days after the death (once every seven days for seven times seven days), so there would be plenty of opportunity to check the carving of the stone. Finally, Mr. Chen checked the map of the cemetery to determine the location of the plot, and the brother and Mr. Chen walked to the site to look it over. Everything seemed in order, so they left the cemetery and returned to the parents' home.

By the time they returned to Mr. Wang's apartment, it was already 2:30 p.m. Mr. Chen's assistant had set up the home altar in the living room. At the photo shop, at a cost of 180 yuan, the phone photo headshot had been blown up into a 40x60cm framed portrait of Mr. Wang. A space had been cleared in front of one of the living room' walls by temporarily moving some chairs into the spare bedroom. The portrait had been hung high on the wall. Below it was a blanket to which was attached a piece of white cardboard with the character 奠 (meaning "in memorial" or "in sacrifice for our ancestors"). Below the blanket was a low table with three plates of sacrificial food on it (贡品). Two plates had apples, and the third bananas. On each plate was an odd number (five or seven) of pieces of fruit. In addition, there were two candles placed on either end of the table, which were to remain lit the entire time the altar was set up. Mr. Chen further instructed that at least one relative of Mr. Wang, preferably male, should stay up all night for the two nights until the funeral. Relatives could take turns maintaining this vigil, but it was important that someone remained awake to keep Mr. Wang's soul company. They were also to leave the doors to the apartment ajar, even though that meant letting in cold air. In front of the table was a pillow for kneeling down and performing kowtows to the portrait of Mr. Wang. In another corner of the living room, the assistant had set up a table with ink brushes and long strips of paper on which he could write calligraphic couplets for those bringing flower wreaths. At the entrance to the apartment, outside of the front door, the assistant hung two black paper lanterns. Finally, a desk with a gift register on it was set up in the adjacent bedroom to record the gifts of anyone who came by and gave an envelope filled with cash.

In the early afternoon, the husband of the younger sister, the wife of the older brother, and her son—the twenty-six-year-old only paternal grandson of Mr. Wang—had come to the apartment. With their help, the mother and the two sisters made a list of all of the people to be notified. These included Mr. Wang's old work unit; the households of Mr. Wang's two brothers and one sister (including those of all their children); the households of Mr. Wang's wife's sister and brother (including those of all of their children); and the households of all of the brothers and sisters of the son-in-law and the daughter-in-law. The daughter-in-law came from a large family with eight siblings, so her relatives amounted to about a quarter of the people to be notified. Because the middle daughter's husband and son were in England, their relatives would not be notified. Though they would not make it to Nanjing in time for the funeral, they did plan to come a few days later to visit the grave with the middle daughter. Finally, the mother asked them to notify the families of three close former friends of Mr. Wang.

The brother, younger sister, and their spouses made the necessary phone calls. Most of the friends and relatives promised to attend the funeral and said that they would visit the home altar either later that evening or on the following day. The family calculated that they would need twenty-two return gifts for the families that would attend the funeral, and that, counting the immediate family members, thirty-four people would attend the funeral and banquet. The number of return gifts needed was determined by counting the number of households who were giving packets of gift money. If a child lived apart from their parents and acted as a financially independent household, then his or her household would give a cash gift and receive a return gift. No one gave a gift as an individual.

They asked Mr. Chen to bring the twenty-two return gifts to the funeral and to arrange a banquet for thirty-four people at a local restaurant for the afternoon after the funeral. They knew the prices at that restaurant and specified that they wanted to order a banquet at a level of 80 yuan per person. Mr. Chen said he would arrange the banquet and tell the cooks which foods were appropriate. In particular, he said, it was traditional to serve stir-fried cabbage and tofu (白菜豆腐) at funerary banquets. The brother paid Mr. Chen the money for the return gifts.

When they contacted the work unit of Mr. Wang, the call was transferred to the head of the workers' union, who expressed his condolences and said that, as city regulations mandated, Mr. Wang's family would receive a final payout in the amount of twenty-four times his monthly pension. Since Mr. Wang's pension was 3,900 yuan per month, the payout would be 93,600 yuan. To receive the payout, the family members would have to bring the mother's ID card, the mother's bank account information, the death certificate, and the certificate of household registration erasure to the work unit's pension office.

Mr. Chen then returned to his shop. He told his assistant to remain with the family until 9:30 p.m., and to return the following day from 8:00 a.m. until 6:00 p.m. to write couplets and to assist the family. Mr. Chen would return at 6:00 a.m. on the morning of the funeral and direct the family through it. On the way to his office, Mr. Chen arranged the banquet.

The first official visitor to the household was the son of Mr. Wang's older brother. Mr. Wang's older brother was still alive but too frail to leave the house in winter himself, as was his wife, so this nephew of Mr. Wang was the official representative of that household. He brought a gift of 1,000 yuan in a white envelope and a flower wreath. Mr. Wang's daughter-in-law made a record of the gift in the gift register, listing it as coming from the household of Mr. Wang's older brother. Mr. Chen's assistant inquired about the name of the visitor and his relationship with Mr. Wang and then wrote out a calligraphic stock phrase on white strips of paper: "Magnificent Uncle (father's younger brother) last forever, your nephew, XXXX" (叔叔大人千古，侄儿XXXX). Mr. Chen's assistant attached the calligraphic strips of paper to the flower wreath and put it in a prominent position in the living room. The assistant then directed the nephew to either bow or use the pillow to kowtow three times to the portrait of Mr. Wang. The nephew performed three kowtows. The assistant then directed Mr. Wang's son to perform three kowtows to thank the nephew. That ended the ritual portion of the visit, but the nephew stayed for about thirty minutes longer to offer his condolences to Mr. Wang's wife and children and to make small talk.

Over the rest of the evening and the following day, representatives of the twenty-two invited households came by to offer their condolences and give gifts. From some households just one person came, but from others couples or even entire nuclear families dropped by. All of them brought envelopes of cash, which ranged from 200 yuan to 1500 yuan. The largest gift was given by the household of Mr. Wang's sister, who were quite well off and had been particularly close to the family. The smaller gifts came from the relatives of the in-laws and a few of Mr. Wang's more distant nephews. Nine of the households also brought flower wreaths, which, with the added calligraphy, were put on display in the living room. Mr. Wang's son, his son-in-law, and his paternal grandson took turns staying up to maintain the night-time vigil. Mr. Wang's wife complained of the cold, but they left the doors open anyway. Mr. Wang's son always performed the return bows and kowtows.

At 6:00 a.m. on the sixteenth, Mr. Chen returned to Mr. Wang's apartment as planned. The three siblings and their spouses and the grandson had either spent the night or had come over early in the morning. Mr. Chen brought with him 30 yuan worth of Chinese ten-cent coins. He explained that they needed to throw these out of the car window on the way to the funeral home whenever they crossed a bridge or passed a major intersection to appease the ghost of Mr. Wang. He also brought a red cloth and the cinerary casket that the family had purchased, as well as some spirit money. He had told the family to prepare some food products and liquor to be used as sacrificial offerings in the burial ceremony, and he placed these into a carrying container. He asked the siblings if they wanted to bury any objects (随葬品) with Mr. Wang's ashes. They chose to bring Mr. Wang's electric shaver, glasses, a package of cigarettes, and a cigarette lighter. Mr. Chen also suggested that they bring Mr. Wang's clothes and burn them at the funeral home. Mr. Chen had driven his own car, and Mr. Wang's son and son-in-law had also driven cars that morning. The three siblings, the son's wife, the younger daughter's husband, and the grandson collected the portrait of Mr. Wang and the flower wreaths, Mr. Wang's clothes, and the other items needed for the rituals, and got into the three cars. Because of her health, Mr. Wang's wife did not go to the funeral. On the road, the caravan tossed coins out of the windows whenever they stopped at a major intersection or crossed a bridge. By the time they arrived at the funeral home it was 7:15 a.m. They had to wait until 7:35 for the people using the room before them to finish, but at 7:40 they were able to enter the room they had reserved for the farewell ceremony. At the back of the room was a place for Mr. Wang's open casket. They hung Mr. Wang's portrait on innermost wall of the room and arranged the nine wreaths that relatives had brought to their home around the other flowers decorating the room. The funeral home workers also rearranged the characters on the door frame to the room so that they announced Mr. Wang's funeral instead of the person who came before him. The family members were given black armbands to wear. Outside of the door was a desk for guests to register.

The other guests arrived shortly thereafter. The funeral home worker who registered the guests passed out white flowers and black armbands to each person. The guests milled about outside the farewell meeting room while the family members and the funeral home workers made the final arrangements inside. Mr. Wang's body was brought into the room in an open casket and placed on the platform, near the back wall, with his head towards the west side of the room (the left-hand side of the room from the perspective of someone standing at the door). The immediate family members looked at the body and had a moment to grieve and collect themselves. Outside of the room, Mr. Chen introduced himself to the guests and said that they should arrange themselves into rows of six people, with those who were more closely related to Mr. Wang at the front, and birth order determining the position of those who were equally related. Following this logic, the households arranged themselves in the following manner: at the front were the families of Mr. Wang's siblings, followed by the families of Mr. Wang's wife's siblings, and then the siblings of the daughter-in-law, the siblings of the son-in-law, and finally the friends of Mr. Wang. Within each group the families of elder siblings came before the families of younger siblings, though the layout of the room required families to mix together to form rows of six.

The master of ceremonies, a woman employed by the funeral home, told the immediate family members to stand in the front row of the room (closest to Mr. Wang's casket) and called for the doors of the room to be opened so that the other guests could enter and assume their positions. She herself stood behind a lectern positioned at the back right-hand corner of the room, facing the audience of mourners. After everyone had assumed their positions, the master of ceremonies began talking: "We are here today to mourn the passing the venerable Mister Wang (王老先生). Our hearts are full of grief because Mr. Wang was a good man, a respectable cadre who contributed to the building of our nation. He was a good father, husband and grandfather. . . ." In all, she spoke for only three minutes and, as had been agreed on beforehand, no other person gave a speech. After her speech, she said, "We will now bow collectively three times to the deceased. Bow once." Everyone bowed. "Bow twice." Everyone bowed again. "Bow a third time." Everyone bowed one more time. She then told the immediate family members to take a step forward, bow three times in front of the coffin, throw their white flowers into the coffin, and walk counter-clockwise around the coffin until they reached the west wall of the room, leaving a space between themselves and the coffin for the other mourners to pass. The two daughters cried quietly while the men stood solemnly. The master of ceremonies then directed each row of mourners to step forward, perform three bows in front of the coffin, throw their white flowers into the coffin, and walk around Mr. Wang's body in a counter-clockwise direction until they reached the line of the immediate family members. When they reached the family members, each row of mourners shook their hands in turn and offered some brief words of condolence. When they finished consoling the immediate family members, they left the room, and the master of ceremonies invited the next row of mourners to step forward. Because there was only one short speech, the entire farewell ceremony took only about twenty minutes.

After leaving the farewell ceremony, the guests went to the parking lot and waited while the immediate family members collected Mr. Wang's portrait, the flower wreaths, and Mr. Wang's clothes. The funeral room workers took Mr. Wang's body to be cremated. With the grandson holding Mr. Wang's portrait, Mr. Chen then led them to a room with a furnace for burning items brought by mourners (separate from the furnaces used to cremate bodies). Mr. Chen directed them to burn Mr. Wang's clothes, the flower wreaths, and some spirit money.

In Chinese cultures, burning is the primary way for mourners to give things to their deceased loved ones. As in many other cultures, it is also possible to bury items with the deceased, but this may only be done once, and, given the size of contemporary burial plots, can only include small items. Foodstuffs are also given

FIGURE 1. Varieties of spirit money. Photo: Andrew B. Kipnis.

to the dead (and to gods) by placing them on altars or on the grave itself. Most of what is burnt, however, are paper replicas of items that might be useful to or give pleasure to the deceased. These can include paper houses, cars, refrigerators, microwave ovens, mahjong sets, and even condoms or beautiful women, but the most common is money. The money is not "real" (the replicas are so fake that no one would consider them counterfeit currencies) and most often take the form of special "spirit" or "purgatory" currencies, but sometimes imitate ancient Chinese forms of money, US dollars, Euros, or other valued currencies, quite often in out-landishly large denominations.[1]

In the case of the deceased's clothes (as well as the flower wreaths), the items burned are real. The logic is partially the same—once burned, the deceased can use or enjoy the items in another world. But another logic also applies, as Mr. Chen explained: some things, if retained by the living, are likely to bring them bad luck. Moreover, retaining the clothes of a deceased person might cause his or her ghost to linger and haunt the house where the clothes are kept. Perhaps as a consequence of such ideas, there are few markets for second-hand clothes in China and few people would ever consider wearing clothes that were once owned by someone who is now deceased.

After the family burned the clothes and other items, Mr. Chen took them to the waiting room of the funeral home's crematorium. They brought Mr. Wang's portrait, the cinerary casket purchased from Mr. Chen, and a red cloth Mr. Chen had prepared. At 10:15 a.m., the crematorium room attendant called for Mr. Wang's family to come to a desk where they would receive Mr. Wang's ashes. First the attendant asked for the cinerary casket and the red cloth. Then he showed the plastic bag with Mr. Wang's ashes to the family members. It had a tag with a number that corresponded to Mr. Wang's number in the record book, which the attendant also showed to the family. Next the attendant placed the ashes in the cinerary casket, closed the lid, wrapped the casket in the red cloth and placed it on an altar. The grandson hung Mr. Wang's portrait behind the casket and Mr. Chen instructed the family members to perform three bows to the casket. Finally, four funeral home workers placed the cinerary casket on a palanquin and carried it to Mr. Chen's car. Mr. Chen instructed Mr. Wang's son to give a 20 yuan tip to each of these workers. With the cinerary casket and the portrait safely placed in Mr. Chen's car, they drove to where the other mourners were parked and then, in a procession led by Mr. Chen's car, to the cemetery.

At the cemetery, Mr. Chen checked in at the office and was soon accompanied by one of the graveyard workers. They picked up a pail for burning spirit money. With the grandson holding the portrait at the front of the line, the daughters carrying the plates of sacrificial food, liquor, and the personal items to be buried with Mr. Wang, and the eldest son carrying the cinerary casket wrapped in a red cloth at the back, they walked in a procession to Mr. Wang's gravesite. When they arrived at the gravesite, the underground chamber on the right-hand side of the site (as the mourners faced it) was open. The right-hand side of the site is the "upper" position in Chinese ritual, and, in a nod to patriarchy, is reserved for the man in dual gravesites. A pillow was placed in front of the open chamber. Mr. Chen directed the immediate family members to stand directly in front of the grave, the other mourners to stand in rows behind them, the eldest son to give the cinerary casket to the graveyard worker, and the grandson to place Mr. Wang's portrait in front of the yet to be carved tombstone.

Mr. Chen then began the burial ceremony: "With sadness in our heart, let us collectively wish the venerable Mr. Wang a peaceful journey. Wealth is the backbone, the cycle of life is eternal (九九归一). Grant the descendants a peaceful life. Five coins placed at the four corners [and the center] guarantee wealth to thrive and a peaceful and stable life."

Mr. Chen placed five 1-yuan coins on the bottom of burial chamber. Then he continued: "The filial piety of the sons and daughters is as deep as the ocean. Kneeling I place the beloved." He knelt on the pillow, took the cinerary casket from the worker, and placed it on top of the five coins. Then he placed Mr. Wang's shaver, glasses, cigarette lighter, and cigarettes into the chamber. Finally, he placed seven more coins on top of the casket and said: "The seven starred coins bring wealth to the entire family. Entering the earth is peace (入土为安). Seal the grave."

Mr. Chen stood up and the graveyard worker placed a lid on the chamber and sealed it with cement, wiped the grave clean, and left.

Mr. Chen then took out the five plates of sacrificial food (rice, meat, tofu, fish, and bok choy) and arranged them on top of the grave. At the center he placed an incense burner with a candle on either side. He lit some incense as well as both of the candles and placed the bucket for burning spirit money next to the pillow. He called up the eldest son and instructed him to first bow three times in front of the grave, to kneel down on the pillow and perform three kowtows, and finally to burn some spirit money in the bucket. Then he instructed the son to walk counterclockwise in a circle around the small section of the cemetery in which Mr. Wang's gravesite was located, and return to the back of the line. Mr. Chen then told the daughters, followed by the grandson, followed by the son-in-law and the daughter-in-law, to do the same. After the immediate descendants had finished, Mr. Chen directed the other mourners to each perform three bows and burn some spirit money and then return to the parking lot. After all of the non-immediate family members had left, he lit a cigarette and placed it on the grave for Mr. Wang's spirit to enjoy. He then got out the liquor and two small glasses. He filled one glass and placed it on the grave. He called the oldest son forward and filled the other glass and handed it to him. He instructed the son to toast his father, drink the liquor, bow three more times, and burn some more spirit money. He then instructed the grandson and the son-in-law to do the same. Next, he told the two daughters and the daughter-in-law to bow three times each and burn some money without drinking. They burned the rest of the spirit money. Next Mr. Chen addressed the neighboring graves—"You have a new neighbor, please welcome him"—and lit some firecrackers to scare away unwanted ghosts. Finally, Mr. Chen instructed the eldest son to give three graveyard workers, who had been watching the whole affair, 10 yuan each. They would be responsible for keeping the gravesite clean. Mr. Chen then picked up Mr. Wang's portrait and led the immediate family members back to the parking lot. The graveyard workers impatiently took the sacrificial foods and items from Mr. Wang's grave (this was the last morning burial of the day and the workers were eager for lunch), threw them in a trash bag with all of the ashes from the burning money, and cleaned the gravesite.

Near the graveyard parking lot was another furnace. Mr. Chen said that the portrait of Mr. Wang should be burned, and the siblings agreed to dispose of the portrait in this manner. He told all of the mourners to burn their black arm-bands as well. The mourners then returned to their cars and drove to the exit of the graveyard, where Mr. Chen had arranged one last act. In a metal platform set up on the pavement, Mr. Chen lit a small fire with dried grass. He told all of the mourners to step over the fire. By doing so they could absorb some of the Yang energy from the fire to counter the excesses of Yin that come from spending time at ghastly places like graveyards and funeral homes.

By the time they finished, it was almost noon. The banquet was arranged for 2:30 p.m. Most of the mourners departed to return to downtown Nanjing and prepare for it. Mr. Chen gave the immediate family members the packets of return gifts, and suggested that they make and drink some hot sugar water after they returned home to further counter the Yin force (气) of the funeral. Finally, he implored them to visit Mr. Wang's grave or at least perform a sacrifice to him at their home on the first seven weekly anniversaries of Mr. Wang's death. On the one hundredth day they should also visit, and after that they could visit on the traditional days for visiting graves in the Chinese ritual calendar, the most important of which is Qing Ming (April 4 or 5). Finally, he told the family members that they should avoid cutting their hair for the forty-nine-day period. Mr. Chen then thanked the Wang family for their business and left. The siblings returned to the mother's apartment.

At the apartment the younger sister prepared some warm sugar water for everyone to drink while the older sister described the funeral to her mother. The mother voiced her approval about most aspects of the ritual, but said that it would have been better to keep Mr. Wang's portrait, as she did not view it as an inauspicious item. She also said that she would like her own funeral to be as simple as possible. The siblings agreed to meet the next day with the mother to settle accounts around the expenses for Mr. Wang's funeral and hospitalization, and the inheritance of his savings and pension payout.

At the banquet, the siblings handed the packages of return gifts to each of the households who had given money during the mourning visits. The packages included a washcloth and some scented soap, which again could be used to wash off the excessive Yin energy generated by the funeral. The three siblings, the son-in-law and the daughter-in-law, and the twenty-six-year-old paternal grandson all sat at one table. During the banquet, the grandson drank close to a bottle of hard liquor (白酒), mostly just drinking from his own glass rather than toasting his relatives, as etiquette would demand. After he finished drinking he said: "Now my paternal grandfather has passed away. I am the only paternal grandson in this family, the last member of this Wang family line. I am the only hope for family continuity and everything my grandfather owned should be mine." His mother told him that now was not the time to say such things; they could discuss them when the funeral was over. But this would prove to be the opening salvo of an inheritance battle among the siblings, especially between the brother's family and the younger sister's.

The next day the siblings met in the mother's apartment as planned. The daughter-in-law also came, but not the grandson or the son-in-law. Unlike many of his peers, Mr. Wang had written a will, which stated that his money should be divided equally among the three siblings and his wife. This will greatly upset the daughter-in-law, who insisted that her household should inherit everything. She shouted: "Wang X"—her son—"is the only one who can continue the Wang family line and he is not yet married. To find a good wife he will need to have his own apartment and significant family resources. Do you want to end the Wang family line?" The younger sister had a stepson who was already married (and had attended the funeral as a related household rather than a direct descendant), while the middle sister's husband and son had still not arrived in Nanjing. The younger sister said, "We all have children, and I am the one who provided the most care for father and who has been doing the most for mother as well. Why should my brother get everything?" The daughter-in-law replied: "Step-children don't count. Is he surnamed Wang? Will his children be surnamed Wang?" Mr. Wang's wife said that he had left a will and that they needed to respect his wishes.

The mother's declaration seemed to settle the matter, but that was only because what they were fighting over now was not really the most important aspect of Mr. Wang's estate. Because he was a former cadre, Mr. Wang had had some health insurance, but still, the hospital costs had eaten away a significant portion of his life savings. What he had left, along with his pension payout, amounted to slightly more than 200,000 yuan. Much more valuable was the decrepit but well-located downtown apartment in which they were now arguing. The siblings thought that it was worth about 1.9 million yuan at that time and that its value would increase significantly every year. After Mr. Wang's death, the apartment belonged to Mr. Wang's wife, but, given her frail health, the real battle among the siblings was over the future inheritance from the mother. The daughter-in-law said: "Just you wait, if anyone tries to deny my son this apartment you will see what I will do." The daughter-in-law also insisted that when they divided the gift money from the funeral, her family should get all of the money given by her relatives, who constituted the greatest portion of the givers. The mother said fine, they could do it that way, but she was obviously upset. The middle daughter also became angry and yelled at her sister-in-law: "Can't you see that you are upsetting my mother, you should stop saying these things and get out of here." The younger sister did some quick calculations which showed that after accounting for the funeral expenses and the final hospital bill, each share would amount to about 53,000 yuan, with the daughter-in-law's household getting about 1500 more because of her relatives' gifts. The brother and younger sister went to Mr. Wang's work unit to get the pension payout wired into Mrs. Wang's account, and then to Mrs. Wang's bank to withdraw the money (with a signed letter from Mrs. Wang); the daughter-in-law left and the middle daughter remained to comfort her mother.

The next day the three siblings met again in the apartment. They gave the middle sister her share in cash; the other shares were already in the respective households' bank accounts. This would be the last time the siblings met together, other than in courts of law. The brother and his household later sued the younger sister to claim rights over the apartment, but the court ruled that the matter could not be resolved until Mr. Wang's wife either passed away intestate or made a final will. Neither of those events has occurred as of this writing. The brother and his household became enemies of the younger sister, and the middle sister sided with her.

FIGURE 2. Paraphernalia stalls at cemetery. Photo: Andrew B. Kipnis.

The evening after the final meeting of the three siblings, the husband and son of the middle sister arrived from England. They rented a hotel room and the middle sister stayed with them for the following week, though they visited the mother each day. On the seventh day after the death of Mr. Wang, the younger and middle sisters arranged for their households to visit the grave together. The younger sister and her husband picked up the middle sister and her husband and son at their hotel at 9:30 a.m. They drove out to the cemetery. In the parking lot, the two sisters inspected a line of stalls selling spirit money, paper houses, mahjong sets, and furniture items, flowers and other funeral paraphernalia.

The middle sister spent 100 yuan on white chrysanthemums while the younger sister spent 20 yuan on spirit money. They picked up a pail for burning spirit money and walked to the father's grave. The tombstone had been properly carved and painted. On the right-hand side their father's name was engraved vertically, with the engraving of his surname painted red and that of his given names painted black. The surname was red because his family still lived on. Above his name stood the character for "father." His birth and death dates were carved vertically to the right of his name. To the left of the sisters' father's name was the mother's, but her name was entirely in red, as she was still alive. The character for "mother" was above her name; her birthdate was also carved and a space for her death date remained. Above the characters for father and mother was the character 先, which in this context means "elder," "ancestral," or "departed." In smaller characters, on the far left-hand side of the tombstones, carved vertically, were the names of Mr. Wang's children, their spouses, and the grandchildren. Each person was labelled with the appropriate Chinese kinship term, which differentiate children from children-in-law and paternal from maternal grandchildren. All of the descendants' names were painted red. The middle sister placed the flowers on the tomb. The younger sister said: "Dad, we have come to see you. Your son-in-law and your grandson (外孙) have come all of the way from England to visit you. Mom is OK. She thinks of you but her health is OK. Don't worry, we will all be fine. Today is the seventh day, we hope you are comfortable. We have brought some money for you." Then she burned some spirit money in the pail. She then told the middle sister's husband and son to perform three bows each and to burn some spirit money in the pail. Finally, she told the middle sister and her own husband to burn some spirit money.

After she finished burning the last of the spirit money the middle sister suddenly began sobbing loudly: "Dad, I should have come and seen you sooner." The younger sister said, "None of us knew he would pass so quickly, there was nothing anyone could do." The middle sister's son and husband put their arms around her and her grief momentarily subsided. They tore the petals from the flowers before they left, so that no one could re-use the flowers and place them on another grave. On the way back to the parking lot they bumped into one of the women who tended the graveyard and they gave her another 10 yuan tip, telling her exactly which grave was their father's and asking her to keep it clean.

The younger sister made two more visits to the grave during the first forty-nine days after death, and also a year after the death and each year in late March, in the weeks before Qing Ming. The middle sister visited the grave whenever she came back to Nanjing.

Of Transitions and Transformations

I began formal research on the Chinese funeral services industry in May 2013. Before then, I had attended a couple of memorial services for friends and relatives in urban China (my wife is from the Chinese city of Nanjing). I had also witnessed about ten funerals in rural China, mostly as part of a research project I conducted in Shandong province during the late 1980s and early 1990s (Kipnis 1997). I had more recently written a book on the rapid urbanization of a formerly rural county in Shandong (Kipnis 2016), and the combination of these research experiences suggested to me that a project on the urban funeral sector would reveal much about contemporary China. Funerals in rural areas had a very local mode of organization. Villagers who suffered a death in their family would ask village or lineage elders to organize the ritual and bury the deceased on village land. But those living in urban areas rarely had any contact with "familial elders" other than their own parents. Consequently, when dealing with the death of a parent they had neither a person to help organize the ritual nor land on which to bury the body.

Urbanization as a social transformation involves the creation of densely inhabited areas without land for burials and the formation of a population of people who live in nuclear families. This transformation requires a total rethinking of the process of conducting funerary ritual. In addition, the organization of urban funerals as a for-profit business is a product of the post-Mao (1978-) era of commercialization and urban social reorganization. During the Maoist era, work units (单位) tightly controlled most aspects of urban Chinese lives, including the conduct of death rituals. The history of the urban Chinese funerary industry thus also illuminates much about transformations in the Chinese economy during the post-Mao era.

Finally, I imagined that research on urban funerals could illuminate several aspects of the political regulation of state-society relations. The death of a loved one pushes everyone to deal with questions of the significance of life, regardless of the presence or absence of particular systems of religious belief. In a country where religious expression is permitted but regulated and "superstitious practices" are supposedly banned, how should the body and soul of a loved one be treated? Tensions around this question pervade the official treatment of funerals. In addition, the strong emotions associated with death can become a source of political energy. Funerals involve semi-public gatherings of groups of people who share a relationship through the deceased. Political movements often transform collective grief into political/moral outrage by turning the deceased into a martyr who died for a particular cause. In a country where all forms of political protest are discouraged, what do the politics of mourning reveal?

To conduct research for this project, I undertook several types of activities. First, I interviewed people involved in the funeral business, including one-stop dragon entrepreneurs; those who worked in state-run funeral homes and graveyards; Buddhist, Christian, and Muslim religious practitioners who sometimes conducted religious rituals in relation to death; nurses and administrators in old-age homes; and those who worked in the government, either regulating the funeral industry or arranging funerals for poor people and party cadres. Overall, I conducted formal interviews with fifty-five such people, in several cases more than once. I also conducted informal interviews with many people on the fringes of the business, such as those who sold flowers in front of cemeteries. Second, inquiring only among my own friends and my wife's relatives, I asked people who had arranged funerals for their parents to share their stories with me. I never approached people who had arranged the funeral for a child or who had recently conducted their funeral, as I imagined their grief would be too severe. I also always shared my own experiences (I, alongside my brother, have arranged the funerals of both my father and my mother). Though the sample of people from whom I collected stories cannot be considered representative, the depictions of fifteen funerals I collected in this manner were an important resource for this book. Third, I visited as many cemeteries as I could. Tombstones provide important clues about the families of the deceased. One can examine who is buried together as well as who is listed on the tombstone as a descendant. In cases where short eulogies or life histories are carved into the tombstone, one can examine what about the deceased—their soul, if you will—was deemed important enough to memorialize. Since different sections of a graveyard include the ashes of people buried at different times, one can make comparisons, examining how memorialization changes over time. Since graveyards can vary widely in terms of the cost of a burial plot, one can also make inferences about class differences in practices of memorialization. In addition, some tombs, mausoleums, and even cemeteries are central sites for state memorialization, state-sponsored political education, and propaganda. By comparing state practices of memorialization with those in graveyards for everyday people, one can trace the mutual influence of state preoccupations and a wider culture of practices of memorialization. In graveyards, one can also witness burial ceremonies. On holidays like Qing Ming, one can witness other practices of grave visiting and cleaning. Finally, as many forms of business in China maintain an online presence, I subscribed to the social media (Wechat) distribution lists of several enterprises in the funerary industry and visited the websites of many others.

In addition to these more formal research activities, I also had the opportunity to attend a few funerals during the course of my research, both because friends or relatives had passed away and because universities sometimes hold open funerals for famous professors, and I was associated with various universities during the course of this research. In all, I completed about eight months of research between 2013 and 2017. About three quarters of this research was conducted in Nanjing, but I also conducted interviews in Beijing, Jinan, Yinchuan, and Shanghai, and visited graveyards in several other cities as well. In 2018 and 2019, I had the chance to conduct research in several southern Chinese cities, including the separately governed Special Administrative Region of Hong Kong, where I was living. During this later period of research, I did not have time for any in-depth ethnography, but I did gain a better appreciation of both regional variation in funerary practice and the continuing evolution of government regulation of this sector.

In China, research on contemporary urban funerals is surprisingly rare. There have been important works in English written about funerary ritual in rural China and funerary ritual in the past (see especially Watson and Rawski 1988), but very little on contemporary urban funerary ritual. Two older works on this topic (Ikels 2004b; Jankowiak 1993) focus on conflicts over the forms of religious or "superstitious" elements to include in a funeral. While such conflicts still exist (see, for example, Colijn 2016), they were relatively rare in my research, perhaps because of the role of experts like Mr. Chen. During the period when Jankowiak conducted his research (over thirty years ago), or even Ikels (over twenty years ago) one-stop dragon entrepreneurs like Mr. Chen were not common. More important, neither Ikels nor Jankowiak focuses on the role of urbanization per se in the conduct of funerals. In the Chinese-language literature, publications on this topic are just as rare. Among academics interested in funerals in China, discourses of tradition and authenticity loom large; since facets of life like funerary ritual belong to the category of "traditional culture," researchers assume that the most "authentic" forms are to be found in the past and among those living in rural areas. Modernity and urbanization are seen as contaminating purer forms of ritual, which derive their authenticity from their association with a rural past. But for me, the clues funerary ritual and memorial culture give us about contemporary processes of modernization and urbanization are more valuable than what they might tell us about Chinese traditional culture. In addition, as one Chinese scholar working on the history of rural funerals told me, for academics in the People's Republic of China, the very factors that make urban funerals politically interesting also make them dangerous to write about, particularly under the repressive academic environment instituted by Xi Jinping.

The funeral of Mr. Wang, as depicted in chapter 1, is both a factual depiction of an actual event and a work of fiction. I selected Mr. Wang's funeral for two reasons. First, it was a funeral about which I collected interview depictions from three separate people (the two sisters plus Mr. Chen) and, thus, one for which I had a relatively complete record. Second, it seemed typical in many ways for a funeral in Nanjing in 2014.

How might the depiction of Mr. Wang's funeral be considered a work of fiction? Anthropologists have often argued that ethnographic writing combines narrative techniques derived from the writing of fiction with factual research experiences (for an excellent synopsis of some of this literature, see Narayan 2012). I created the narrative of Mr. Wang's funeral from the narratives told to me by three people. Like many news stories and ethnographic depictions, it is a story based on stories told by other people, though the fact that I heard the story told by three different people does increase the reliability of my version. The elements of dialogue I present in my narrative are based on moments of dialogue told to me by those three people, but, by the time I translated them into English and recorded them on the pages above, that dialogue is already several degrees removed from what actually took place. The depiction is also fictive because for purposes of maintaining anonymity I changed a few details (Mr. Wang and Mr. Chen, for example, are both pseudonyms). In addition, in places where I did not have enough detail to tell the story properly, I filled in details based on what I knew to be typical of the ritual process in Nanjing from other rituals I had seen and heard about. In this sense, the story of Mr. Wang's funeral might be seen as 90 percent coming from the funeral of a particular individual and 10 percent coming from my research in general.

In what ways was the funeral of Mr. Wang typical? First, consider the place and time of the event. In Nanjing, most people conduct the farewell meeting, cremation, and burial in the morning of a single day, an odd number of days after death. This was not the case in Beijing and Shanghai. In Nanjing, I was told that the reason for completing the process before noon was that the soul of the deceased was a "Yin" entity that would be damaged by the strong "Yang" that emanates from the afternoon sun. I suspect that this belief and practice were once fairly widespread in China, but that in large cities like Shanghai and Beijing, it is no longer practical. In Shanghai, the state-run funeral homes and the state-run crematorium are not usually located at the same facility (there are several funeral homes). Moreover, the graveyards are a long way from the center of town. Most critically, the ratio of the number of deaths on an average day to the number of time slots available for farewell meeting rooms at the state-run funeral homes is higher; consequently, it is not possible for all of the farewell meetings to be arranged in the morning. In Shanghai, I never heard anyone say that the entire funerary process should be completed before noon. But in many other smaller cities I visited, they also completed the entire process before noon. In Jinan they completed funerals for young people (those with a parent who was still alive) in the morning and old people in the afternoon. In Chongqing, according to the experience and research of a Chinese student of mine (Duan 2018), people set up tents in the public spaces between apartment buildings rather than constructing home altars.

The amounts of money involved in the economic transactions depicted in Mr. Wang's funeral also vary by place and time. In China's most expensive and coastal cities—like Shanghai, Beijing, and Guangzhou—everything would be more expensive. In cities further inland, prices would be lower. Moreover, the economy all over China has been growing. Prices for everything have risen, and the amount of money given for gifts has also increased. Twenty years ago, people would not have given cash gifts at funerals in Nanjing, but rather blankets or pieces of cloth. Since cash gifts at funerals became the norm, the amounts of money given have increased over time. In short, the funeral depicted in the last chapter was at best typical for a funeral conducted in Nanjing during the period of my research, though I think that people in many large Chinese cities would see significant similarities to funerals they have attended.

Other aspects of typicality have to do with the particularities of Mr. Wang and his family. Funerals for younger people can be radically different. Those who die in the prime of their working lives often see greater involvement of their employers in their funerals and a large number of colleagues attending. Funerals for the young are more painful affairs and can involve classmates and teachers if they are still at school. But old people pass away at a greater rate than the young, and husbands die before their wives more often than the other way around, so Mr. Wang's funeral was "typical" in the sense that he was an older man who passed away before his wife. Having three children and many nieces and nephews is also typical for urban Chinese people of Mr. Wang's generation. Those who were in their seventies and eighties at the time of my research had their children during the Maoist era, before the onset of China's birth planning regime, and typically had many children. They also worked during the peak of the urban planned economy and, thus, under the work unit structure of that era. As a consequence, they usually have reasonable pensions and often own apartments to which they gained rights during that era. The combination of multiple children and apartment ownership implies, unfortunately, that inheritance struggles are all too common in contemporary urban China. Several one-stop dragon entrepreneurs told me that incipient inheritance struggles were visible to them in over half of the funerals that they organized. One-stop dragon entrepreneurs also told me that religious practitioners are hired in less than 5 percent of the funerals that they organize, so Mr. Wang's funeral was also typical in that it did not involve any overtly religious elements, though it did involve many practices that could be considered "superstitious" from an orthodox communist point of view.

Mr. Wang's funeral was also typical in terms of its size, level of expense, and grandeur. Mr. Wang and his children were neither particularly wealthy nor impoverished. As an older man, many of Mr. Wang's friends and colleagues were either dead or unable to leave their homes for extended periods in the winter, so most of those attending the funeral were Mr. Wang's younger relatives. According to interviews with people involved in the organizing of funerals at graveyards and funeral homes, as well as one-stop dragon entrepreneurs, larger funerals typically involve famous academics (who have taught many students who themselves are now academics), powerful cadres (who have appointed many people and thus have large networks of underlings, some of whom themselves are now powerful), rich businessmen, or people whose children occupy one of these positions. Mr. Wang and his children did not belong to any of these groups of people. Extremely impoverished people, or those with no living relatives, might have a state-sponsored ceremony which only a couple of people attend, but such funerals are also not so common. The types of funeral plots available and the style of tombstones at elite graveyards can differ drastically from those at Mr. Wang's graveyard, but, of the thirteen public cemeteries around Nanjing, only one was truly elite; the extent of variation among the rest was limited. Some impoverished people, or those particularly concerned with the ecology of wasting land for graves, might opt to have their ashes, or those of their loved ones, disposed of in a manner other than burial in a regular plot; they could, for example, have the ashes buried in a small wall vault or even scattered in the Yangtze River from a boat specifically designated for that purpose in a ceremony organized by the Nanjing Funeral Home. But, according to officials in the Nanjing funeral home, over 85 percent of Nanjing residents have their ashes buried in a regular sized plot.

Finally, many of the particular details of Mr. Wang's funeral, such as the throwing of coins from car windows, or the words spoken by Mr. Chen at the burial ceremony, would have been slightly different if a different one-stop dragon entrepreneur had organized the ritual. Many one-stop dragon entrepreneurs came from the rural areas surrounding the city. Often they got into this field of work because they or someone in their extended family had been involved in arranging funerals for their village. Since village custom can vary from place to place, the ritual particulars they bring with them can also vary. But the extent of this variation is easy to overstate. Though one-stop dragon entrepreneurs would claim that customary rural practice shifted every few kilometers, many of the logics behind particular forms of practice were consistent across places even when the details varied. Moreover, there have long been forms of state "orthopraxy" (that is, state sanctioned forms of orthodox funerary practice) in China.[1] In addition, many current one-stop dragon entrepreneurs get ideas about how to arrange funerals from internet sources. Consequently, notions about what constitutes a proper ritual are widely shared. Few in the funeral industry would find the particular ritual prohibitions Mr. Chen admonished against, or the particular manner in which he arranged things, to be strange.

OF TRANSITIONS AND TRANSFORMATIONS

This book is about transitions and transformations of many types, but most basically about the relationship between the transition that a funeral marks—from a social situation in which a person is alive to one in which they are considered a memory or an ancestor—and the transformations in Chinese society that occur as it urbanizes, commercializes, and becomes more wealthy. The words transition and transformation have much in common, but are not quite the same. What do they share? Both words imply an entity shifting from one state to another, suggesting both change and continuity. The entity in its new state must differ from its old state, but must carry forward at least some of the aspects of its original being. Elsewhere, I have analyzed urbanization as a form of transformation and argued that all transformations are recombinant (Kipnis 2016). In transformations, elements organized in a particular way are recombined with some new elements to form an entity in a different state. While some of the elements from the pre-transformation entity are recognizable in the new entity, their position within the whole may have changed, or shrunk, or grown. The same might be said of a transition. What is different about the words, at least as I use them here, is that transitions are regular occurrences. The transitions of death in any human society are regular enough to be marked by a ritual, which we call a funeral. Transitions are transformations that occur so regularly, that are so expected, that we have standardized ways of dealing with them, even though their effects in any given instance might be shocking or revolutionary. Transitions tend to have clear temporal markers. Death occurs in moments and it is generally easy to mark the precise day and even hour at which death occurs. Puberty may take a bit longer, but generally takes place early in the second decade of a human life. Transformations are more open-ended. It is hard to say exactly when something like "urbanization" begins and ends, though we can point to moments when it seems to progress more quickly. Transitions themselves may transform. This book depicts transformations in funerary ritual, and the relation of ritual transformations to the transformations of urbanization.[2]

The transformation of funerary ritual in China is an ongoing affair that has neither a clear beginning nor a clear end; nevertheless, some of the broader transformations funerary ritual in Nanjing involves can be given a periodization. The rapid growth in the urban areas of China's largest cities has been especially apparent in the twenty-first century. In Nanjing, urban growth was strong but steady during the early reform era (with the urban area expanding at a rate of slightly over 1 percent a year), but really took off after 1995. Since then growth rates have exceeded 5 percent annually (Chen, Gao, and Yuan 2016). The geographic expansion of Nanjing has affected funerary ritual in many ways. The expansion of the city has involved the establishment, re-establishment, and relocation of the city's graveyards and the crematorium itself; shifts in the ways in which people move around the city; re-workings of the borders and relationships among the rural and urban districts of the wider urban area; the expansion of the population of the city, and the redefinition of citizenship in the city—that is to say, the extent to which Nanjing is a city of recent migrants versus a home to people who grew up in the urban area. It has also involved an increasing segregation of the spaces of the living from the spaces of the dead. Chapter 3 examines the relationship of these changes to the transformations of funerals by focusing on the spatial organization of death and death ritual.

Urbanization and modernization in Nanjing have been accompanied by transformations in the practices and patterns of kinship as well as the wider field of social networks in which people live. Household units have become smaller, and structured primarily around nuclear families, as many modernization theorists would suggest (Goode 1963; Yan 2003). But transformations in kinship patterns in China are much more complex than a straightforward modernization theory could predict. As Davis and Harrell (1993) pointed out over two decades ago, Chinese families have been shaped by the drastic policy shifts of the People's Republic of China as much as by processes of urbanization and industrialization. As is the case for Mr. Wang's family, family demographics have been strongly influenced by the generally pro-natalist policies of the early Maoist era followed by a gradual increase in inducements to reduce the number of children during the 1970s and a strictly enforced birth planning policy during the post-Mao era. The result is a generational structure in which those born during the 1920s, 30s, and 40s often have several children, while those born in the 1950s, 1960s, and 1970s only have one. In addition, the privatization of the economy, especially of the housing stock, has meant that issues of inheriting property from parents have gone from being crucially important to one's class position during the pre-communist era (before 1949), to being unimportant during the Maoist era, to being of gradually rising importance during the post-Mao era. Today, after forty years of rising gradually, the inheritance of parental property has again reached a level of crucial importance. Contradictions between patrilineal ideologies of inheritance and a legal system that is not patrilineal result in considerable tension. Other shifts in social and familial relationships can likewise be seen as arising from a combination of urbanization and government policies. Yunxiang Yan has argued that both individuation (2009, 2010) and descending familism (2016) (a form of familial commitment which prioritizes the development of youth over the authority of the elders) are becoming more prevalent.

Closely related to the rise of individualism (that is, the decreasing importance of familial relationships) is the rise of importance of relationships to strangers. As the funeral of Mr. Wang demonstrates, former strangers, like the one-stop dragon entrepreneur Mr. Chen, now often play a crucial role in these familial rituals. Chapter 4 explores transformations in the patterns of familial and wider societal relationships, as they are revealed in practices of death ritual and memorialization.

The urban economy has also transformed dramatically over the past forty years and this transformation both involves and goes beyond the specific policy measures national and local governments have taken to shape the economy. As might be expected in an economy that has steadily grown and become more unequal, there has been both an overall increase in the amounts spent on funerals and a greater degree of divergence between high-end and low-end practices of memorialization. During the Maoist era, funerals were often organized with the help of representatives from work units. As the work unit economy has gradually given way to the private economy, fewer and fewer people have work units to help organize funerals. This has created a business opening for one-stop dragon entrepreneurs. Before the twenty-first century, very few such businesses existed. At first they were even illegal, but over the first decade of the twenty-first century they were tolerated and gradually became ubiquitous. The state-run crematoriums and funerals homes have also undergone considerable economic reorganization. They are increasingly asked to make themselves profitable at the same time that they are tasked with regulating conduct at funerals and providing low-cost funerals for the impoverished. Finally, as society becomes wealthier and older, larger companies are looking to move into the industry. They work closely with the government to both open new graveyards and disrupt the one-stop dragon industry by introducing new web-based platforms to the funerary market sector. The economic transformations of funerary rituals are examined in chapter 5.

Politically, funerals are sensitive occasions. Death can be an occasion for protest, for assigning blame or responsibility for the death to political actors. The strong emotions of grief can be transformed into forms of political passion. For this reason, the Chinese Communist Party regulates death and death ritual carefully, imposing its priorities wherever it can, but negotiating with other actors when the imposition of strict regulation threatens to result in too much resistance or indignation.[3] In addition, when confronted with death, most families seek the expertise of people like Mr. Chen to obtain guidance on how to follow proper customary procedures. The tangle of rules, laws, and customs that govern funerary procedure are the topic of chapter 6.

A final aspect of the transformation of funerary ritual has to do with conceptions of soul. This aspect of funerals is more abstract and difficult to pin down than funerary businesses or familial relationships, but still reveals much about contemporary Chinese society. The transition that funerals manage requires a concept of soul, of the animating spirit that seems to depart the body of a loved one when she or he dies. If funerals are about the reconstruction of social and cultural relationships among a group of people after one of its members is lost, then this recreation requires an assertion of continuity. How can the family continue when the deceased is no longer present? How can the values, the mission, the purpose for which the deceased stood for continue? How can the future remain connected to the past after the demise of the deceased? Thomas Laqueur (2015) suggests that all human societies use mortuary ritual to connect the past with the future. Imagining a soul allows something of the deceased to remain after his or her body perishes. The soul of Mr. Wang was addressed by his daughters, asked to last forever by the mourners, and given spirit money and flowers on several occasions. But exactly what this soul consists of, how it interacts with the living, and what sorts of agency it is seen as exerting all shift over time. Ideas about soul are often political because powerful people and organizations assert that they represent something that is immortal, unchanging, and everlasting. Such permanence adds to their mystique. Especially in a country like China, where "superstitious" activities are forced underground, explicit discussions of concepts like soul are quite rare. But they are nonetheless implicit in both funerary ritual and acts of memorialization at graveyards. They are also present in the widespread ideal of filial piety, which makes remembering deceased ancestors a form of moral obligation. Transformations in the treatment of the soul form the topic of chapter 7.

The final chapter of this book analyses ghosts. Ghosts haunt. They are present but not present, both real and figments of our imagination. Through the presentation of a ghost story, I return to the question of the relationship between fictional writing and truth and examine the psychological realities of haunting as they relate to processes of urbanization and political repression. From a secular, psychological point of view, souls can be seen as the aspects of a human that should persist over time, that should be memorialized to help us connect the past to the future. In contrast, ghosts haunt our memories whether we think they should be remembered or not. They remind us of that which is repressed, ignored, and forgotten.

3

Of Space and Place

Separation and Distinction in the Homes of the Dead

Urbanization in most places involves the segregation of the dead from the living, and such is the case in China today. Different aspects of this segregation have separate causes. Regimes of urban sanitation remove the slaughtering of live animals from the home; the increasing availability of hospital care shifts human death from the home to the hospital; the lack of space for burying the dead shifts burial to cemeteries located far from city centers and the places where most people live. The segregation of the living from the dead leads to new attitudes towards death and new practices of memorialization, which in turn reinforce the segregation. But the segregation of the dead from the living does not always mean relegating the dead to second-rate places. Elite cemeteries are often spectacular locations which maintain tombs and gardens meticulously, even when they are neglected by family members. Non-elite cemeteries, however, can be desolate places.

In rural China many aspects of death were and are close to home. Most rural old people die in their homes and express a preference for doing so (Cai, Zhao, and Coyte 2017). In the rural funerals I witnessed in the 1980s, or read about in the anthropological literature, the body would remain in the home for several days after death while people paid their respects, and the funeral itself would be held in the home. After the funeral, burial would take place in either the fields around the village if the village were located in the plains, in the mountains surrounding the village if people had access to mountainous land, or perhaps in a village grave-yard.[1] When I was doing research for this project in 2015, such practices continued in the villages around Nanjing. Refrigerated caskets allowed the body to be kept at home for five or seven days after death even in the peak of summer. During this period, friends and relatives of the deceased stopped by to pay their respects to the deceased, give a gift to the family, and be treated to a banquet and perhaps other forms of entertainment (such as traditional opera performances). These practices resemble those that occurred during the visits to the home altar of Mr. Wang, but, in the peri-urban villages around Nanjing, the respects are paid to the body of the deceased itself rather than a photo on a makeshift altar. Though residents of these villages must still have the body cremated, they bring the ashes back to be buried on village land or in a village cemetery.

In the mountainous areas of China, one can still see tombs scattered across the hillsides. Very often villagers in such places have consulted geomancy masters to help their families locate graves in places thought to be the most propitious, that allow the spirit of the buried ancestor to bring good fortune to future generations. Villages and families sometimes fight over favorable burial sites, or attempt to alter the landscape to destroy the favorable geomancy of places where their rivals' ancestors are buried. But whether the dead are buried in family fields, in family tombs in the mountains around the village, or in a village cemetery, in rural China the site of burial remains close to the home and is shared not by strangers but by agnatically related kin or at least fellow villagers. Moreover, the burial of the dead and the productivity of the land are intimately related. Either the dead are literally buried in the fields where crops are grown, or the burial sites are linked to the productivity of the fields through the forces of geomancy.

I do not mean to idealize rural life here. As in urban areas, in rural China there were and are people who died away from home or at a young age, people who were too poor or marginalized to be given a dignified burial, and periods of war, famine, epidemic, and other forms of mass death that led to irregular forms of funerary ritual, burial, and memorialization. However, for those fortunate enough to see their elders die a good death and properly become an ancestor, land and family, the dead and the living, the generation of food through agriculture and the recreation of community are intimately inter-related. In urban China today, the spaces of the dead are not so intimately connected to those of the living. Rather, from the moment of death to the time of burial, the dead are sequestered in their own spaces, and this segregation feeds psychological fears of death and dying.[2] Cultural analysts in many other parts of the world argue that this segregation has led to a rising fascination with death in popular culture—an increasing focus on zombies, vampires, and ghosts (Khapaeva 2017).

HOSPITALS AND THE MEDICALIZATION OF DEATH

That Mr. Wang died at a hospital speaks both to general trends of mortality in urban China and the class circumstances of Mr. Wang and his family. Mr. Wang was a low level cadre during his working career and hence a relatively educated person with a regular pension and some limited health care coverage. In China, rural people and people of lower socioeconomic status are more likely to die in their homes than middle-class urbanites (Cai, Zhao, and Coyte 2017). In part, this is because they cannot afford hospital care. But in a city like Nanjing, most of the elderly with urban household registrations, even if they used to be factory workers, have regular pensions and some health care coverage. They worked during the socialist period of economic policy in China and their status in retirement is not so different from that of Mr. Wang.

In China as a whole, the number of hospital beds has more than doubled between 2007 and 2017.[3] In most urban areas, the heavy regulation of the public hospital sector, along with the lack of development of non-hospital primary health clinics, has made public hospitals the main site of health care for urban residents (Wang et al., 2018). Those with cancer or severe heart problems, like Mr. Wang, often spend their last days in a hospital.

Hospitals make death less visible in several ways. First, they are segregated social spaces in themselves, with walls and admittance procedures. Hospitals separate the sick from the well. Second, death, for hospitals, is failure. Their purpose is to cure people and hospitals do not like to advertise their failings to the public. When a patient dies, curtains are drawn around the bed as quickly as possible and the dead person is transferred to the hospital morgue. Morgues are located in the part of the hospital least likely to be seen by visitors and other patients. Throughout China, public funeral homes arrange for cars to take the dead from hospital morgues to government-run funeral homes with a minimum of fanfare. Hospitals might declare that death is a private matter for the family of the deceased, but it is also in their interests to remove death as much as possible from the public view. Too much attention to those who die in their care damages reputations and generates lawsuits.

Advanced medical technologies make the determination of death an increasingly difficult matter. With the availability of cardiopulmonary resuscitation, the simple cessation of breathing cannot be considered an irreversible death. Doctors must certify a death according to legal definitions that vary from country to country. Neither the legal definitions of death nor the technological means of determining death are transparent to the majority of people.

In the context of the United States, Helen Chapple (2018) argues that the invisibility of death in hospitals has led to numerous medical scandals and even murderous episodes. The American nurse Charles Cullen was convicted for killing forty patients over a sixteen-year period while working at seven hospitals. Because death is a commonplace but hidden phenomenon in hospitals, no one noticed the patterns behind Cullen's activities for many years. Hospitals have little incentive to vigorously audit all of the deaths that occur on their premises, and considerable reason not to let news of wrongful deaths become public knowledge.

Though some urbanites do die at home, in all of the cities I visited, urban residents were not legally permitted to keep dead bodies in their apartments for the period leading up to cremation. Upon discovering a lifeless body in an apartment, urban residents must call an ambulance if they think there is any chance that the person might be resuscitated. If the ambulance workers determine that the body is dead and beyond resuscitation, they will take the body either directly to the state-run funeral home or first to a local hospital so that the cause of death may be certified. If the person discovering the body is confident that it is dead, she or he may instead notify the local neighborhood committee (社区), who will send someone from the local health service to certify the death and arrange for the funeral home to pick up the body. In urban China, these services are available twenty-four hours a day, seven days a week.

When I discussed the rural practice of keeping a body in a coffin at home with urban residents, all I spoke to said that the practice would be unthinkable in an urban context. Not only might the stench upset the neighbors, but even if there were no smell, the idea of having a dead body in the same apartment building would make people feel uncomfortable. "It would be inauspicious" (不吉利) was the most common way of describing this discomfort. One man said "keeping bodies at home is a result of rural people's superstitious beliefs." Urban people, he added, have "higher quality" and would not think of keeping a dead body in their apartment.[4]

A young woman extended this argument to the setting up of a home altar. She said that home altars reeked of superstition, were disrespectful to neighbors (who would not want to think about the fact that there had been a death in their building), and demonstrated the "low quality" of the people who did so. While I did not conduct surveys that would enable me to say how common such attitudes are, I found that the larger and wealthier a city was, the less extensive the practices associated with home altars were. In Nanjing, home altars were common, but not the erection of large tents or platforms outside of apartment buildings for the purpose of staging performances or entertaining large numbers of people. In Shanghai, both another researcher[5] and a one-stop dragon entrepreneur told me that the setting up of home altars was unusual. But three of my students who hailed from poorer, smaller urban areas in Western China told me that both home altars and large tents or stages for opera performances were common. When I conducted research in 2019, I found that more and more cities were taking steps to discourage home altars, encouraging families to instead set up their altars at specialized rooms designed for that purpose, available for rent in state-run funeral homes.

Common forms of ideology in China suggest that people living in large, wealthy, Eastern cities are more civilized, less superstitious, and "higher quality" than people from other parts of the country. These forms of ideology, in turn, are used to justify how funerary practice is regulated in various Chinese cities. In the next chapter, I will explore how hyper-urbanization influences social relations in ways that might explain the elimination of home altars in the largest and wealthiest cities; here, I just want to note how practices of keeping death hidden from public view are supported by ideologies of establishing a "civilized society," disparaging people of "low quality," and eliminating "superstition." These ideologies are mobilized by many of the officials in charge of dealing with death in urban contexts, who continually remind urban citizens to conduct their funerals and funerary activities in a civilized manner.

Practices and ideologies of hiding death can be self-perpetuating. Disgust at the smell of dead bodies may be a cultural universal (Robben 2018, xxxi). But such disgust is minimal in people who work regularly with dead bodies. Moreover, extending this disgust into an exaggerated fear of death and corpses occurs most commonly among those who rarely if ever have seen even an odorless corpse. In modern urban environments, lack of experience and discomfort with death become commonplace. The existence of such discomfort makes neighbors who fail to hide death and dead bodies from public view seem un-neighborly and encourages the further segregation of the dead from the living. In China, the ideologies that link "superstitious" and "uncivilized" behavior to lower-class and rural people of "poor quality" reinforce this segregation.

FUNERAL HOMES, CREMATORIUMS, CEMETERIES, AND URBAN REAL ESTATE

The separation of the dead from the living also occurs by moving funeral homes, crematoriums, and cemeteries further and further away from the center of the city. As the boundaries of cities expand, ever greater efforts are required to create this separation. In Nanjing, the first state-run funeral home was built in 1937 by the Republican regime, and was located in Qingliang Shan (清凉山), which at that time marked the outskirts of the city. But now this park is located in the Gulou (鼓楼) district of the city, one of the most central parts of Nanjing. In 1980, the state-run funeral home and crematorium were relocated to new facilities in the Andemen (安德门) area, which constituted the southern fringe of the city through the 1990s, but became a relatively central district after the subway opened in 2005. In 2012, the state-run crematorium and funeral home were again relocated, to a massive new facility nearly twenty kilometers further to south, in what is still a rural area, near several cemeteries. The new location cannot be reached by subway, but is served by a public bus route. During the 2000s, as people's wealth increased, many new cemeteries were built. But all of these were located far from the city center. Some of the older cemeteries were completely relocated; the cinerary caskets were dug up, and family members were given some minimal compensation (usually not enough to cover the costs of a plot in one of the newer cemeteries). The only graveyard that has been allowed to remain near (what are now) the central districts of the city is Gong De Yuan (功德园), the cemetery that is devoted to Party-designated martyrs and heroes of Nanjing origin. It is a site of patriotic education, and is by far the most expensive and exclusive cemetery in Nanjing. Most cemeteries in Nanjing are located in the outlying Qixia and Jiangning Districts. In Jinan and Shanghai similar patterns can be observed. Cemeteries, funeral homes,

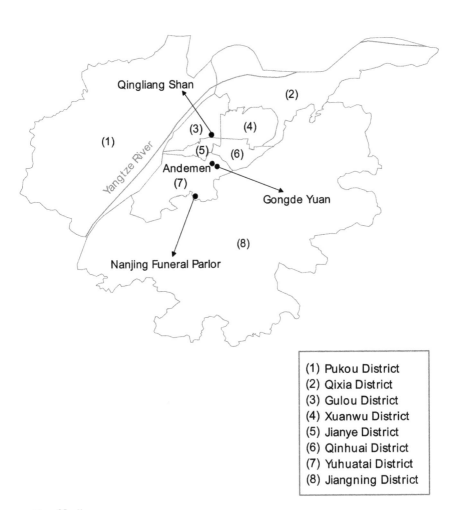

MAP 2. Nanjing.

and crematoriums are gradually relocated to the outskirts of the city, though a few historical leftovers remain in districts that were once at the outskirts but are now relatively central parts of those cities.

Part of this relocation may be attributable to the value of the land on which the cemeteries are located. No matter how much is charged for a cemetery plot, if the value of land increases rapidly, the income from cemetery plots cannot equal the amount that could be earned from erecting a shopping mall or a high-rise office or an apartment building. But another aspect of this relocation relates to desires to separate the dead from the living. One official in charge of arranging funerals at a large work unit in Nanjing told me: "People are still afraid of ghosts; the value of real estate near cemeteries and funeral homes is always lower than in the central districts, so, to protect the value of its real estate, the municipal government attempts to keep funeral homes located far from the city center." An official in the Office of Funerary Regulation (殡葬管理处), told me: "We cannot allow people to dispose of their parents' ashes in public parks. People fear ghosts. One person's ancestors are another's ghosts. People would not like Nanjing's parks if they thought they had ghosts, so it is illegal to scatter cinerary ashes there even if they do not pollute the environment and are indistinguishable from the rest of the dirt." The operator of a one-stop dragon business told me, "sometimes if I have done funerals for many days in a row, I will feel like I have been exposed to too much *Yinqi* (Yin energy, 阴气). Then I will go someplace that is full of life and *renao* (热闹, social activity, literally heat and noise), like Xinjiekou (新街口, the most central shopping area of Nanjing), and get warmed up by the *Yangqi* (Yang energy, 阳气)." In all of these statements, we can hear an ideology that insists on the separation of the spaces of the dead from the living. To protect the living (from their fear of ghosts), the dead must be kept far from the center of the city. To recover from too many visits to the spaces of the dead (which produce Yin energy in the Yin/Yang dichotomy), one must visit a place that is brimming with life, crowds, and human activity.

Hong Kong provides an example of how this separation has been enacted in another Chinese environment, but under a completely different set of governing rules. In Hong Kong, places of burial have also progressively moved towards the outskirts of the city (Yuan Wufeng 2013). The largest public cemetery is located in the New Territories, close to the Chinese border and far from the city center. In Hong Kong, there are seven licensed funeral parlors, places of business that can conduct funerary services on their property and store dead bodies for the purpose of holding such rituals, and approximately 120 licensed undertakers who, like the one-stop dragon entrepreneurs in Nanjing, help with funerary arrangements and sell coffins and other funerary paraphernalia, but do not have the facilities to conduct funerals themselves. What is interesting about these businesses is not so much their location, which can be explained by historical factors, their establishment occurring at times when locations that are now central were peripheral, or at transportation hubs that connected easily to cemeteries in peripheral areas, but the conditions of their licensing. Only those undertakers who began their businesses before the current regulatory regime began in the 2000s can openly advertise the nature of their business, display coffins in their shops, and store crematory remains. These businesses have what are called type-A undertaking licenses. Those with type-B licenses cannot store ashes or display coffins in their stores if any other business or homeowners in their vicinity object. Those with type-C licenses are even further restricted. They may not use the word "funerary" (殡仪) in the signs displayed publically in front of their stores. The logic here is the same as the one voiced by my interviewees in Nanjing. If any neighbor either fears death or dead bodies, or fears that other people's fear could affect the value of their business or property, then this neighbor has the right to restrict the activities of the undertaker. In practice this means that business activities of all proprietors with type-B and type-C licenses are affected. For this reason as well, the only funeral parlors in Hong Kong are older ones that established their businesses long ago.[6] The new restrictions on licenses further freezes the business locations of the current funeral parlors and type-A undertakers. If they were to move their businesses, they would face further restrictions, so they remain where they have been historically located.

Currently, most of the undertakers with type-A licenses are located in the area of Hong Hom, near the terminus of the East Rail line which connects to mainland China and the areas of Hong Kong furthest from the downtown core. In Hong Hom, many apartment buildings are located in the vicinity of these undertakers. Those apartments which have a window from which one can see an undertaker's shop (and shop sign) rent for less than apartments which do not feature such a view.

In Guangzhou and many other large mainland Chinese cities, land use laws prevent the establishment of new cemeteries or the expansion of old ones. While these laws are justified in terms of saving land, their effect is to shift the location of cemeteries further from the city center (to a location outside of the city's jurisdiction) rather than eliminating them altogether. But these distant cemeteries market their gravesites to families from those very cities that exclude them. The location of cemeteries outside of large cities results in customers needing an automobile to visit, but that is not necessarily an obstacle from the point of view of either the customers or the cemetery owners. Driving to a countryside grave can make for a nice family outing, and customers who can afford their own cars are also those who can pay the most for gravesites.

RELOCATING THE DEAD

The rapid pace of urbanization in China has resulted in a massive number of grave relocations. Thomas Mullaney (2019) suggests that over ten million graves have been relocated in the past decade alone. He has documented the original sites and the number of these relocations by mapping grave relocation notices, which must be published in local newspapers, onto a digital platform with a map of China. Christian Henriot (2019) has researched over a century of such relocations in Shanghai and notes that procedures for these relocations during the twenty-first century at least improves upon those of the Maoist era, when graves were simply flattened and built over rather than relocated. Nevertheless, the current procedures rarely seem just in the eyes of those people whose ancestors' graves are being relocated.

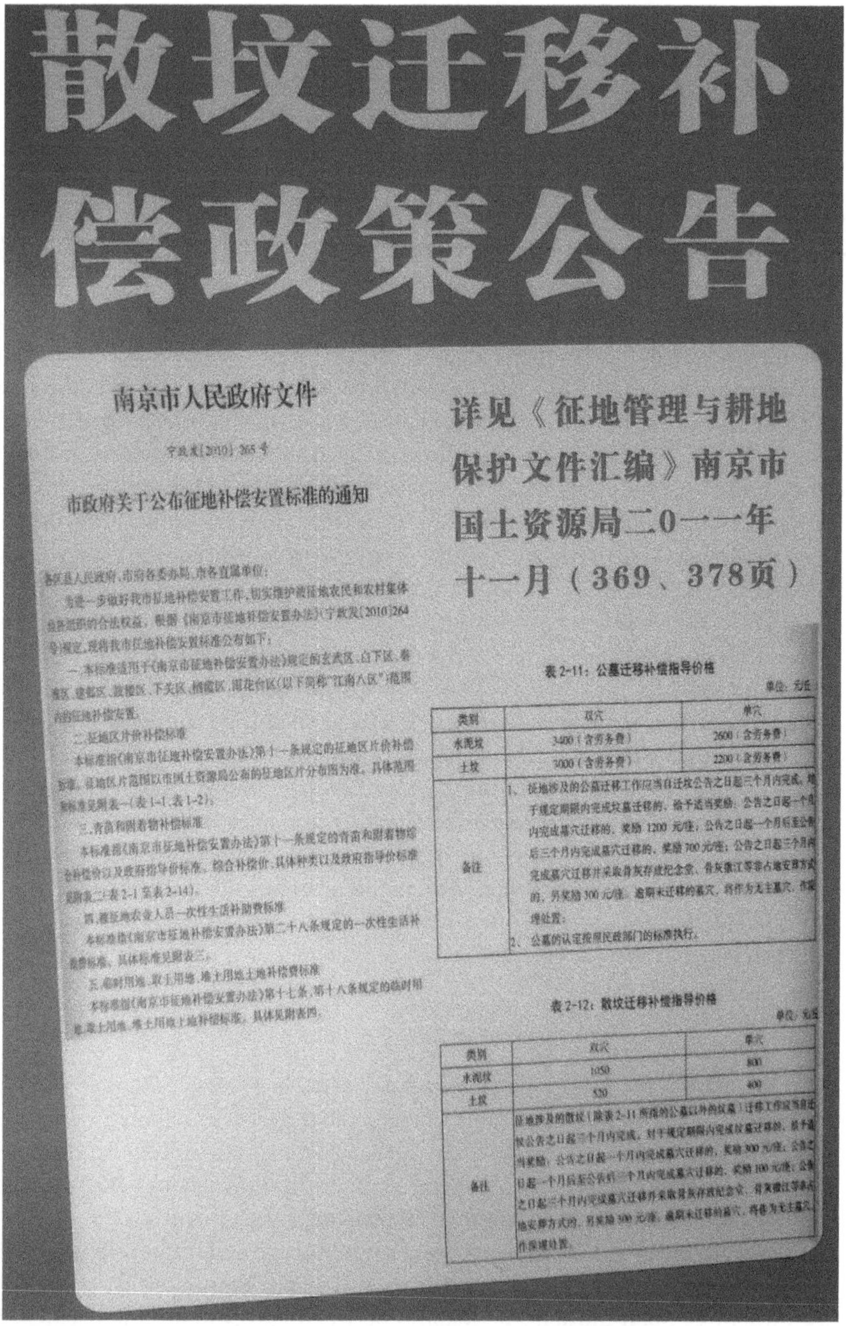

FIGURE 3. Grave relocation compensation notice. Photo: Andrew B. Kipnis.

Often villages situated in what was the outskirts of a given city had small collective graveyards. In other cases, individual families buried their dead in their own fields, with or without tombstones. But regardless of whether the relocation involves scattered individual graves or a collective cemetery, the procedures individualize those families whose graves are relocated. Descendants must come forth separately to reclaim the cinerary caskets of their relatives and receive compensation. When, where, and if to rebury the cinerary casket is a decision for each individual family, so collective gravesites can never be reconstituted. The community of the dead as well as the community of families who bury their dead together is dispersed. Second, the amount of compensation is not enough to purchase a new plot in one of the newer cemeteries. In Nanjing in 2015, the maximum amount of compensation to be received for a relocated grave was less than 5,000 yuan, while the least expensive plot in a new cemetery was over 15,000 yuan.

In Nanjing, I came across an announcement for an impeding grave relocation near a park in the Yuhuatai District in 2015. One man there complained of the amount of compensation he would receive for his father's grave. He said that he could not afford a new grave and tombstone with the amount of money he would receive, so he would be forced to relocate his father's ashes in a tree burial, a form of burial without a tombstone in which the ashes of many unrelated people are scattered into the ground in front of a tree.

But new construction projects are not the only cause of grave relocations in urbanizing China. Urbanization in China has also entailed a vast amount of geographic mobility. Many rural families have relocated and bought property in urban areas far from their original homes. At a cemetery on the outskirts of Nanjing, I met a man who had just conducted a grave relocation ceremony for his parents. His parents had been buried in a village cemetery in Shanxi province. He said that he felt like he had no connection to his home village anymore. He spent most of his childhood in boarding schools outside of his village in the county seat where he lived. He went to university and then got a job in information technology in Taiyuan (the capital of Shanxi province); he married and had a child there in his twenties and was transferred by his company to Nanjing in 2009. His father died when he was in his twenties and was buried in the village cemetery; his mother had lived with them, helping with the care of their son until she died in 2008. They buried the mother with the father in 2008, but, in 2013, they purchased an apartment and formally moved their household registration to Nanjing. He said that they now felt like Nanjing residents and that it was too inconvenient to go all the way back to Shanxi every time they wanted to visit his parents' grave. So, in 2015, they purchased a cemetery plot in Nanjing and had the cinerary caskets of their parents relocated there. He personally went back to Shanxi to carry the caskets to Nanjing, and arranged a reburial ceremony through the cemetery office. The cemetery manager told me that they regularly conducted such rituals for customers that were relocating their parents' ashes from another place.

Another three-generation migrant family I knew was having conflicts over where the parents were to be buried. They had migrated to Nanjing from Anhui province and ran a successful pet grooming business. The grandparents were in their seventies and seemed well adapted to urban life, but still said that they wanted to buried back in their village in Anhui. The father thought that he would be well-remembered by the descendents of the fellow villagers with whom he had grown up, many of whom belonged to his lineage. But the son and daughter-in-law were less certain. "Our future is in the city," the daughter-in-law said; "how can we be filial in tending our parents' grave if it is so far away from where we live?"

CEMETERIES AND CLASS: DISTINCTION IN THE SPACES OF THE DEAD

If cemeteries are being pushed further and further away from the centers of the city and the spaces of the dead are being increasingly separated from the spaces of the living, that does not imply that the spaces of the dead are shabby. Rather, the beauty of the spaces of the dead varies greatly with the prestige of their families and the amount of money that is spent on their funerals and gravesites. Graves are often called "residences for the deceased" (阴宅), especially when using the logics of a real estate market to discuss the buying and selling of gravesites. Just as many people pay more for an apartment on a higher floor with a beautiful view and an aspect that receives sun at the right time of the day, so do cemetery salespeople justify charging more for graves higher up the slope of a hill or with a nicer view or aspect. In some cemeteries, there are opportunities to consult an expert in geomancy about the exact location of one's grave. While in earlier dynasties geomancy was considered particularly important for locating graves in a manner that would bring good fortune to the descendants of the deceased, geomancy experts today often frame their art in much less "superstitious" terms. They offer "scientific" advice about all manner of practical problems such as the location of apartments for the living, the arrangement of furniture within homes and apartments, and the architecture of buildings. Their practice reinforces the comparison of real estate for the dead and the living. Moreover, just as upscale apartment complexes include beautiful landscaping around their buildings and a workforce of landscapers to maintain it, so do elite graveyards manicure their gardens with great care and precision and hire a large number of caretakers to tend the grounds. Finally, just as residing in an expensive apartment complex ensures that one's neighbors will not include people of the lower classes, so does being buried in an expensive cemetery ensure that you will be buried among other relatively wealthy people. In China, I have heard both residential apartments and gravesites marketed in terms of the "quality" of those residing in the same "neighborhood."

The word "quality" in China often has a political connotation as well, with one's loyalty to the Communist Party being a crucial dimension of one's supposed overall quality. Those who are high-ranking cadres within the Communist Party are assumed to have the highest political quality of all. This sort of ideology permeates elite cemeteries, as many cemeteries become elite when a large number of high-ranking Party members are buried there. Babaoshan cemetery in Beijing is the national political cemetery, memorializing the bodies and the ashes of the highest-ranking deceased Party members and national heroes. While most countries may have something like a national cemetery for war heroes and political leaders, in China the logic of the national cemetery is reproduced at many political levels, with almost all major cities having cemeteries devoted to local Party leaders and martyrs. All such cemeteries are meticulously maintained, as they enshrine both the respect and obedience of the local population to the local branch of the Party and the loyalty of the local Party to the Party leadership in the national capital.

The Communist Party regulates cemeteries and funerary ritual fairly strictly in China, and one of the ways in which the owners of cemeteries attempt to ensure that their businesses will not be adversely affected by government regulation is to reinforce the ideology that political quality is the most important component of one's overall quality. Cemeteries express this ideology by going out of their way to memorialize the people and the ideals that the Propaganda Department of the Party would like to see memorialized, and transforming their cemeteries into museums that depict the historical events that this Department wants the public to remember. Schools often arrange for students to take fieldtrips to such cemeteries for classes in patriotic education, and local governments often stage wreath-laying ceremonies at such cemeteries on national holidays.

In addition to advertising the quality of the people residing in their neighborhoods, elite cemeteries ensure political backing for their continued existence by reproducing political messages supportive of the current regime. In these cemeteries, ideals about quality, devotion to the Party, and respect for the dead blend. Catherine Bell (1992) suggests that ritualization is a political act in which one defines ideals, symbols, or people as sacred, placing them beyond criticism and making them unquestionable. Respect for the feelings of the grieving make it unthinkable to criticize a dead person in front of mourners at her or his funeral. The separation of death from life in urban contexts furthers the sacralization of the dead. Fear of the dead leads to a silence that can be read as deference. The government forces the public to be respectful to the symbols of the Party and country. Elite cemeteries reinforce the sacralization of the idea of "quality," respect for these symbols, and respect for the dead by blending them together.

The Gong De Yuan (Garden of Merit) in Nanjing is one elite cemetery that utilizes this form of sacralization. As its promotional materials explain, in 1954,

Party leaders selected a majestic spot at the edge of the city to create a burial ground for revolutionary martyrs. In 1956, the first burials were held there in state-sponsored ceremonies. Over the decades, other city leaders and martyrs were buried there, and, in 1992, the organization that maintained the site was declared a "work unit protecting high level cultural relics" (高级文物保护单位), giving the site political protection from redevelopment by real estate interests while the city expanded. In 1999, to enable the government work unit that ran the site to be less economically dependent on funds from the city budget, the Garden of Merit was allowed to operate as a public cemetery. It started selling gravesites to whomever could pay the price, in addition to continuing to bury heroes and leaders designated by the Party-State of the Municipality of Nanjing. It became by far the most expensive cemetery in Nanjing, charging prices many times higher than the least expensive cemeteries. It also became the best maintained cemetery in Nanjing; throughout the day scores of workers tending the gardens are visible. After the opening of the subway line in 2005, the cemetery's location became a relatively central part of the city, but, as a protected site for cultural relics, it could not be relocated or redeveloped. As of 2016, it was the only large cemetery accessible by subway in Nanjing.

There are many types of burial available at the Garden of Merit. The most common forms include wall burial cubicles and regular gravesites. In 2015 the prices for a wall burial cubicle could cost as much as 100,000 yuan (generally spots higher up the wall cost double those near the bottom), which was five times the cost of a regular gravesite at the least expensive cemeteries in the vicinity of Nanjing. Because land for burials is limited at the Garden of Merit, most of the available slots are of the wall burial type, but their ability to sell these cubicles, and for such a high price, demonstrates the premium some people are willing to pay for the opportunity to be buried or to bury their family members at the Garden of Merit. Other than the Garden of Merit, no cemetery in Nanjing has been successful in selling wall burial cubicles, as most people prefer to purchase regular burial plots with headstones and would economize by looking for a plot in a less expensive cemetery rather than by accepting a wall burial.

A one-stop dragon entrepreneur explained to me, "In China, people believe that entering the earth brings peace (入土为安), so they prefer their ashes to be buried in the earth rather than a wall cubicle." But official policy now promotes wall cubicles because wall burials use less land than burial plots. The government and the cemeteries market them as a form of green or ecological burial. When I asked a salesperson at the Garden of Merit why so many people chose wall cubicles there, he linked the acceptance of green forms of burial to ideas of human quality and loyalty to the Party: "The people who choose to be buried at the Garden of Merit are of high quality. They have a high level of ecological consciousness and are loyal to the Party. Therefore, when the government promotes the idea of green burial, they are receptive to the message."

FIGURE 4. Wall burials at the Garden of Merit. Photo: Andrew B. Kipnis.

FIGURE 5. Gravesites at the Garden of Merit. Photo: Andrew B. Kipnis.

FIGURE 6. Grave of Communist martyr at the Garden of Merit. Photo: Andrew B. Kipnis.

The Garden of Merit also earns money by offering elaborate services. These include burial ceremonies, decorating tombs with flowers when family members are not able to come themselves to place flowers on a grave, and ceremonies on various anniversaries of the death of the person buried or on Chinese holidays. For heroes of the Communist Party from the 1950s, many of whom no longer have family members living in the Nanjing area, the cemetery regularly places large batches of expensive flowers on the tombs to make it look as if someone had just visited the grave.

Perhaps the most spectacular cemetery in China is the Fu Shou Yuan (福寿园), located on the outskirts of Shanghai. Founded in 1994 as a joint venture between the Shanghai Municipal Government and a private company, the company has since expanded and restructured to open cemeteries (in partnership with other local governments) in eight cities across China. The history of the Fu Shou Yuan is very different to that of the Garden of Merit. Because it was founded after the Maoist period, it does not have a long history of burying communist martyrs. Moreover, because it was founded in a period of rapid urbanization, municipal officials were very cautious about using land that might interfere with the expansion of the city, and located it far from the city center. Despite these differences, the political and ideological strategies of Fu Shou Yuan resemble those of the Garden of Merit. As a joint venture between the local Party-State and private capital, it can count on local state support while it pursues profit. Like the Garden of Merit, it bridges the public/private divide. Though it started out with no Maoist-era national martyrs buried on its land, it has aggressively pursued the ashes of celebrities, high-ranking officials, and national heroes, with the result that it now claims to have more than six hundred famous people buried on its grounds. Many of these celebrities died well before the founding of the cemetery, so Fu Shou Yuan had to entice the families of these people to relocate their ancestors' ashes to the cemetery's premises. It now aggressively markets its ability to provide "residences for the deceased" in the same "neighborhood" as these celebrities. It also promotes communist heroes and national martyrs as the most important form of celebrity of all, politically supporting its existence with the twin ideological pillars of nationalism and loyalty to the Communist Party.

A tour of the cemetery illustrates the extent of these strategies. The entrance to the cemetery is lined with paired statues of mythic and real animals, in the style of the statues on the entrance roads to the tombs of Ming dynasty emperors. Since Ming dynasty tombs have been preserved as historical relics and reconstructed as tourist attractions in both Nanjing and Beijing, this style is familiar to many Chinese visitors. The statues announce that one is entering an elite memorial space, and that the elite-ness of the space relates to the memorialization of the government in power. In addition to tombs, the site houses a columbarium, a building for storing boxes of ashes before they are buried in a grave, a museum, a memorial to the New Fourth Army, a monument to model workers with the names of all model

FIGURE 7. Humanism Memorial Museum. Photo: Andrew B. Kipnis.

workers buried in the cemetery, a Buddhist temple, gardens filled with statues, a hotel, extensive office and meeting facilities, and a coffee bar. All of these cater to the ideology of Party-supporting social distinction described above.

The museum, called the "Humanism Memorial Museum,"[7] is a large three-story building that displays the life stories of many of the most famous of the celebrities who are buried in the cemetery, and a few others who have close ties to Shanghai. It includes over three thousand relics from their lives as well as a movie theater, a gift shop, a lecture hall, a library, artworks, and a collection of over 150 epitaphs, carved in wood, taken from the tombstones of people from around the world. Some of the people featured in the museum include Chen Duxiu (1879–1942), one of the founders of the Chinese Communist Party; Cai Yuanpei (1868–1940), former president of Peking University and founder of Academia Sinica; Deng Lijun (Teresa Teng, 1953–95), a famous Taiwanese pop singer, who, though not buried in the cemetery, was so popular in Shanghai during the 1990s that a popular saying went "Deng Xiaoping rules China during the day, but Deng Lijun rules at night"; Feng Zikai (1898–1975) a famous artist, intellectual and cartoonist;[8] and Wang Daohan (1915–2005), a communist official credited with the economic planning behind Shanghai's rapid development in the 1980s as well as a former mayor of Shanghai. Throughout the museum, famous intellectuals, party officials, and popular figures (singers, artists, actors, and athletes) are mixed together and presented as a unified elite devoted to Shanghai, the Party, and the nation.

FIGURE 8. Section of New Fourth Army Memorial. Photo: Andrew B. Kipnis.

The New Fourth Army was one of the two main components of the Chinese Communist Party's army during the civil war with the Nationalists in the 1940s. Appropriately, it was the section of the army that was located close to Shanghai, and many members of the army became Shanghai residents after the war. Fu Shou Yuan's New Fourth Army Plaza includes a long, low wall with the names of all the soldiers who participated in particular campaigns near Shanghai (in a style that reminds me of the Vietnam War Memorial in Washington, DC), as well as statues of men at battle and of children saluting soldiers. The site has been declared an area for "red tourism," and Shanghai schoolchildren are regularly taken to the memorial as part of their patriotic education. According to publicity material released by Fu Shou Yuan, this "base of red tourism" receives 400,000 visitors a year.[9] When I visited the cemetery just before National Day (October 1) in 2019, the local government was rehearsing a to-be-televised wreath-laying ceremony complete with speeches, an honor guard, and military personnel.

The museum, New Fourth Army Plaza, tombs of famous people, and statues are scattered across the grounds of the cemetery, which is divided into different sections for different types of people and different types of burial. Maps enable tourists to find the tombs of their favorite celebrities when visiting the grounds. Near the New Fourth Army Plaza is a section for military men. Separate sections for children, intellectuals, artists, and devout Buddhists and Christians are dispersed around the cemetery. There are also sections for highly individualized "artistic tombstones," as well as sections for eco-burials and a large area for wall burials. There are both tombstones that give elaborate biographies of the people whose ashes are buried underneath, and, much more commonly, tombstones that simply present the names of the deceased (usually couples are buried

FIGURE 9. Chen Duxiu's tomb.
Photo: Andrew B. Kipnis.

FIGURE 10. Wall burials in Fu Shou Yuan. Photo: Andrew B. Kipnis.

FIGURE 11. Children's section of Fu Shou Yuan. Photo: Andrew B. Kipnis.

together) and the names of their descendants. Like the Garden of Merit, the Fu Shou Yuan also offers a wide range of services including making offerings at the grave, placing flowers by the grave, interment ceremonies, and rituals led by clergy from the attached Buddhist temple. Specific sorts of food offerings are permitted to be placed in front of graves, as is the burning of candles, but not the burning of the types of paper products prevalent at many other cemeteries. Perhaps because the cemetery is located on a completely flat plot of ground, there are no offices offering advice on grave location (geomancy consultation). The grounds are kept spotless.

The particular mix of memorial activities, museum displays, and Party-loving patriotism at the cemetery reflects the social conditions of Shanghai's elite at this moment in history. Shanghai identity itself is a form of elite identity, as Shanghai has been a symbol of wealth, cosmopolitanism, and successful commercial cultural endeavor for the entire reform era, if not longer. The actors, artists, singers, and intellectuals memorialized at the cemetery help distinguish such an elite Shanghai identity. The trick is to merge this identity with one of patriotism and love of the Party. To do so, key aspects of the lives of those memorialized are elided. Chen Duxiu's intellectual life and career as a communist are memorialized, but not his conflicts with Mao Zedong. Teresa Teng's commercial career and ties to Shanghai are memorialized, but not her support for the student protestors in Tiananmen Square in 1989, or her concert of "Democratic Songs Dedicated to China" performed in Hong Kong in May of that year. Feng Zikai's cartoons and lay Buddhism get a mention, but not his persecution during the Cultural Revolution. Communist party officials and war-time martyrs are blended together with these cultural figures as a singular cultural elite.

The second aspect of Fu Shou Yuan's elite identity is the manner in which it draws distinctions between proper religious activity and superstition. Space is made for a Buddhist temple and both Buddhist and Christian burials, as these two religions claim many adherents among Shanghai's elite and are officially recognized by the Chinese Communist Party. Daoism is also recognized as an official religion in China, but is more often associated with less elite and less urban temples than Buddhism. Buddhist priests offer to chant scripture for the souls of the deceased, a relatively intellectual activity. The associations of Buddhism with Buddhist philosophy enhances its status as an elite religion. While the cemetery offers an extensive range of flower products and living plants to be used in memorial services and to decorate graves, it does not sell paper houses, appliances, or mahjong tiles to be burnt in sacrifices to the ancestors, as such forms of memorialization reek of their association with low status, "low quality," rural people. Such practice is often labelled as "superstition," in contrast to the more elite forms of religious activity permitted at Fu Shou Yuan.

Non-elite cemeteries make no attempt to articulate the elitist ideologies apparent in Fu Shou Yuan and the Garden of Merit. They are not sites of patriotic education, and have no memorials dedicated to communist or nationalist martyrs, model workers, or celebrities. They have very few eco-burials or wall burial slots, as most people prefer to be buried in a traditional tomb. They do not divide their cemeteries into sections for people with different types of careers. At most, sections of such cemeteries may be differentiated by the period in which the tombs were sold or the design of the tombs. The tombs rarely display information on the careers of those buried there. Rather they memorialize the dead as family members: as mothers, fathers, aunts, uncles, brothers and sisters. At less elite graveyards, a wider range of sacrificial activities, such as burning paper offerings and setting off firecrackers, is accepted, and fewer workers are employed to keep the grounds spotless. In most of the non-elite cemeteries I visited, the grounds were relatively clean, but in a few of the least expensive ones there were weeds growing between grave plots, leftovers from sacrificial offerings scattered about (if foodstuffs placed on graves are not removed soon after they are offered, animals will approach and make a mess), and even litter. Those who cared about the upkeep of their family members' tombs and the adjacent grounds sometimes gave small red packets of money to graveyard personnel, as did the daughters of Mr. Wang. But not everyone did so and some tombs received little care.

Perhaps the ultimate contrast to cemeteries like the Fu Shou Yuan are those that memorialize events and people that the Communist Party would like to be forgotten. In Chongqing there is a small cemetery devoted to Red Guards who died during armed battles during the most violent year of the Cultural Revolution (1967). At the time, their bodies were given rushed burials in a park in an out of the way location. During the Cultural Revolution decade (1966–76), the work units of the dead built large tombstones for many of those buried there, as they had died in battles fought on behalf of those units. Many of the tombstones have

FIGURE 12. Tombs in a non-elite graveyard. Photo: Andrew B. Kipnis.

FIGURE 13. Trash in a non-elite graveyard. Photo: Andrew B. Kipnis.

Cultural-Revolution-era sayings etched onto them, and treat the deceased like wartime martyrs. During the 1970s, there were more than twenty such small cemeteries in Chongqing, but most were razed. The one that survived was located in a relatively remote corner of the city and received the support of a tolerant Party Secretary during the 1980s. After a period in which it was forbidden to mourn the dead in the graveyard, during the late 1990s and early 2000s families with loved ones buried there began to visit and conduct sacrifices and other mourning activities more openly. In 2009, the park in which the cemetery was located even managed to have the cemetery declared a local level site for historical preservation. However, since then, restrictions on visiting the cemetery have re-emerged. Under Xi Jinping, the cemetery has been surrounded by barbed wire. It is completely closed except for the Qing Ming holiday, when only relatives are allowed to visit. No photography of the tombstones is allowed.[10]

CALENDRICAL CYCLES IN THE SPACES OF THE DEAD

Activity at cemeteries follows an annual cycle. For much of the year, the only people there are those burying their relatives or visiting on death anniversaries (commonly observed dates include the seventh day and every seven days after that for seven weeks, the hundredth day, and the yearly anniversary). Often only a few groups of people will visit a cemetery on a given day. But on certain days marked in the Chinese traditional calendar, including Dong Zhi (the winter solstice), Zhong Yuan Festival (the fifteenth day of the seventh lunar month), Chong Yang Festival (the ninth day of the ninth lunar month), Winter Clothes Day (*Hanyi* 寒衣, the first day of the tenth lunar month), and Qing Ming (April 4 or 5), grave visits are common. Of these Qing Ming is by far the most important.

As China has urbanized, Qing Ming has become a more important holiday. While it has long been an occasion for "sweeping graves" (that is, cleaning and tidying up tombstones and carrying out simple ancestral sacrifices at gravesites), when graves were located close to the home, these activities were relatively routine. They could be done by a single person in the family (often the eldest woman able to walk), hardly interfered with her daily routine, and were activities that might be carried out on many other days during the year as well. But for people who live in a part of the country that is distant from their ancestral home, perhaps even in another country, or even for those who live in the city where they were raised, but whose parents are buried in a cemetery far from the urban center, visiting the grave becomes a major outing. It is often combined with visits to relatives living in the place where one's parents are buried, or family outings to urban gravesites with siblings, children and spouses. China made Qing Ming into a national holiday in 2008.

On Qing Ming, traffic jams around major cemeteries become so intense that many people elect to do their grave visits during the preceding weeks. Even then, on weekend days during the month before Qing Ming, traffic jams are common. Vendors line the streets near the entrance to the cemetery selling flowers and (at non-elite cemeteries) spirit money and other paper offerings. Families will often buy some flowers or paper offerings and bring some sacrificial food (fruit, rice, steamed bread, or dumplings, and the favorite dishes of the deceased), and sometime liquor and cigarettes for male ancestors. They will clean up the grave a bit, removing any leaves that have fallen on it and pulling up any weeds that are growing near it. They will lay the food and flowers on the grave and bow or kowtow in front of the grave, usually one at a time in age order. While performing bows, they will often speak to their deceased ancestor, using an appropriate kinship term to address her or him, announcing who they are, and perhaps telling the ancestor a bit of family or personal news. If the cemetery is a non-elite one that allows the burning of paper offerings, they will take turns burning paper offerings in a bucket (provided by cemeteries at the entrance) that is placed in front of the tombstone. Finally, they might give a graveyard attendant a tip in a red envelope and ask him or her to keep the grave clean during the coming year. Afterwards, those who have come by car in family groupings will often go out to a rural restaurant or another rural destination in the vicinity of the graveyard, turning the outing into a day-long event. Those who are not able to visit their ancestor's grave on Qing Ming might hire someone else to do the grave sweeping and sacrifice for them, and many cemeteries have even set up ways of doing so by smartphone.

It is difficult to say exactly what percentage of urban people who visit graves on Qing Ming literally believe that their ancestors are present in another world or that the items burned for them and sacrificially placed on graves actually do these ancestors any good. But the practice is taken as a display of filial piety, and many Chinese do believe this virtue is an important one. The link of ancestral sacrifice to filial piety is a delicate issue for the Chinese Communist Party. On the one hand, it wants Chinese adults to take good care of their aging parents, as the government fears needing to provide healthcare and significant pensions for all aged people. On the other hand, some in the Party have long campaigned against spending money on funerary activities, and try to dissociate filial piety from activities devoted to the care of ancestors after their death, constantly repeating the slogan "Thick Care, Thin Funerals" (厚养薄葬). Nevertheless, cemeteries often claim that they are promoting the virtue of filial piety in their attempts to legitimate themselves in the eyes of the government, and the public itself clearly views proper treatment of deceased ancestors as an outward sign of filial virtue. The internet is full of advice on how to act properly during Qing Ming grave visits.

Just as elite cemeteries reveal complex mixtures of Party propaganda, strategies of social distinction, and popular desires to memorialize ancestors, so does the rise in importance of Qing Ming as a national holiday involve an intricate mixture of commercial, popular, and state support. The popularity of the festival suggest that people embrace certain forms of filial piety and familial activity. The

OF SPACE AND PLACE   51

state itself promotes filial piety and has made Qing Ming into a national holiday. Commercial actors, from cemeteries to street vendors, seek ways of profiting from the enthusiasm.

CONCLUSION

As China urbanizes, the spaces of the dead have been increasingly separated from the spaces of the living. This separation is a global phenomenon. Philippe Aries (1975, 1983) depicts death as becoming invisible in Western societies, while Thomas Laqueur (2015) traces the rise of the modern cemetery as a sanitized, park-like space in the nineteenth and twentieth centuries. As death is separated from life, it arguably becomes more fearsome, more unknown, and more haunting.

But this separation should not only be seen in a negative light; it is also productive. Cemeteries are spaces to contest the politics of memory. In the case of Fu Shou Yuan, a cemetery actually houses a museum. In providing a platform for public memory, cemeteries also provide a platform for practices of social distinction. Claims to elite status can be made by memorializing one's ancestors in a glorious manner. Finally, the very fact that the spaces of the dead are haunted creates the need to deal with ghosts. This makes visiting cemeteries a semi-heroic deed in itself, a sacrifice that is worthy of being labelled with the virtue of filial piety. It also creates the grounds for practices to neutralize the haunting, such as visiting a bustling district of the city or stepping over fire and consuming warm sugary drinks after visiting a cemetery.

Though the separation of life from death in urbanization is a global phenomenon, we should note the ways in which this transformation involves culturally specific Chinese elements. The concepts of filial piety and Yin energy have long histories in China, while the role of Communist Party propaganda in cemetery construction and management reflects the place of the Party in twenty-first century China.

4

Of Strangers and Kin

Moral Family and Ghastly Strangers in Urban Sociality

In a famous essay on the religious landscape of Taiwan during the 1960s, Arthur Wolf (1974) argued that the types of supernatural entities worshipped there (gods, ghosts, and ancestors) mirrored the categories of people salient in people's lives: government officials, strangers, and kin. Gods were like officials in that they possessed the power to greatly alter the life circumstances of families and communities, for both better and worse. Ghosts resembled malevolent strangers who wreaked havoc in the lives of anyone that they came across. Like aggressive and potentially violent beggars, they needed to be appeased just to prevent them from causing harm. Ancestors resembled familial elders who worked for the benefit of their descendants, though they could become angry if neglected. Wolf's discussion of the distinction between ancestors/kin and ghosts/strangers provide an excellent lens for considering the relationship of funerary ritual to the categories of strangers and kin.

Wolf's essay has been discussed by a number of scholars. Three of those discussions relate directly to the category of ghosts and resonate with the topics of this chapter. First, Stephan Feuchtwang (2010) argues that ghosts can be kin as well as strangers. In his analysis, ghosts are dead people who have not been given proper funerary rites and thus do not become ancestors. Feuchtwang suggests that the entire purpose of a properly conducted funeral and burial is to transform the dead into ancestors rather than allowing them to become ghosts. Second, Robert Weller (1987; 1999) points out that in rural Taiwan, in addition to wreaking havoc, ghosts can bring benefits to individuals if worshipped properly. However, transactions with ghosts must be done on a contract basis, benefit an individual rather than a family or community, and are often immoral. Finally, in a book about Chinese urbanization as a transformation from a society of kin to a society of strangers (and, hence, about the importance of the forms of morality that apply to strangers for modern China), Haiyan Lee (2014, 59–70) notes that urban interactions with ghosts (and strangers) can be spiritual, erotic, and energizing as well as dangerous, and that urbanization itself is often accompanied by a transformation of ghost stories from a depiction of the dangers of the world to a type of entertainment.

This chapter uses death ritual and memorialization as a lens to examine how relationships within families and with strangers have transformed during the process of urbanization. It focuses on the social roles strangers and various types of kin play in life, on the construction of "strangers" and "kin" as categories for thought and social action, and on the role of imagining ghosts in contemporary societies. It sees urbanization not as the simple replacement of a society of kin by a society of strangers, but as a transformation in the places of kin and strangers in our lives, as well as a transformation in our imagination of ghosts. Like Wolf, I argue that there is a strong overlap between the imagination of ghosts and strangers, but I see this overlap as increasing in strength in the process of urbanization rather than as a vestige of a traditional, rural society. Feuchtwang's arguments about the relationships among ghosts, ancestors, and funerary ritual may accurately reflect traditional rural Chinese society. But I see urbanization as involving a shift in imagining ghosts away from the way that Feuchtwang depicts them. In urbanized China, ghosts seem more like strangers than like kin who have not been treated properly. From Weller, I borrow the insight that urbanization is often accompanied by increasing commercialization and a deepening division of labor, both of which increase the importance of strangers and contractual economic relations in our lives, but I do not see these relationships as necessarily amoral. From Lee, I build on the insight that ideas about ghosts also transform in the process of urbanization and that this transformation resonates with the roles that strangers come to play in our lives.

TRANSFORMING KINSHIP AND SOCIAL RELATIONSHIPS IN URBAN CHINA

Much has been written about how family life in China is changing as it urbanizes.[1] Household size is decreasing, birth rates have fallen, age of marriage is rising, and patriarchal, patrilineal family structures are losing their importance. While these broad trends are accepted by most scholars, the causes of these changes, as well as their implications for social relations, childcare, and gender relations, and the way these changes differentially affect families of different class and social backgrounds, remain issues for debate. For example, while some scholars emphasize the importance of conjugal relationships, love marriages, and a culture of dating and individualism, others point out that the extremely high cost of housing in China's large urban areas gives parents an important role to play in the lives of their adult children. Since they must be relied upon for the financial resources to purchase housing, parents often have a voice in decisions about who to marry. Moreover, if the family is not wealthy, and cannot afford separate apartments for grandparents and parents, three-generation households are not uncommon. Finally, grandparents often provide childcare for their grandchildren, so that both husband and wife can work to pay off the mortgage. Class and social variation is important here. Families that have migrated to cities from the countryside differ from families that have a multigenerational history of residing in the same urban area, and wealthy families have different familial strategies than impoverished ones.

While some scholars debate the extent to which the birth control policy or "modernization factors" are the primary cause of China's rapid reduction in birth rates (Whyte, Wang, and Cai 2015), it is clear that family life in urban China has been shaped by government policy. From 1980 to 2016, urban China was under a one-child policy. As a consequence, the one-child family has become a social norm. Rather than simply an overall low fertility rate, in which the average is about one child per couple, but some couples have no children, some have one, some have two, and a small minority have three or more, in urban China almost every couple has exactly one child. Moreover, in urban China retirement ages are relatively young, usually under sixty, so that grandparents have much time to devote to their families. In addition, expectations for marriage are high. Through the institution of "fake" marriages, even the majority of gay and lesbian urbanites are able to present themselves as belonging to a "normal" family. The 4:2:1 family structure, in which four grandparents and two parents dote on one grandchild, is "normal" both in the statistical sense and in the expectations of urban dwellers. As was the case for Mr. Wang, many of the people in their late seventies and eighties during the second decade of the twenty-first century have several siblings and children, but one grandchild per child.

For anthropologists, kinship is an expansive social category. It includes a broad range of social relationships beyond those based in birth and marriage. Some anthropologists thus prefer the word "relatedness" rather than "kinship." The analysis of relatedness includes both those who count as "family members" and those, who, technically, do not. In China, such a conception of kinship is bolstered by the fact that many people use kin terms like auntie, uncle, sister, and brother to address people who are not literally their kin. Fei Xiaotong (1992), perhaps the most famous Chinese anthropologist of all, conceptualized Chinese social relations as a series of concentric circles; starting with the self and close relatives, one's social network branched out in rings to include ever more distant friends and acquaintances. In constructing these networks, sharp lines were never drawn between kin and non-kin. But in some contexts, the distinctions between kin and non-kin matter, and both the shape of the networks of urban Chinese and the importance of the distinction between kin and non-kin have evolved as China has urbanized.

Two shifts in the way China is governed have had a heavy influence on general patterns of relatedness in urban China since 1978. First has been the reduction in importance of the work unit. During the Maoist era, work units structured all aspects of their employees' lives, including housing. As people lived in housing blocks alongside those who worked in the same work unit, and as school districts were often aligned with housing arrangements (some schools were even directly controlled by the work units themselves), the categories of colleague, neighbor, and classmate often overlapped and community relationships could be as close and complicated as kinship relationships. Now that work units have become less important and housing has become a matter of private ownership, relationships within apartment blocks have become less important. Neighbors often do not know each other. Though wide-ranging social networks can be important for finding jobs, the distinction between kin and other forms of social relationships has increased in importance because the stability of communities has declined and few other than kin maintain lifelong relationships. Moreover, the demise of the work unit as a provider of so many goods and services has led urbanites to rely on commercial businesses, leading to an increased role for strangers and acquaintances in everyday life.

Yet the legacies of the work-unit era have not completely disappeared. There are still a few large employers that act in ways similar to traditional work units, including universities and some other government sector employers. Moreover, for urbanites of Mr. Wang's age, employment during the work-unit era resulted in a wide array of privileges, including generous pensions and apartment ownership, that influence their relationships with their children and raise issues of inheritance.

The second factor shaping social relations in urban China today has been a loosening of the household registration policy and the resulting high rate of rural-urban migration. Chinese cities are increasingly populated by people who were neither born nor raised there. In many cases the relationship of these people to the cities where they live is tenuous. They do not hold local household registrations. They do not belong to networks of classmates who graduated from the same local schools, though some might form networks of people who migrated from the same place. Generally speaking, if such people die in the city, their funeral will not be held there. Overall, both the demise of the work unit and rise of migration have dis-embedded Chinese urbanites from previously existing communities. Especially for those unable to form new communities in urban areas, the absence of non-kin-based networks or communities makes the distinction between family members and non-family members more important.

RELATEDNESS IN DEATH RITUAL

The study of how funerary ritual constructs family contributes nuance to our understanding of relatedness. Urban funerals are increasingly family affairs rather events for a community. In some western Chinese cities, as well as places where work units remain important, urban funerals can become community events. Work units or well-organized communities set up entertainment tents outside of apartment blocks during the period between a death and the funeral; work units may also organize transportation for large groups of colleagues to go to the funeral home. But in cities like Jinan and Nanjing, several one-stop dragon entrepreneurs told me that funerals increasingly only involve small groups of relatives. Without a work unit organizing the event, the only people who attend are those invited by the children of the deceased, and these are usually only close relatives. Moreover, as Chinese urbanites live longer lives, they become more socially isolated. Their friends, siblings, and spouses might be too old and frail to leave the home and attend a funeral. In this way, Mr. Wang's funeral was typical.

The dynamics of funeral attendance in urban areas reverse those of rural China, both past and present. In rural China, the older a deceased person, the more likely that a large number of people would attend the funeral. In rural China only those who were younger in a genealogical sense (belonging to a younger generational cohort according to lineage systems of generation names) would attend funerals. But because the manner of calculating genealogical relatedness could be quite expansive, and because members of extended families often live in the general vicinity of the deceased, rural funerals for elder people could be quite well-attended events. In some rural communities, the number of people attending a funeral reflects the prestige and importance of the family of the deceased. Invitations are not required to attend a funeral, or at least to pay respects to the family of the deceased before the funeral, and some families arrange activities to attract acquaintances and even strangers to the funeral. There could be stages with opera performances. Even more surprisingly, in some rural Taiwanese burial processions, "electric flower cars" (motorized stages like those used in parades) with strippers on them follow the line of cars to a cemetery where the deceased will be buried. Attracting a crowd as well as entertaining the ghosts are the stated functions of the performances.[2]

While I did not come across any funerals with strippers in the course of my research, I did hear about several well-attended funerals in villages on the outskirts of Nanjing. In one case a rural family kept the body of their deceased father at home in a refrigerated casket for five days while friends, relatives, and well-wishers dropped by to pay their respects. Everyone who came gave a cash gift (which was recorded in the gift register) and was treated to a banquet. A stage for opera performances was set up in the courtyard of one of the father's five children's houses, while banquet tables were set up in the other homes. The one-stop dragon entrepreneur who organized the event told me that there were more than a hundred banquet tables, each seating up to ten people, and that over the five-day period several thousand people consumed more than five thousand meals. The five children and their spouses had all set up successful businesses and had widespread social networks as a result. Though this funeral may have been an extreme case, three one-stop dragon entrepreneurs who worked in both rural and urban Nanjing told me that rural funerals were generally larger than urban ones. At the least, most people who lived in a given village would attend the funerals of all elderly people who passed away there.

In urban China too, exceptionally privileged or famous people might hold well-attended funerals. All of the urban funeral parlors I visited had at least one or two large rooms designed for such funerals. In 2014, a one-stop dragon entrepreneur told me:

> Three types of people have large funerals. First are important government officials who have appointed many underlings. Then all of the people this person appointed and their family members are likely to come to the funeral. The second is someone who currently holds considerable power in either government or a large business, whose father or mother passes away. Then all of the people who wish to network with the person in power, no matter how weak their relationship is with that person, will try to come to the funeral and give a cash gift or at least present a flower wreath. The third type are academics who had many students and trained many successful people. Then all of the students of the academic will come to the funeral.

In the case of famous professors, universities often will often work with the family of the deceased to help organize the funeral. Through its union (工会), it will pay for most of the expense of the funeral, publicize the funeral to all staff at the same university, invite staff members to attend, and even arrange transportation from the university to the funeral. As I was affiliated with various universities during the course of my research, I also attended several funerals in this way. Once the funeral is publicized by the university, former students who work outside of the university will learn of it and publicize it to their networks on social media. At one of the university-organized funerals I attended, I counted over 130 people.

For high-level cadres who work in government work units, funerary committees are in charge of determining the level of grandeur and relative size of the funeral. For powerful Party members whose parents pass away, funerary committees would not be involved if the parents themselves were not officials. But, often enough, powerful cadres are also the children of powerful officials. Under Xi Jinping, there has been an emphasis on restricting the size of such funerals to prevent corruption. In Nanjing, funeral home workers told me that spending on funerals for mid- to high-ranking cadres dropped from about 200,000 yuan in 2012, to about 50,000 yuan in 2014 (Xi came to power in 2013; an average funeral cost in the range of 10,000–20,000 yuan during that period). Demand for the largest rooms at the funeral parlor also dropped. In 2016, the government further tightened the regulations surrounding the family rituals of Party members. In the city of Harbin, for example, funerals for the parents of Party cadres were supposed to be limited to one hundred people, all of whom had to be relatives (Piao 2016; Zhao 2016).

The overall trend towards smaller funerals in urban areas reflects the declining importance of broader forms of community in urbanizing China, but it also reveals several nuances and inverted patterns within this overall trend. Particular forms of community can still be important and funerals can be platforms for building these communities. These include the communities related to "lineages" of professionals as defined by students taught by a particular professor, the communities formed by still intact work units, and the communities formed by villages-in-the-city and villages on the outskirts of urban areas. These villages are often empowered during processes of urbanization; villages-in-the-city can receive forms of compensation which transform them into corporate entities (see Kipnis 2016, 52–62, 174–180), while villages on the fringes of cities may experience increasing chances to develop real estate and other business opportunities. Finally, many people would like to construct relationships with powerful people in business or government. The anti-corruption policies of Xi Jinping have the effect of limiting these networks for the families of Party cadres, but the incentives for constructing these relationships remain. Ironically, the policies of Xi may have the effect of making social relationships for high-ranking cadres resemble those of more ordinary people. For both groups, the demise of various forms of community mean that very few social relationships occupy the space between kinship and the relationships among acquaintances and strangers. In this sense, the stranger/kin dichotomy is reinforced. For such people, as was the case for Mr. Wang, all those who attend funerals are family.

Funerary ritual also tends to present familial relationships in patriarchal ways. It reinforces age and gender hierarchies. Such hierarchies may not be so important in many aspects of urban life, but funerary ritual is a time for respecting elders, and, hence, certain patriarchal arrangements that are imagined as tradition. Most one-stop dragon entrepreneurs are men from the countryside, and they will usually try to arrange those attending a funeral to stand and bow to the deceased in age-ordered groupings, with the eldest children going first. For roles involving carrying items to the gravesite, or performing particular ritual actions at the grave or with the cinerary casket, sons and their sons are usually chosen over daughters, granddaughters, and the sons of daughters. However, many urban families confound typical patriarchal arrangements. There may be daughters and no sons, sons who produced no grandsons, or assertive elder daughters who insist on age-order groupings that place them above their younger brothers. Some one-stop dragon entrepreneurs also give advice on gendered forms of taboo and ritual preference. For example, at one burial ceremony I witnessed, the family, following the instructions of a one-stop dragon entrepreneur, had brought bananas, dumplings, and a tofu dish to be used as sacrificial offerings on the grave. After the interment, the entrepreneur told the daughters of the deceased to take the bananas home and eat them, and the son to consume the dumplings. These foodstuffs, now blessed with the ancestor's energy, would be respectively most beneficial for female and male reproductive health.

Social media (Wechat) feeds from funeral homes likewise provide gendered advice. One described how to properly visit graves over Qing Ming. It instructed families visiting graves to bow in the following order: eldest son, eldest daughter, second son, second daughter, and so on. It also urged women not to wear brightly colored clothes when visiting cemeteries and stated that pregnant women should never visit graves. Finally, when registering the names of the families who give "white envelopes" at funerals, or writing the names of those who give flower wreaths at funerals on couplets that are attached to the wreaths, it is often the name of the ritually designated "head of household" that is used, and usually that is the eldest man in the family.

Weeping also constructs kin relations in a gendered way. In some parts of rural China, families paid professional mourners to attend funerals and sob loudly. In most parts of rural China, weeping at funerals was considered to be a female responsibility. In urban China, however, loud or excessive crying is considered uncivilized. Buddhist priests say that excessive sobbing is likely to make the soul of the deceased too attached to this world, and unable to make the transition to Western Paradise. In the urban funerals and interment rituals I witnessed, daughters would often visibly cry at their mother's or father's funeral, but not very loudly. I did not see any urban men cry at funerals.

KINSHIP ON TOMBSTONES

Another way of understanding how kinship is changing in China and how kinship is affected by urbanization is by examining tombstones and wall burial plaques in cemeteries. These forms of memorialization display whose ashes are buried together in the same place, and usually list the names of the descendants of those whose ashes are buried. Tombstones can also pay homage to the deceased for being loving or caring fathers, mothers, grandparents, aunts, or uncles.

Contemporary tombstones reveal a few general patterns, which were exemplified in the case of Mr. Wang. Most people are buried with their spouses, on tombs that give the names of all of their children, their children's spouses, and their grandchildren. Names are carved vertically, with the man's name on the right of tombstone or plaque as you face it and the woman's on the left. As was the case with Mr. Wang, in some regions and cemeteries, the surnames of the deceased are painted in red rather than black, to indicate that the family lives on even though the individual has passed away. These patterns indicate a general shift away from traditional patterns of patrilineal Chinese kinship to a more bilateral method of reckoning who belongs to one's family. On the tombstone, sons, daughters, sons-in-law, and daughters-in-law all have equivalent positions. Paternal grandsons, maternal grandsons, and granddaughters through either sons or daughters likewise have equivalent positions. The names of deceased women use their natal surnames, and these surnames are often painted in red, which makes the tombstone as much a homage to the family indicated by the wife's surname as to the family indicated by the husband's.

FIGURE 14. Tombstone with names painted in red and black. Photo: Andrew B. Kipnis.

But despite a shift towards bilateral kinship, a close reading of tombstones suggests that traditional Chinese patriarchy still leaves a legacy. First, placing the man's name on the right gives him the hierarchically upper position. Much rarer, but more interesting, are those cases where a threesome of a man with two wives are buried together. On such tombstones the names of all of the children and grandchildren by both of the wives are typically displayed. Such families exist either because the man had two wives before the founding of the People's Republic of China in 1949, when polygyny was legal, or because a man's first wife died at a relatively early age and he remarried and also had children by a second wife. As might be expected, such tombstones are more prevalent in historically older sections of graveyards (because of the end of legal polygyny in 1949), and more prevalent in rural cemeteries than urban ones. But in my examination of close to ten thousand tombstones in many cemeteries, I have never seen a tombstone over a grave shared by a wife and both of her husbands. While the Han-dominated regions of China never practiced polyandry, there both were and are many cases in which a woman's first husband dies and she remarries a second man. Indeed, widowed women remarrying are probably almost as common as widowed men doing so, and I even know of several cases in which women had children with both their first and second husbands. But to memorialize a woman as having had two husbands, or to list the children she had by her first husband and second husband as all belonging to the same family, define "family" in ways that are too scandalous to permanently carve into memory on a tombstone. Such a form of memorialization would violate basic principles of patrilineal familial formation.

Though most people are buried with a spouse, a substantial minority are not. This is because either they were not married at the time of death or because the living spouse chooses to leave open the option of being buried separately. Many surviving spouses who plan on being buried with their partners—women more often than men—will have their names carved on the tombstone but left in red. In a section of a working-class cemetery in which people who passed away during the 1990s had their ashes buried, I counted eighty-one tombstones with a dead husband and the name of a still-living wife, but only twenty-two with a dead wife and a still-living husband. In a section of the same cemetery with people who passed away roughly a decade later, I counted 153 tombstones with a dead husband and a still-living wife, but only seventy-five with a dead wife and a still-living husband. Each of the two graveyard sections had approximately eight hundred tombstones in total. As might be expected, there are more tombstones with surviving spouses in the newer section, but the changing ratios of husbands to wives can be interpreted in several ways. First, men die before their wives more often than women die before their husbands. According to World Bank data available online, in China as a whole during 2016, 88 percent of women survived to the age of sixty-five, but only 84 percent of men.[3] I suspect that this fact accounts for some but not all of the disparity. Second, the cemetery workers I asked about this phenomenon suggested that men whose wives have passed away are considering remarriage more often than women whose husbands have passed away. I find this suggestion quite reasonable. To be buried with one's spouse suggests a form of permanent union that potential new partners might find objectionable. We should note, however, that even if men consider remarriage more often than women, men do not necessarily remarry at greater rates than women. Remarriage takes a man and a woman, and, in most cases I know of, remarriage involves couples in which both members were married once before.[4] Finally, the decline in the ratio of the number of tombstones with a surviving wife to those with a surviving husband (81:22, or nearly 4:1, from the 1990s, reducing to 153:75 or just over 2:1 during the 2000s) could indicate that preferences for remarriage are becoming more gender-balanced.

During the imperial period before 1911, widows in China were actively encouraged not to remarry. Women who lived many years as a widow and then died without ever having remarried could be memorialized as "chaste widows." While the government no longer encourages this practice, and while contemporary women remarry almost as often as contemporary men, idealizations of proper behavior for women seem to have had a lasting, but perhaps diminishing influence on practices of memorialization. Complementing the data from tombstones with couples' names on them are data from tombstones with just one person buried. In the two cemetery sections discussed above, I found fifty graves for a single woman, but only twenty-nine for solitary men. Many of these tombstones listed the names of the children of the deceased individual, but not his or her spouse. In a wall burial section of the Garden of Merit, I counted ninety-five plaques with the name of a solitary woman, but only sixty-eight for a solitary man. In short, women are more likely to be buried without a partner than men, and only men can be buried with two partners.

In addition to hints about gender relations and patterns of remarriage, cemeteries reveal the central place of children in contemporary Chinese families. During the imperial period, children were almost never memorialized. Classical ritual texts suggest that children who died before the age of eight should receive no funerals, while older children were to receive limited funerals. In practice, most poorer people simply abandoned the corpses of young children and babies in open fields to be eaten by animals. Though Confucian scholars sometimes criticized the practice, many rural people felt that dead babies or children harbored fearful spirits that would return to the family if the children were given a proper burial. At the end of the Qing dynasty, some officials constructed "baby towers" where people could place the bodies of deceased infants. These towers could accommodate thousands of small corpses in deep pits with a tower constructed on top. Though they offered no place to memorialize the names of the deceased and were not the site of any ritual, they kept animals away from the corpses (for more on baby towers and the late-imperial treatment of dead infants see Snyder-Reinke 2019).

In an extremely poor country where the majority of children died before reaching maturity, it is perhaps not that shocking that dead children were treated this way.[5] But over the twentieth century, China has undergone a demographic transition. Many fewer children are born, almost all of them survive, and the death of a child has become the most severe form of tragedy that a family can face. Yunxiang Yan (2016) calls the central place of children in contemporary Chinese households "descending familism." The 4:2:1 family structure makes these sentiments especially important for urban households. Now some of the most elaborate tombstones in Chinese cemeteries are reserved for children. They can contain carvings of toys and etchings of children's characters from popular culture, as well as epitaphs declaring the everlasting love of the parents and other relatives who cared for them. In cemeteries like the Fu Shou Yuan, graves for children are given a separate section of the cemetery (see figure 11 in chapter 3). What is so striking in the Chinese case is the way that these forms of memorialization completely reverse the customs of a pre-urbanized, pre-demographic transition China. They vividly illustrate both the continuing importance of family in urban China, and the shift of the symbolic center of contemporary families from the ancestor to the child. Such a reorientation also speaks to the simplification of familial structures that has occurred during the post-Mao era. Many people could be descended from a single ancestor. Consequently, conducting funerary rites for an extremely elderly person could involve a large extended family or even an entire community. Families centered around a single child are much smaller.

A final trend observable in a minority of cemeteries is a rise in individualism. While some analysts describe rising individualism as a China-wide phenomenon (see, for example, Yan 2010), in the cemeteries I visited, individualism on tombstones existed only in a few cases in the most elite graveyards, though it did seem to be a rising trend there. In non-elite graveyards, almost everyone was buried with someone else. Single people were often buried with another single person from the same family—an aunt with a niece, for example. Sometimes two men could be buried with a woman, but they would not be her two husbands. Rather it would be a husband, a wife, and a single brother of the husband. When an individual was buried alone, the tombstones would always list the relatives who grieved the deceased and had paid for the burial and tombstone. Finally, as described above, many tombstones of individual people would still leave the surname of the deceased person in red, implying that their family lived on and framing the life of the deceased as one of sacrifice and devotion to the family cause. But in elite graveyards, I not only noticed more single burials, but also counted that the number of single burials increased from about 3 percent to 10 percent when comparing graveyard sections from the 1990s and the 2000s. Moreover, among those buried after 2015 in the Garden of Merit, I even noticed a few wall burial plates that had nothing inscribed but the name of the person buried there. The plate gave no indication that the person had ever belonged to any family. In short, memorialization is overwhelmingly a family affair, especially for lower- and middle-class people. Individualized memorialization, however, has become a small but growing trend among the elite.

STIGMATIZED STRANGERS IN THE FUNERARY INDUSTRY

As urbanization proceeds, as commercialism becomes the predominant form of economic exchange, and as family structures evolve and reduce in size, strangers come to play a larger role in the average person's life. Such is particularly the case in the funerary industry. Rather than being directed and enacted by family members, the ritual is entrusted to the strangers who work in funeral homes, crematoriums, cemeteries and one-stop dragon businesses. Not only has urbanization in China allowed for the rise of this entirely new industry, it also has given birth to the business of training and certifying workers for this sector.

Most of the small private businesses in the funerary sector are run by the rural-urban migrants who undertake the majority of the dirty, dangerous, or despised occupations in urban China. The large cemeteries and state-owned funeral homes, however, tend to hire graduates of the technical school (大专) or, now, university (本科) programs that specialize in training workers for this sector. Because work for any aspect of the funerary industry tends to be stigmatized, these graduates also tend to be rural-urban migrants. Their migration, however, takes a detour through a formal stint at a university.

The establishment of tertiary courses for funerary workers began at the Changsha Social Work College (长沙民政职业技术学校) in 1995.[6] During the 1990s, a history and literature professor with interests in traditional funerary rites, Wang Fuzi, noticed the increasing number of funeral homes and cemeteries in China's rapidly growing urban areas. He visited many funeral homes and cemeteries around the country and, in 1993, wrote a formal report on establishing a course in funerary studies. He received permission to do so at the secondary specialized level (中专) and took in his first class of almost one hundred students in September of 1995. The course added a few specialized classes in funerary ritual, presenting and cremating corpses, and funerary business management to a large range of general education courses in Chinese, English, history, business management, and politics. It also arranged for students to do internships at funerary industry businesses during the summer months. In 1999, the teachers of the course were able to organize themselves into a separate department, and in 2000 they upgraded the course from a specialized secondary course to a specialized tertiary course. In the same year they divided the course into two majors—one in funerary ritual technology and management and one in cemetery design (including both landscape and tombstone design). In 2006, they split up the funerary ritual technology and management major into three separate majors—one in funerary service (殡仪服务), one in funerary equipment (especially the operation and repair of crematory ovens), and one in embalming and preparing corpses for viewing—to arrive at the present arrangement of four majors in total. In the twenty years between 1995 and 2015, over five thousand students graduated from its courses. As of 2017, the school was admitting close to 350 students per year. In 2012, the Department of Funerary Studies was upgraded to the School of Funerary Studies (殡仪学院), in recognition of the large number of students it was educating. In 2017, the school was also in the process of upgrading the degree from a three-year tertiary short course to a four-year university degree. As the first and by far the largest such program in the country, the School of Funerary Studies has also been active in accrediting other courses around China, as well as providing teaching materials and textbooks for these courses.

The strength of the program can be seen in the networks of its graduates around the country. Located in Hunan province, the school gets about half of its students from Hunan and the rest from all over the country. Its graduates have set up formal alumni associations in twenty-seven of China's thirty-two provinces, and act as the top leader or vice leader of more than three hundred municipal funeral homes across China. Its students have the opportunity to serve as summer interns in more than twenty funeral homes around China. They work at graveyards, funeral homes, crematoriums, and funeral equipment manufacturers, and many have set up their own businesses. Often, alumni in charge of hiring new funerary workers call up the School to lure students to leave for work opportunities before they even graduate. Those that offer internship opportunities for students from the school often hire their interns after they graduate.

The success of the program can be credited to the foresight of Professor Wang, or simply to being in the right place at the right time. The rate of urbanization in China directly correlates to the overall size of the funerary sector, as rural people do not need professional funerary services. The fact that China's urbanization has also been associated with rapid economic development has given the funerary services industry a second source of growth. The sector is growing both because the urban population is expanding and because the per capita income the population has to spend on funerals swells each year.

The careers of the following two students are typical.[7] Mr. Zhang (a pseudonym) came from a village in Hunan province. His family was poor, so he was attracted to the major for the economic benefits it could provide. He graduated in 1997, when the program offered a specialized secondary degree. He completed a summer internship in a municipal funeral home in Nanjing after his second year, and secured a job there after graduation. The job gave him Nanjing citizenship rights, an indication that his employer was willing to spend a considerable sum of money to sponsor his application for urban citizenship. He worked a series of different positions within the funeral home before rising to management in 2013. When I asked him about discrimination against funerary workers, he emphasized that though some people do discriminate against those working in the sector, by behaving in a dignified manner, you could demonstrate that you were a "quality" person and gain people's trust most of the time.

Ms. Bao (also a pseudonym) came from the western Chinese city of Wulumuqi (Urumqi). She graduated from the school in 2004, when it was a tertiary program, and was attracted to the major because it offered excellent chances of securing a permanent, high-paying, urban job. She married a classmate and said that she was one of eleven couples from her class who married. She joked that "people say that in this profession men can't find wives and women can't find husbands, so the best solution is to devour (消化) each other." She and her husband both managed to find jobs in her home city, and her husband had just passed a test to become a permanent worker there, so now they are both permanent residents of Wulumuqi. In 2012, they had twins.

Two aspects of these brief life histories deserve emphasis. First, in both cases, men from the countryside (Mr. Zhang and Ms. Bao's husband) were able to secure permanent citizenship rights in major urban centers. The men secured local citizenship rights through the sponsorship of their employers, indicating that their workplaces highly valued their services. While not all rural-to-urban migrants working in the funeral industry can secure urban citizenship rights, success in this regard is more common for funerary sector workers than for migrants working in other sectors. Second, both had internalized an awareness of the stigmatization of funerary workers. A study of funerary sector workers in Anhui province concluded that this stigma leads to widespread psychological problems for those working in the sector (Ren 2017).

A third example, this time of a one-stop dragon entrepreneur who never received any formal training, likewise reveals the dynamics of stigmatization and upward mobility. Mr. Cao came from a village on the outskirts of Yancheng, a mid-sized city in Jiangsu province about 250 kilometers from Nanjing. His father had been a lineage elder who arranged funerals for family members in the same village for free. During the 1980s, the father started helping distant relatives who lived in Yancheng with their funerals, often receiving gift payments in return. The work developed into a small business and the son was brought in to help during the mid-1990s. In 2002, the younger Mr. Cao decided to try to his luck in Nanjing. At first the Nanjing municipal government considered his business to be technically illegal; the state-run funeral home and work units were supposed to be in charge of arranging funerals. Nevertheless, Mr. Cao got some business by passing out business cards to nurses in hospitals, but he was not willing to risk renting a shopfront or advertising to the general public. As more and more work units went out of business, however, a larger percentage of people had no one to help arrange their funeral, and Mr. Cao's business boomed. By 2006 he was arranging close to six hundred funerals a year. He hired relatives from his hometown to help him with the business, bought two apartments in Nanjing, and, as the owner of urban apartments, was able to formally transfer his household registration to Nanjing. In 2012, the municipal authorities acknowledged the legitimacy of his line of work, and he began renting a shopfront for his business so he could display the cinerary caskets, longevity clothes, and other funerary paraphernalia he was selling. In 2016, he rented a more expensive shopfront, completely remodeled the interior, and moved into the upgraded facilities. Despite his successes, Mr. Cao has also felt the stigma associated with his occupation. He said that soon after he moved to Nanjing, he learned not to attempt to shake hands with any of his customers, as many of them shrunk away. He has never become friends with any of his former customers. He added that he never told his neighbors at his apartment building in Nanjing what he did for a living, and told his daughters that if anyone asked about their father's occupation, they should say that he was in the restaurant business. Despite moving his household registration to Nanjing, he kept his daughters in school in Yancheng to insulate them from the stigma of the family business. After they graduated from high school, he brought them to Nanjing and helped them get jobs in the real estate sector. Finally, Mr. Cao said that since he did not personally handle dead bodies, people did not discriminate against him as much as they did against people who worked in the funeral homes and crematoria.

The stigmatization of funerary workers was part of the reason that Professor Wang founded the program in Changsha during the 1990s. By making funerary work into an occupation that required a university degree, he hoped to raise the "quality" of the people involved in funerary work, thereby diminishing their stigma. As described in the last chapter, quality is a key concept in contemporary Chinese society. The government has dedicated itself to "raising the quality" of the population and uses the term in many of its policy documents and propaganda campaigns, especially those related to educational programs. People often use the term to discriminate against those whom they feel are below themselves, mocking them with the term "low quality." Most people also accept that education raises the quality of those who attain it. So Professor Wang's strategy was not illogical.

However, despite its desire to reduce stigma, the program owes its existence to, and feeds off of, the economic implications of this prejudice. Work in the funerary industry is easy to find not only because the sector is expanding, but also because many urban residents fear the stigma associated with the work. For the same reason, salaries and money-making opportunities are relatively high. Students who come to the program are often those with very low test scores on the university entrance exam, who could not have gained admittance to any other tertiary program. They are also often from relatively impoverished rural families, and find the promise of easy employment after graduation (or, in many cases, even before graduation) alluring. After graduation, many funerary workers marry other funerary workers so that they will not be subject to stigmatization during familial negotiations over marriage. They also often meet their spouses either at the School of Funerary Studies or through its alumni networks. The school's alumni associations thus become both socially and professionally important to the school's graduates, and the school benefits greatly from the contributions of its alumni.

STRANGERS, STIGMA, GHOSTS, AND THE IDEALIZATION OF FAMILY

Why are workers in the funerary industry stigmatized? A common anthropological answer would be that funerary workers are contaminated by the pollution of death (Bloch and Parry 1982). As a generalization, such an answer may be correct, but it does not explain how this pollution was managed differently when funerals were conducted by relatives. My speculations in this area return to the relationships among ghosts and strangers, as well as ideas about family and strangers in a rapidly urbanizing society.

In the last chapter, I suggested that the segregation of the living from the dead increases the fear of death, dead bodies, and ghosts in urban settings. But in addition to sheltering us from experiencing death and dead bodies, the segregation of the dead into the spaces of cemeteries also makes visits to the graves of one's own dead relatives into occasions when one must pass near the graves of complete strangers. When I did research in rural China during the 1980s, in a village where people buried their ancestors in the fields where they worked, I never heard stories about ghosts in the field (Kipnis 1997). But then and there, all of the people buried in the fields were considered to be ancestors. In urban settings, not only is the city a society of strangers, but the cemeteries are also full of dead strangers. The presence of unknown dead people makes cemeteries spookier than agricultural fields, even if people are also buried in the fields. References to the spookiness of cemeteries come in many forms in urban China. During the funeral of Mr. Wang, Mr. Chen formally introduced Mr. Wang to his new "neighbors" in the cemetery.

He also directed all of the participants in the funeral to step over fire at the end of the funeral, to counter the "Yin energy" of the cemetery they were leaving. The spookiness also stigmatizes workers in the funerary sector, who handle both the dead people of one's own family and those of strangers. A comparison with sexuality resonates: women who have sex with their husbands are looked upon as normal, moral, upright citizens, while women who have sex with strangers for money are looked upon as degenerate prostitutes.

James Watson (1982; 1988a) has argued that paid and stigmatized funerary workers were a standardized part of traditional Chinese funerals. But he did his research in a town in peri-urban Hong Kong that was already subject to the pressures of urbanization and modernization. Susan Naquin (1988, 54) suggests that in rural North China during the late nineteenth and early twentieth century, assistance at funerals for the great majority of non-wealthy farming households was provided by unpaid relatives and neighbours rather than paid specialists, while Zhou Shaoming (2009, 118, 130, 210) says the same about Eastern Shandong in both the pre- and post-revolutionary periods. I suspect that urbanization exacerbates the stigmatization of funerary workers, though there may also have been some regional diversity in the ways in which funerary rites were conducted in China.

In the categorization of Arthur Wolf, we could surmise that working with ancestors (that is, dead people in one's own family) contaminates the body less than working with ghosts (dead strangers). But, with reference to Feuchtwang, we would also need to acknowledge that the very meaning of being a ghost evolves. In traditional rural China, fearsome ghosts and spirits might be one's own kin who were not treated fairly in life or not given proper funerals. The babies who were thrown into baby towers or left for the animals in the fields were one type of fearsome spirit. In contemporary urban China, dead children receive top-grade funerals; it is only strangers who become ghosts. Moreover, the dead of urban cemeteries might be haunting ghosts even though they have had funerals. Strangers cannot be relied upon to either treat family members well in life or conduct their rituals properly.

Note also the construction of the categories of family and strangers in these conceptions of ghosts. In traditional Chinese society, one's extended family constituted most of one's social universe. But in such a society, or in a society that is imagined in this fashion, both good and evil would have to be located within the social universe of the extended family. Family members could become either harmful ghosts or benevolent ancestors. Familial relations themselves could be both good and bad. In contrast, in contemporary urban China, familial elders always become ancestors. While children who die before their time might not be considered ancestors, they at least become spirits who represent only the familial love that was devoted to them and the joy that they brought to the lives of family members. Evil and conflictual, exploitative relationships are imagined as occurring only with strangers (and those strangers who have become ghosts). As Robert Weller suggests, ghosts can help you gain fortune by successfully exploiting strangers, but not to enjoy harmonious relationships within your own family. Between 2017 and 2019, I often asked groups of Chinese students about ghost stories. While the students had many stories they could tell, none of the students I asked either told or had even heard of a ghost story in which the ghost was one of their own dead relatives. To depict a deceased relative as a ghost would imply that one's own family was a site of evil, a blasphemy against the sacred value of family.[8] The idealization of family and demonization of ghosts is a second way in which the process of urbanization dichotomizes the categories of family and strangers. Not only does the shrinking of forms of community beyond close family members make the distinction between kin and non-kin more clear, but the distinction between benevolent and exploitative relationships is also imagined as corresponding to the distinction between kin and strangers. In the social imaginary of funerary ritual, cemeteries, and memorialization at least, family is moral, while strangers are ghastly.

In urban settings, ghost stories narrate ghosts who harm strangers. Sometimes they are taken seriously. In the last chapter, we saw how the location and visibility of funeral homes affected real estate values in Hong Kong. But funeral homes are not the only macabre influence on real estate there. In addition, apartments, homes, or sometimes even entire apartment buildings where murders, suicides or unexplained accidental deaths have occurred rent and sell for discounted prices. There are numerous online databases that help real estate shoppers keep track of these places, known as "haunted dwellings" (凶宅). Like the spirits of deceased children who were thrown into baby towers, the ghosts who reside in haunted dwellings are a source of recurring forms of bad fortune. They speak to or possess the strangers who come to live in the haunted place in order to convince the new occupants to commit the same actions that led to their own downfall. But instead of harming members of the family into which they were born, these ghosts harm strangers. The prices for haunted houses are often 20 percent lower than for other houses; in some extreme cases they can be 50 percent lower.[9] In addition to haunted dwellings, there are also haunted places in Hong Kong that are associated with sites of mass death, where natural disasters or wartime executions occurred (see, for example, B. Chan 2016).

Of course the ghost stories themselves were often told in a playful manner, and most people I spoke to would not admit to believing in ghosts. Even the smartphone applications for locating haunted dwellings in Hong Kong use a symbol for haunted dwellings that looks more like the American cartoon character Casper the Friendly Ghost than any truly fearsome entity. In addition to a playful side, Chinese ghosts can have an erotic dimension. Stories in which beautiful female ghosts assume a human form to seduce unsuspecting men are common, and form the basis for the most popular Chinese movie about ghosts ever produced,

A Chinese Ghost Story.[10] As Haiyan Lee (2014) suggests, however, the playful, erotic sides of ghosts do not negate the imaginative association of ghosts with strangers, but rather give us a more nuanced appreciation of the role of strangers in urban life. Positive relations with strangers require an open mind, a playful attitude that welcomes the other to enter one's social universe. Non-arranged marriage, or forming new sexual relationships of any sort, necessitates leaving the confines of one's family and reaching out to strangers. Eroticism itself thrives on the unfamiliar and the erotics of urban living can include the erotics of mixing with strangers in public space (Pile 2005). Despite the possibilities of eroticism, the majority of the most downloaded ghost stories on popular story telling websites in Hong Kong (such as https://www.discuss.com.hk) feature two narrative elements. First, those who become ghosts are those who have been neglected by their families in both life and funerary ritual. They become "wandering ghosts" (游魂野鬼), precisely because of this neglect. They are metaphorically "homeless" in both life and death. Quite often they haunt public housing estates, where the elderly are sometimes given shelter for their last years. Second, even though the cause of their homelessness was familial, the people they end up harming are strangers. Such narratives speak to fears engendered in the process of urbanization, both about transformations in familial relations and the growing role of strangers in daily life. That is to say, they tell us both that the demise of extended families and communities increases the chances that we will die alone, and that as we depend more and more upon strangers in all aspects of our life, we become more vulnerable to harm.

5

Of Gifts and Commodities

Spending on the Dead While Providing for the Living

Economists often talk about "the economy" in the singular. The economy is where goods and services are exchanged for cash. Since cash is countable, by examining the economy as a single field, economists can mathematically analyze universal economic rules. Anthropologists, however, tend to see a diverse array of partially separable economic processes instead of a singular economy. They are interested not only in mathematical flows of money, but also in the moral rules and social logics that inform patterns of exchange. Some productive activities, like housework and childcare, may not involve the exchange of cash at all, but do involve strong moral norms as well as value creating forms of labor. In the case of the funeral of Mr. Wang, we saw how his younger daughter provided a great deal of care work in the hospital for free, partially because she saw this work as her moral duty as a daughter. But even if we restrict ourselves to discussing activities where cash is exchanged, we can observe differing social, moral, or legal frameworks that structure the ways in which exchange takes place. Giving cash as a gift, as occurred when the households of Mr. Wang's nieces and nephews visited the Wang family home altar before Mr. Wang's funeral, involves different expectations than paying cash to a funeral home for the services it provides. Giving cash as a gift recreates kinship relationships between households of givers and receivers. Paying cash to the funeral home, in contrast, does not establish a kin-like relation between the funeral home and the family holding the funeral. As they involve different types of social relationships, the two types of cash exchange also involve different sets of moral expectations.

My point here is not simply that the economists are wrong and the anthropologists are right. The whole point of money is to transcend difference. Money received as a gift can be turned around and spent at a funeral home. But even though money can be used to do almost anything, people tend to use money in specific ways, to categorize money according to specific purposes, and then to attach different moral and social rules to differing categories of money. There can be rent money, drinking money, lottery money, gift money, money for the grandchildren etc. This is as true of modern money as it was true of the so-called traditional, special-purpose currencies, like cowrie shells in New Guinea.[1] It is also as true in the formal economic realms of state taxation and business accountancy as it is in the informal economies of households or street peddlers. But alongside the relative universality of categorizing money, there usually exist forms of inventive morality, novel rule interpretation, or creative accounting that allow money of one type to be used as if it were money of another type. A strong analysis of the economic activities, moralities, and processes involved in funerals should depict both the different moral shapes this economic activity takes and the ways in which actors switch from one type of economic morality to another.

Distinctions among different forms of exchanging money often involve different ways of defining the social relationships between the people involved in the exchange. In the last chapter, we saw how patterns of kinship and modes of interacting with strangers have evolved as China urbanizes. This chapter carries this theme forward from an economic perspective. Funerary economic transactions influence four types of socioeconomic relationships. These are those within the household (defined here as a group who pool economic resources and share a common budget), the extended family (potentially including distant relatives, friends, and fictive kin relations), strangers who are to remain strangers, and the overarching political nation, that is, those who participate in markets regulated by the People's Republic of China.

Different forms of social relationships can be seen as involving different forms of capital. In pooling a budget, households are held together by economic capital—money. Extended families are held together by social capital, a form of trust extant in long-term social relations. The larger political regime is held together by political capital, that is, loyalty to the Chinese Communist Party. Large firms, like the cemeteries examined in chapter 3, secure favorable conditions for conducting business by bolstering the legitimacy of Party rule. People who want to keep strangers at arm's length, to make them remain strangers, strategically avoid sharing any form of capital. In manipulating their social relationships and forms of capital, economic actors sometimes attempt to transform one form of capital into another, thus blurring the boundaries among different types of economic morality.

The diversity and transformability of economic moralities in China today is driven in part by the legal ambiguity under which much economic activity takes place. Three types of legal ambiguity influence funerary economic activity: the ambiguity of ritual activities involving gods, ghosts, ancestors, or other "religious" or "superstitious" actors that could be labeled as illegal superstitions; the ambiguity of gifts given between households when the household receiving the gift could include a cadre or a business leader and the gift could be labeled as a bribe; and the ambiguity of small-scale businesses that neither obtain state licenses nor pay taxes. I begin by briefly reviewing patterns of urban economic development during the post-Mao era. I focus on the types of economic shifts that have affected most of China's larger urban areas. Then, I examine five forms of economic morality and exchange involved in funerals during the period of my research. This material constitutes the bulk of the chapter and derives mostly from my research in Nanjing, where I was able to collect relatively detailed economic data. Finally, I analyze the failed attempt of a large insurance firm to disrupt the entire funerary industry. Despite the failure of this particular attempt, the strategies and thought processes of the insurance company reveal much about patterns of economic exchange in contemporary urban China.

FROM PLAN AND WORK UNIT TO HOUSEHOLD REGISTRATION AND MARKET

During the Maoist era planning dominated the Chinese economy. Urban residents worked in work units. Housing was provided either through work units or the municipal government. Migration from rural areas was strictly regulated. Cities had many factories, and factory workers were considered both the largest and most important sector of urban employees. Almost all consumption took place in state-run stores. Though service in such stores could be poor, and often depended upon establishing some sort of relationship with a store clerk, the only alternative was to purchase goods illegally on the black market. Income levels were low, but alongside the poverty was a relatively high level of economic equality, at least among those who were official urban residents of the same municipality.

During the post-Mao era, economic reforms have come one on top of another. While a detailed history of these reforms is beyond the scope of this study, exploring a few of the major trends provides a context for the discussion of funerary economic exchanges. As described in the last chapter, the role of work units has declined. The majority of young and middle-aged people no longer work for a work unit that provides all-inclusive lifelong benefits. To lessen urban pollution, factories have been pushed out of large city centers; more importantly, the biggest cities in China envision themselves as entirely post-industrial, middle-class spaces, rather than industrial, working–class ones. Overall, economic growth has been strong and rapid, with the result of increasing spending in most sectors of the economy, including funerals. As people become wealthier, they rely more and more on cash to purchase goods and services from strangers rather making do with what they have, constantly repairing old items themselves, or undertaking almost all of their own cooking, cleaning, sewing, and shopping. Commercial enterprises compete to provide good service to customers. Increasing wealth has also allowed cities to grow in size, expanding their borders and developing their infrastructure; almost all large Chinese cities now have extensive subway systems. Housing has been privatized and the price for apartments has skyrocketed, especially in the largest cities in the eastern part of the country. As municipal governments rely on profits from selling and rezoning land, they have developed interests in both continuing urban expansion and maintaining high real estate prices. Many young people are unable to afford apartments and must rely on their parents for living space. Inequality has increased, with the emergence of both impoverished urban residents and migrant workers from the countryside, who undertake most of the dangerous, despised, and most poorly paid occupational niches. The experience of rapid increases in living standards in a context of growing inequality and expensive housing makes many fear the possibility of being left behind. Because many urbanites see housing as a necessary precondition for marriage and forming an independent household, fears of being left behind economically and fears of not being able to continue the family line intertwine.

As migrant workers move to the city from the countryside, they have come to dominate certain sectors of the economy, including funerary services. Though some manage to get their household registrations transferred to the cities where they live, many do not. One result of this lack of registration is that many migrant workers either choose or are forced to spend their old age and then die in the place where they come from. All of the one-stop dragon entrepreneurs I asked said that they only did funerals for people who had either a local urban household registrations or a rural household registration in one of the villages at the edge of the urban core.

Finally, social media and new communications technologies have rapidly influenced the way urban Chinese, and almost everyone else, lives their lives. Information and services that used to require travel to a physical store are now often accessed through social media. The last section of this chapter explores how the digital revolution might affect funerary economies.

THE FIVE ECONOMIES OF URBAN FUNERALS

As Caroline Schuster (2016) points out in her analysis of death ritual and credit in Paraguay, funerals are moments for a settling of accounts for the dead and an opening of new accounts for the living. In contemporary urban China, this settling and opening of accounts takes place across (at least) five different forms of economic interaction: the inter-household gift economy, the intra-familial inheritance economy, the state redistributive economy, the small-scale informal market economy, and the large-scale formal market economy. Because funerals are complex economic affairs, I illustrate these five modes of exchange with data from different funerals. I could not simultaneously follow all five processes in a single case. While the five modes of economic exchange proceed under differing moral codes, the codes are all shaped by the forms of socioeconomic grouping described above: the household, the extended family, and the political nation.

Inter-Household Gift Economy

Funerals across China involve gift-giving. As we saw in the funeral of Mr. Wang, in the city of Nanjing, relatives of the deceased often give cash gifts and flower wreaths when they come to visit the home altar of the deceased during the period before the farewell meeting. The hosts of the funeral (typically the children of the deceased) keep a gift register in which the names of all those giving gifts and the amount they give is recorded. Those who give gifts will usually be invited to a banquet after the funeral and be given a small return gift at the banquet.

While I never saw the gift register for Mr. Wang's funeral, another Nanjing household showed me the gift register from their eighty-year-old father's funeral in 2015. At that funeral, thirty-five people gave slightly more than 25,000 yuan in gift money. The father had two brothers and two sisters who had a total of seven children. The brothers and sisters themselves each lived with one of their children, so there were seven gift-giving households from the father's side of the family, each of whom gave between 1,000 and 2,000 yuan. The surviving mother had one sister who was still alive and five nieces and nephews, making a total of five more households who also gave between 1,000 and 2,000 yuan each. The deceased had three children—two sons and a daughter—and a total of twenty additional households, including relatives of the children's spouses as well as a few close friends, gave between 100 and 500 yuan each. Finally, three neighbors who had been friends of the father gave 100–200 yuan each. The total amount given at this funeral was slightly more than what was given at Mr. Wang's funeral, but similar to most other middle-class urban families I heard about.

This amount would have been much larger at the funeral of an important government official, at least before the Xi Jinping-instituted crackdown on giving gifts to cadres at the funerals of their parents. Gift-giving relationships imply an indebtedness that can encourage corruption, but it is not only powerful cadres and anti-corruption agencies who worry about the implications of indebtedness. The household of the eighty-year-old father also refused one gift. An associate of one of this household's sons-in-law attempted to give the deceased's wife a gift of 3,000 yuan (larger than any other) three days after the funeral. He was not particularly close to the family and had not been invited to the funeral, but wanted to deepen his business relationship with the son-in-law. The mother declined the gift, saying that the funeral had already passed. She told me that the families were not close enough to know of each other's funerals and that the morality of exchange demanded that they would have had to return a larger gift in the future, but they would not know when to do so. Without the ability to reciprocate, the gift would become a burden, an unrepayable debt, hanging over the head of the son-in-law. This example demonstrates that the legal ambiguity in drawing the line between gifts and bribes reflects a serious moral problem: how to separate economic relations based on moral ideologies of fairness that require all to be treated equally with social relationships in which economic obligations for some people are greater than those for others.

The logic of inter-household giving at urban funerals closely resembles that already depicted in the literature on gift-giving in China,[2] but a few points deserve reiterating. First, as the mother's comment indicates, gift-giving involves a logic of continual inflation. If one of the households that gave a gift at this funeral were to hold a funeral in the future, then the mother's household should give an amount larger than the amount they received at this funeral. To return the same amount would cancel the indebtedness between the households and thus end the relationship. Second, none of the households who might inherit something from the deceased (the mother, the three children, and various grandchildren) could give a gift at this funeral. They were the direct mourners and thus constituted the group of gift-receivers at this funeral. Third, the practice of giving gifts draws economic boundaries around households. Gifts are understood as coming from a household. In no case do different members of a household give two separate gifts. Though the receiving unit could be seen as comprising several households, the key members of those households were originally all members of the deceased's household. That is why they could inherit. Households form and break up over time, but while they are intact they have strong economic boundaries. Because funerals mark a time for potential shifts in household structure, they become important moments for recreating kinship bonds among households. New accounts of indebtedness and relatedness are created.

Three forms of economic grouping are visible in these transactions. First are the households themselves, defined as gift-giving and gift-receiving units. Second is that of the extended family defined by the networks of debts recorded in the gift register. Third are those non-family members who are excluded from the bonds of social capital shared by family members. The example of the refused gift shows how the morality of maintaining relationships of indebtedness through gift exchange can be manipulated to influence wider forms of economic exchange. The mother feared that the social capital gained by the man who wanted to give 3,000 yuan would one day require her son-in-law to give the man a form of economic benefit that was even more valuable. The man was forced to remain in the category of non-kin.

Tensions over defining the boundaries of extended families go to the heart of the moral problems of economic exchange in urbanizing China, and perhaps throughout the contemporary world. As urbanization increases the space for strangers in our lives, fairness, or treating everyone the same, becomes the predominant moral guideline for economic interaction. But logics of family or community require treating in-group members with higher levels of generosity and compassion, and the lines distinguishing in-group and out-group members become starker. Friends occupy a potentially uncomfortable moral place in the logics of exchange, destabilizing the distinction between kin and strangers. Governmental and corporate agencies, as well as familial elders, all have a stake in defining who does or does not belong to the extended family. Funerals are one of many moments when such boundaries become explicit.

Intra-Familial Inheritance

As we saw in the case of Mr. Wang, the death of a parent often marks the start of struggles over inheritance. In urban China during the period of my research, several factors exacerbated such tensions. First, the generation of people passing away in urban areas typically had their children before the birth planning policy was implemented in 1979; they often have three or more children. Second, this generation worked in an era when work-unit employment was the norm. Most, even if they were factory workers, own apartments and receive pensions and, thus, have significant assets to leave to their children. Third, the 1990s, 2000s, and 2010s have been periods of rapid increase in urban real estate values. The value of apartments has increased much more rapidly than incomes, and even the small dingy apartments of former factory workers can be worth a fortune, especially in relation to the income levels of their children. For many urban families, the value of the property to be inherited is many times larger than the annual incomes of the heirs. In addition, many elderly people in China do not want to think about the fact that their children may be preparing to fight over their inheritance. They avoid the issue by not making out a will. Finally, the moral logics around inheritance (but perhaps not so much the legal logics in this case) can be contradictory and ambiguous. Many sons and daughters-in-law argue for a patrilineal logic of inheritance. Daughters tend to suggest that inheritances should be split evenly among all the children of the deceased, and the law generally agrees with them. Finally, many people feel that inheritance should depend on the quality of the relationship between parents and their children and the amount of physical and emotional care and financial support a particular child gives to the parents in their old age. The courts also consider this support in their rulings.[3]

During my research, I learned of many conflicts that ended up in the courts. A man who ran a small business arranging funerals in Nanjing told me:

> It seems that more than half of the funerals I do involve siblings quarrelling over the inheritance. They will try to keep the hostilities under control for the three days between the death and the funeral itself, as quarreling at the funeral is inauspicious. But some cannot even keep their tempers in check for that long. I know many families in which the siblings no longer speak to one another.

In one case, a long-retired factory-working couple passed away together in an auto accident. They owned a ninety-square-meter apartment in a former work-unit housing complex that was centrally located near downtown Nanjing, close to parks and a subway stop. Though not fancy, the apartment was worth over 2 million yuan. In addition, the family received a pension payout of over 200,000 yuan. The couple had two sons and a daughter. All were married; the sons had one child each but the daughter was childless. The mother had been ill before the auto accident and the daughter had provided most of the care. None of the children had attended university and all worked service-sector jobs, earning between 2,000 and 4,000 yuan per month. The value of the property to be inherited was more than forty times greater than the annual incomes of the children. The sons claimed that the daughter should not receive any inheritance, as she was childless while they were continuing the family line. The daughter claimed a share because she had spent considerable time caring for her mother. The case went to court, which ruled that the inheritance should be split evenly. The sons were appealing the case when I finished my research, and the siblings only communicated through their lawyers.

In this case, differing moral logics of inheritance conflicted. The logics of continuing the family line (which are often patrilineal, although not in this case as the daughter was childless) conflict with logics of reciprocity which dictate that those giving care to the elderly should receive an inheritance. In the case of the funeral of Mr. Wang, we saw how the son and daughter-in-law invoked patrilineal logics. They insisted that since only the patrilineal grandson of Mr. Wang would have the surname Wang, all of Mr. Wang's wealth should pass to him. They raised another point as well. In contemporary urban marriage markets, the marriage-ability of a young man is very often tied to his ability to provide an urban apartment for the new couple. Since women do not face such expectations, in a family with many grandchildren, grandsons should have preference over granddaughters and paternal grandsons absolutely must have access to an apartment (or the wealth to purchase one) if there is any hope for continuing the family line. I often heard such logics spoken when asking about issues of inheritance.

In rural China, both today and in the past, formal practices of dividing the household (分家) usually kept such conflicts under control.[4] But in contemporary urban China, traditional ways of dividing the household are largely lost and conflicts often end up in the courts. The existence of these disputes shows the importance of economic capital in the constitution and reproduction of households. The fact that strict patrilineal logics of inheritance are being successfully challenged by daughters on the basis of their care work (where such challenges would not have been entertained in a relatively recent past) is evidence of the changing moral and economic structures of the basic unit in Chinese society (the household). Nevertheless, the claims of sons are not, either socio-morally or legally, dismissed outright; patriarchal assumptions persist.

Finally, note the differing economic moralities of the inheritance and the gift economies. The inheritance economy is primarily about forming households, and it is in this context that patrilineal arguments hold their greatest moral sway. In the inter-household, intra-familial gift economy, relatedness defined in a patrilineal fashion matters little. Households strive to maintain connectedness with other related households regardless of whether those relations are through men or through women. In a context of disintegrating urban communities, relatives often constitute the only community one can sustain. In addition, the birth control policy has yielded many households with single daughters, and the parents of such households are especially reluctant to give up their connections to other households.

The State Redistributive Economy

As the pension payout to Mr. Wang and the above case demonstrate, the state, or, more precisely, municipal governments play a heavy role in governing death. In Nanjing the economic governance of death flows through two channels. First the Civil Affairs Bureau (民政局) regulates the state-run funeral home/crematoriums as well as the urban graveyards. It forces these institutions to keep prices artificially low for their most basic services (while allowing them to profit from everything else), regulates the types of rituals that can proceed at these places (recently banning firecrackers used to scare away ghosts, for example), and provides free basic funeral services for impoverished households without pensions. Second, work units, or the government units that have taken over their pension burdens if they no longer exist, provide pension payouts and additional services to the families of dead people who originally worked at their unit. Under 2016 Nanjing municipality regulations, upon the death of a pensioner, the families of the deceased receive a payout equivalent to twenty-four months of pension payment. Pensions vary greatly in Nanjing—as low as 1000 yuan per month, or higher than 10,000 yuan for high ranking cadres. Because pensions have gone up regularly over the years, people who retired long ago often receive higher pensions than those who retired recently. In 2015, factory workers who retired at the age of fifty in the 1980s often received pensions of 3,000–4,000 yuan per month. The politics of pension reform is a fraught area, but most cities in China pay out retirees for life at state-regulated levels rather than giving workers Individual Retirement Accounts. Pension levels have been a cause of protests in many cities, and relatively high pensions are often seen as a way of maintaining social stability (维稳). Some people suspect that pension payouts are a strategy for buying political peace (see Hurst and O'Brien 2002). They encourage people to report the deaths of their aged parents—in the past there were rumors of people continuing to collect pensions while storing their dead parents in refrigerated caskets—and give families an immediate payout at a time when they face funeral expenses and may be feeling strong emotions that could turn against the state. In addition to the pension payout, certain work units provide other benefits at the time of death, such as transportation to the funeral, small cash gifts to the family when a representative is sent to visit the home altar, and help with arranging the funeral. The families of high ranking cadres receive even more types of benefits. As Martin Whyte (1988) details, during the Maoist era, most urban funerals were arranged by work units. In contemporary urban China, the role of the work unit has diminished for most people, but is still crucial for state employees.

Two forms of moral logic inform the state redistributive economy in relation to death. First, as with all forms of state benefit, bureaucratic logic demands the pigeonholing of people into different categories to determine what sorts of benefits they should receive. Migrant workers in Nanjing, for example, are not eligible for any sort of death benefit. While the construction of the pigeonholes may be unfair, bureaucratic morality requires that the pigeonholing itself be done fairly and accurately. Such an explicit logic of fairness distinguishes state-led economic activities from the logics of inter-household gift exchange. But a second logic of reciprocity also emerges: families should express gratitude towards the state and its bureaucratic workers for the payouts by not using funerals as an excuse for an outpouring of anti-state emotion. In this sense, the pension payout is a way for the state to transform economic capital into political capital and reproduce the loyalties that link households to wider structures across society. Access to state payouts also helps define those who receive the payouts as citizens of a particular municipal area in China, and, by extension, as citizens of the People's Republic of China. In this sense, political loyalty at death is not only a matter for large companies, but also for urban households with local household registrations.

Small-Scale Informal Economies

Funerals can involve many small-scale businesses. There are vendors who sell flowers, spirit money, and other items for burning from carts on the street in front of cemeteries and funeral parlors; religious practitioners who offer services such as chanting sutras for the dead; musicians who play dirges in funeral processions; and, most importantly, one-stop dragon entrepreneurs like Mr. Chen. Almost every community in Nanjing has a one-stop dragon entrepreneur. Other one-stop dragons open small shopfronts near major hospitals. Most families will employ such a person when faced with death. In Nanjing, these businesses typically price three days of service at about 1,000 yuan, which is well under cost. But they require the customers to purchase cinerary caskets, longevity clothes and sometimes packets of return gifts from them, and make their profit selling these items.

While some such businesses have shopfronts which display these items, others just have a phone number and business cards. Many do not bother obtaining business licenses, and even those with licenses and shopfronts only pay taxes on those rare transactions when a customer demands a receipt. Though the busiest of these businesses can do hundreds of funerals a year, and often require two people for a single funeral, they rarely formally employ anyone. Everyone who works at such an establishment does so as an independent contractor and has no insurance or pension payments made by the business.[5] The businesses also pay kickbacks to those who refer customers (often nurses at the hospitals), and sometimes receive kickbacks if they direct customers to particular graveyards. Most of their informal employees are relatives and all transactions are in cash. Of the twelve such entrepreneurs I interviewed, all came from rural areas near the cities where they worked.

In addition to the funeral of Mr. Wang, Mr. Chen shared with me the financial details of another funeral. In this case, I was at his shop one afternoon when a woman approached. Her mother had just passed away one Tuesday in the early afternoon. She had learned about the business from the helper who had provided night care for her mother. After a brief negotiation the woman agreed to pay 900 yuan for three days of service, purchase a 1,000 yuan longevity clothes set, spend 800 yuan for twenty return gift packets, and buy a cinerary casket (which ranged from 1,500 yuan to 10,000 yuan), though she wanted to consult with her family about which one to buy. Mr. Chen then took his son-in-law with him to accompany the woman to her home. After they arrived in the woman's apartment, they met the woman's husband and child. Mr. Chen then went with the woman's husband to drive to various offices to make arrangements and obtain certificates. He accompanied the husband for two hours that afternoon and six hours on the following day. After some direction from the entrepreneur, the woman made a list of people to be notified and began contacting them. Mr. Chen's son-in-law stayed at the home to set up the home altar and to write calligraphy for visitors who came with flower wreaths. The son-in-law spent six hours in the home on Tuesday and twelve hours on Wednesday. The farewell ceremony, cremation, burial and banquet took place on Thursday (the third day) and Mr. Chen accompanied the family for the entire morning (from 5 a.m. until the banquet at noon). The son-in-law convinced the family to purchase a 2,800-yuan cinerary casket. In all, the family paid the entrepreneur 5,500 yuan in cash. The wholesale cost of the items sold was about 1,200 yuan. Mr. Chen gave a 500-yuan kickback to the referring nurse (double the usual amount because this case was the first referral for this nurse) and 1,000 yuan to his son-in-law (500 of which was a commission on the cinerary casket). He also drove his own car to some of the offices, paid for some small items used in setting up the home altar, and had expenses related to renting his shopfront, but he still estimated that he made close to 2,000 yuan on the funeral.

Two moral logics inform the process. The first is that of immediate cash payment for all services, with a short time-frame around each transaction. Opposite to the logic of the gift economy, the norm here involves clearing all debts as soon as possible. There is no attempt to create social capital by maintaining relations of indebtedness. Trust is possible because payments come quickly. The second is one of kinship. Mr. Chen hired his son-in-law and often used idioms of kinship, or at least friendship, when addressing the people with whom he did business. A basic paradox of relatedness emerges here. On the one hand, part of the spirit of the economic morality involved in these transactions was that of family. Households gave and received payments in economic transactions, while forms of fictive and real extended family relations were invoked to establish the trust or social capital that enabled economic transactions to take place with minimal reference to the state. Though Mr. Chen's relationship to his son-in-law was clearly ongoing, the use of fictive kin terms among the other actors allowed only for transactions in which service was performed on one day and payment was received a day or two later. Formal, state-related economic processes were avoided at every turn, in part because many aspects of Mr. Chen's business were technically illegal. He did business in cash only and did not pay taxes. Businesses like his thrive in a legally ambiguous environment in which the municipal government desires a dynamic economy and high levels of employment, but also wants all businesses to register.

On the other hand, the quick cash payouts make it possible for the relationships involved in these economic transactions to be severed at a moment's notice. As noted in the previous chapter, workers in the funerary sector, including Mr. Chen, are often stigmatized. Many of their customers do not want to have any ongoing relationship to them. For the customers, the use of idioms of friendship or distant kinship are at best necessary fictions to enable the transaction to proceed. They imply nothing about their relationship to the entrepreneur.

Formal State-Regulated Business Economies

There are three types of formal enterprises involved in the funeral industry. The first are the state-run funeral home/crematoriums, usually run by the city's Civil Affairs Bureau. Second are the cemeteries, more often privatized but always run by large corporations approved by the Bureau. Third are one or two large insurance companies who are attempting to establish nationwide markets in funerary insurance and pre-paid funerals. All of these types of businesses either formally hire their employees or go through officially regulated employment agencies which pay the insurance fees of their employees. Though some of the employees are given incentives to sell the most expensive of services, most of the employees' income comes from their regular salary. The prices these companies charge are fixed and publically displayed. They issue receipts after customers make payments and pay tax regularly, though they also occasionally pay cash kickbacks to one-stop dragon entrepreneurs who steer business to them.

Though these enterprises operate in the formal, legal, state-regulated economy, contradictions between their state affiliation and their customer orientation shape their economic interactions. The graveyards and the insurance agencies require long-term economic trust from their customers, who buy graves for twenty to thirty year periods (with options to extend) and can pay for pre-paid funerals or funerary insurance decades before the funeral is carried out. In presenting themselves to their customers, these companies emphasize their size and state affiliations to suggest that they will be around for the long haul. The funeral home /crematoriums are run by the state, and many of their prices and services are directly shaped by state regulations. But because funerary ritual often involves activities that could be construed as "religious" or "superstitious," all of these companies must negotiate the line between shaping funerals according to state aesthetics and shaping funerals according to customer desire. In addition, because the state subsidizes cremations and basic services for the poor, the funeral homes must sharply distinguish pricing strategies for basic and optional services. For example, in Nanjing in 2016, the price to rent a small room to hold a farewell meeting was only 100 yuan/hour. But the price to decorate the room appropriately with flowers started at 3,000 yuan and could go as high as 50,000 yuan.

The contradictions regarding "superstitious" activities are even starker. Funeral homes have rules about the types of ritual, religious, and "superstitious" activities they will allow, drawing lines that can seem arbitrary. Graveyards commonly provide burial services during which the master of ceremonies may refer to various ghosts, gods, and ancestors, as well as Buddhist notions of heaven and hell, and even ideas from Western astrology. The master of ceremonies may also make reference to practices that are said to bring good luck to the deceased's decedents. Such references were visible in the burial ceremony of Mr. Wang as well as at several other burial ceremonies I witnessed. Cemeteries also can employ geomancy masters to help people choose gravesites. But they still ban certain activities when required, such as setting off firecrackers (used to scare away ghosts) or burning spirit money. In addition, as discussed in chapter 3, some graveyards go to great length to bury Party and national martyrs, reserving special sections of their graveyards for them, devising elaborate memorials, and opening the cemeteries to the public to offer lessons on the glorious history of the Party to tourists and visiting groups of schoolchildren. Such actions both curry favor with Party officials and demonstrate their relationships to the Party-state to customers. Some customers will pay a premium to be buried (or bury loved ones) at a cemetery that is also home to Party heroes.

In short, these formal enterprises blend two political-economic moral logics. For their economic stakeholders (stock owners for the private corporations and those employees who share in the profits for the state-run funeral homes), they must do whatever it takes to make a profit—charging as high a price as the market will bear and providing whatever services customers demand. But they must also politically support the local branch of the Communist Party, regularly performing their loyalty and enacting any policies the government demands. At times these enterprises find ways of seamlessly blending the two missions, as when the Fu Shou Yuan or the Garden of Merit build memorials for Party designated martyrs, whose presence then attracts high-end customers to purchase plots. But in other instances the two imperatives contradict one another and compromises are reached. The relationship between the two types of logic is often seen as a type of reciprocity: the companies perform loyalty to the Party and the Party gives the companies the regulatory space to be profitable. As many scholars have noted, large capitalists in China almost always forge alliances with state cadres in the districts where they operate (Dickson 2008; K. Tsai 2007). In these examples, the social entity of the Party (with its claims to represent the nation as a whole) and the political capital of those who can build a relationship with the Party-state loom large. But the moral logics of these processes differ from those of the technically illegal small-scale businesses described in the last section.

DISRUPTION AND EMERGENT DIGITAL ECONOMIES

The five types of economy described above provide a snapshot of monetary interactions at funerals during the period of my research. The general economic shifts described at the beginning of the chapter provide some historical context for those inclined to imagine how aspects of this monetary economy may have waxed and waned over the proceeding decades. In this section I examine a case of an attempt to disrupt the entire funerary industry. Such an attempt turns our attention to the future of funerary economies.

"We are going to do to the funerary business what Uber did to the taxi business," declared an enthusiastic recruit at what I took to be a funeral business office in Beijing in September 2015. The recruit invited me into his office when he saw me speaking to a neighboring funerary services shop and showed me a website that his company, Love Convergence (a pseudonym), was developing to enable browsers to scroll through a menu of elements to include in a contemporary urban funeral. The recruit explained that until his company came along, people wanting to arrange funerals did not understand what to do with a dead relative and were at the mercy of unscrupulous funerary parlor workers and one-stop dragon entrepreneurs. By developing a website, Love Convergence would modernize an ancient and corrupt industry and bring transparency to what had been an opaque process. "But how can your company provide this range of services across the entire country?," I asked. "We are not a funeral business, ourselves," he answered, "but a life insurance company. We want to be the first company to open the funerary insurance market in China."

Anthropological discussions of the insurance industry have consistently argued that cultural context has a powerful influence on the way insurance markets develop in a given country. Viviana Zelizer (1979) shows how insurance companies in the United States had to overcome moral reservations about putting a price on life by inventing moral discourses about responsibilities towards children and dependents in the case of death. In China, Cheris Chan (2012) found that life insurance companies had to overcome taboos about talking about death to establish their market. They did so by promoting insurance as a type of investment rather than as a form of protection against an unfortunate early demise. While Chan's and Zelizer's insights illuminate Love Convergence's plans, I later came to question whether their plans had anything to do with "insurance" at all. At the heart of the company's business model was a scheme for raising capital, rather than a plan for sharing risks (as insurance is often depicted). The scheme itself evolved rapidly, as the company adjusted its services in response to problems that arose while setting up the business.

The Rapid Evolution of an Insurance Vision

Love Convergence was founded by Longevity Life Insurance (also a pseudonym), one of the largest life insurance companies in China. In 2013 the company founded a subsidiary to service China's elderly. The subsidiary provides four types of service: retirement homes and communities in China's wealthiest cities; medical services for those living in its communities; financial and legal services for older people with money to invest and give to heirs; and funerary businesses, with cemeteries and the web platform described above. Love Convergence was a subsidiary of this subsidiary. With three hundred employees in five cities across China, it was merely the tip of the iceberg of Longevity Life (which employs millions of people across hundreds of Chinese locales).

Love Convergence evolved rapidly after its establishment in 2015. The website I was shown in September 2015 quickly lost its specific menu for services. By October 2016, the website instead explained how the contract for "funeral insurance" works. A person may buy the policy for oneself or a close relative, most typically an elderly parent. The website is full of images suggesting a caring, filial relationship between an elderly parent and a middle-aged son or daughter. The purchaser specifies whose funeral the contract is for and who will be the "beneficiary," that is, the person who will be in charge of the funeral once the elderly person has passed away. The purchaser specifies the exact level of service she desires for the funeral and pays the full price for this funeral in advance. Upon the death of the insured person, the beneficiary has the option of either carrying out the funeral as specified in the plan or getting the money back with 3 percent annual interest added. In the USA or Australia, such a contract would be called a type of prepaid funeral, rather than funeral insurance. When I asked why Love Convergence markets these policies as a type of insurance, I was told that the contracts insured against both the inflation that might occur in the price of the funeral between the time the policy was drawn and the time the policy was carried out, and also against the fact that someone might carry out the funeral in a manner that the purchaser or the insured person would find distasteful. While I would agree that the policy does insure against extreme inflation, the latter claim seems slightly exaggerated. The beneficiary could still take the money back with 3 percent annual interest and then carry out the ritual in a manner that did not reflect the original contract, though having everything spelled out in a contract could serve as an explicit guide for those designing a funeral.

Further interviews with mid-level company managers I conducted in 2016 suggest that the company had to abandon the menu for services they had originally showed me because the typical services desired and prices charged varied from city to city in China, making a uniform website impossible. The price of a funeral in China's wealthiest cities (Beijing, Shanghai and Guangzhou) average about 20 percent higher than in the other provincial capitals and 50 percent higher than in many smaller cities. As of October 2016, the website urged visitors to contact one of their service "angels" any time, twenty-four hours a day, though telephone or the website. The angels can explain the options available and their cost and even come to your home to help you plan the funeral and choose a gravesite, should you desire.

Also in 2016, a manager in Love Convergence's Shanghai office explained that they had standardized their funerals into two packages—a basic-level funeral for 18,000 yuan and a high-level funeral for 35,000. To hedge against inflation, these prices were about 20 percent higher than current costs. Standardizing the insurance packages into two levels, the manager explained, was a reaction to their customers: "Few people have very specific ideas for their own funerals. What customers want is either a good basic funeral which will not stigmatize them as poor or stingy in the eyes of their friends and families, or a high-level funeral which will distinguish them as being either wealthy or filial." But beyond the basic expression of either standard but respectable or distinguished and special, he added, most customers desired expert advice about the specific items to be included to mark these particular levels of ritual.[6]

During their first ten months of business, Love Convergence sold roughly one hundred such policies in Shanghai. Given the population of Shanghai (over 20 million), this number of policies did not even amount to 0.01 percent of the city's elderly population. The customers were primarily people who worried about not having someone to arrange their funeral. These included the children of elderly Shanghainese who lived abroad, who would attend the funeral but feared that rushing home to attend it would be difficult enough and wanted all of the arrangements in place. Alternatively, the policies were purchased by elderly Shanghainese who had no children and who did not have a living spouse.

During the short period between 2015 and 2016, the entire depiction of insurance provided on the initial website was reversed. The initial website was based on the premise that the current funerary services industry was corrupt, opaque, and not oriented towards the customer. Love Convergence planned to supply detailed information about the ritual process to maximize customer choice and transparency of pricing, while minimizing the chances of salespeople to profit by selling overpriced funerals. But the company soon discovered that it was not practical to list explicit prices. Likewise eliminated was the detailed menu for funerary services, as this had simply raised more questions than it answered for the customers who called in. The opacity of the industry no longer seemed to be an issue. In reaction to customer behavior, the managers decided to reformat the website; at the same time, the product itself evolved. The option for customers to take a 3 percent annual return on the prepaid price recalls Cheris Chan's findings: insurance in

China is best marketed as a type of investment rather than a form of protection. The filial imagery on the website appealed both to anxieties common in modernizing countries with Confucian heritage and to government concerns about the neglect of the elderly. In addition to fitting China's economic, political, and cultural contexts, the filial imagery on the website contributed to the ideological work of making the provision of a good funeral a sacred form of familial duty.

The methods that Love Convergence used when dealing with the businesses that actually provide funerary services also evolved rapidly. Tom Baker (1994) points out how insurance companies often use different visions of insurance when processing claims than they do when selling insurance policies (see also Heimer 2002; Stone 2002). When processing claims, the emphasis is placed on preventing insurance fraud, rather than providing for loved ones. Likewise, Love Convergence expressed a different vision of insurance to these businesses than it did on its website. In 2015, I attended some meetings at which the company pitched their business model to invited groups of funerary services providers. Their presentations suggested that the technology of a highly developed web-based platform, combined with the reputation of a well-established, well-resourced life insurance company, would revolutionize the industry. Customers would trust the reputation of an insurance company worth billions that had repeatedly paid out claims in the past; moreover, customers would be drawn to their expertly designed website. Consequently, people around the country would start prepaying their funerals with Love Convergence. Companies that actually provided funerary services (one-stop dragons) would have no choice other than to work with Love Convergence if they wanted to stay in business. Love Convergence also suggested that even though the companies might have to accept less money for their services than they had in the past, they would gain the security of having business lined up for funerals many years into the future. While the service providers who attended this meeting were polite, several follow-up interviews suggested that none of them signed a contract with Love Convergence. In 2016, Love Convergence managers told me that they no longer had any need for such contracts. There would always be funerary service providers and Love Convergence would simply line up the necessary services for its customers when the time arrived. Their experience in arranging funerals would allow them to know which providers gave good service at a reasonable price.

This change reverberated throughout their business model. Rather than contracts that bound service providers to conduct funerals at relatively low prices, Love Convergence hedged against inflation by charging 20 percent more than existing price levels. Their business visions changed even more radically. In 2015 the enthusiastic new recruit imagined a future company that would dominate funerary services as Uber dominates the taxi business. The web platform was the key to channeling customer demand through them and reducing other actors in the industry to accepting terms that Love Convergence dictated. This vision of their business was most likely pitched to investors, shareholders, and higher-level executives in Longevity Life, as well as the new employees. In practice, the web platform was not so successful and the business only attracted a certain niche market. Consequently, the managerial vision of the company shifted from one in which it dominated all other players in the industry to one in which it could easily work with the other players because there were many of them who competed against one another.

Adopting and Adapting Business Visions from Elsewhere

Love Convergence did not develop its insurance vision in a vacuum. Executives in Longevity Life constantly studied, visited, and held negotiations with other large companies, both overseas and in China. The establishment of Love Convergence involved three inter-related trends in contemporary capitalism and the funerary industry in particular. The first is the attempt to use internet technologies to "disrupt" existing sectors. The second is the consolidation of the funerary industry by large firms that see the potential for profit in death. The third is the search for new sources of profit by large financial and insurance businesses which often leads to new ways of defining what basic financial products such as insurance actually are.

Other attempts in China have been made to revolutionize the funerary business by establishing a web platform. A smaller-scale, more local attempt was made by the company Bi An in Beijing.[7] The claims Bi An made in relation to the existing industry in China closely resembled those made by Love Convergence (Kaiman 2015): they argued that other primary service providers were either seedy small-scale entrepreneurs or bureaucratic non-customer focused state-run businesses, neither of which provided transparent pricing or good service. On the surface there is a bit of truth in these claims. The stigmatization of funerary workers in China makes advertising difficult and causes funerary sector workers to be reluctant to discuss their work. Consequently, many people do not know where to go when they need to arrange a funeral. Moreover, for differing reasons, both small-scale entrepreneurs and state-run funeral home/crematoriums overprice some items to make up for the aspects of the service which are priced well under cost. But I would not go so far as accuse businesses of seediness because of these situations.

Bi An has been more successful in providing transparent pricing than Love Convergence. It does list explicit prices for many of its services on its website, perhaps because it only provides services in one city. But there are limits to this transparency and its ability to revolutionize or disrupt the industry. Even though many customers are happy with standardized packages, funerals can be highly individualized events, and Bi An, like all other companies in this industry, suggests contacting the company for an in-person consultation to determine the exact needs and price of a funeral in a specific instance. Second, like Love Convergence, Bi An does not advertise prices that are noticeably lower than other providers.

Finally, all players in the funerary industry seem to agree that a web-based presence is important for the business. For an industry in which stigma can make traditional forms of advertising problematic, a web presence allows potential customers to search for information. But the usefulness of web advertising to the funerary industry does not necessarily make web platforms disruptive to the existing industry. Hundreds of one-stop dragon entrepreneurs and state-owned funerary parlors are all establishing web platforms.

In its original business vision, Love Convergence borrowed some of Bi An's rhetoric about the shortcomings of the funerary services industry, adding the language of sector-wide, nation-wide dominance and industry disruption. Since Longevity Life already was a huge company, with national coverage, ample capital to invest, and a reputation as an insurance company too big and safe to fail, it hoped to scale up Bi An's intentions in a revolutionary way.

The vision of how the scaling up of Bi An's rhetoric might work also drew from the experience of large companies in other countries that were consolidating the funerary industry. In the United States, for example, Service Corporation International (SCI) has been buying up small family-run funeral homes for decades and is now said to control over two thousand funeral homes (Barrett 2013). As Love Convergence is attempting to do, SCI offers standardized funeral service packages, which are advertised and depicted on websites, which can be prepaid, and which can even be carried out at any of the firm's funeral homes across the country should a family move or an individual die away from home. But also like Love Convergence, SCI has raised rather than lowered prices.

Unlike SCI, Love Convergence does not itself provide funerary services. It instead takes money from customers, invests it in its other businesses, and guarantees that it will find a reputable business to provide the services when the time arrives. Here it seems that Love Convergence did borrow from the model of Uber. It channels customers to independent contractors rather than providing service. One factor in Love Convergence's failure to disrupt and consolidate the industry may be the different financial environments in China and the United States. In the latter, there are estate planning benefits that encourage the prepaying of funerals. By prepaying a funeral, elderly people can spend down their assets in a way that makes them eligible for state benefits (places in nursing homes, for example). If heirs simply paid for the funeral out of the money they inherited, the net position would not be as advantageous. The existence of a financial environment which favors prepaying funerals in turn encourages the growth of large-scale funerary companies, who are in a better position to guarantee the provision of services many years into the future and in many locations across a given country. In China, at present, there are no financial advantages to prepaying a funeral.

Why does Love Convergence call their product a form of insurance? While there are forms of funeral insurance in the United States, such insurance is different to prepaying a funeral. My point is not to criticize a Chinese firm for using financial terms differently than they are used elsewhere. Rather, I wish to point out that the meaning of these terms is quite flexible, that it depends on the evolving legal, tax, and financial environments in which the terms are used, and that large companies often actively seek to stretch the meanings of such terms in their search for new products and modes of profit. In American financial terms, Love Convergence's product is halfway between a pre-paid funeral and a straight-forward investment like a certificate of deposit. As Spencer Kimball (cited in Baker and Simon 2002a, 7), a leading American insurance law scholar puts it, "there is no good definition of 'insurance' for any purpose." As Baker and Simon (2002b, 27) argue, "insurance is not a unified institution."

CONCLUSION

As China's urban economy grows, as more and more goods and services are purchased from businesses staffed by strangers rather than provided by family members, work-units, or thrifty households, and as inequality grows and housing becomes more unaffordable, several trends in the economic transactions surrounding funerals emerge. Communities shrink, but the maintenance of social relations among related households remains important. Families may be careful about who they allow to enter their relatively private circles, but strive to keep some sort of familial network alive. Inheritance battles proliferate in part because of rapidly changing demographic patterns, but also because of the price of housing in relation to average incomes. As the population of those who are passing away comes to be dominated by the parents of only children, inheritance battles will wane, but the relative importance of the economics of inheritance is likely to remain high as long as apartments cost so much in relation to salaries. Though the importance of work units in the lives of urban people diminishes, the economies of government-dispensed benefits has not become less important. While China may attempt to privatize the businesses of providing health insurance and pensions, government regulation of these sectors will remain important. As long as the Chinese Communist Party is governing the country in an authoritarian fashion, it will want to use its association with these sectors to promote political loyalty.

The future of small- and large-scale businesses in China is harder to predict. The retreat of work units in the urban sector, coupled with the opening of migration from rural to urban areas, created the conditions for an explosion of small-scale entrepreneurship, as the one-stop dragon sector illustrates. However, as the economy continues to grow, as many urban business sectors become dominated by established players, and as emerging digital economies offer opportunities to a few large-scale players in a winner-take-all fashion, the space for small-scale business in large Chinese cities may shrink. Love Convergence attempted to squeeze space and profits out of the market currently dominated by one-stop dragon entrepreneurs. At least for the moment, this attempt appears to have failed, but that does not mean that future attempts will also fail. In addition to whatever other advantages they may hold, in China, large-scale businesses often have state backing, and this political capital could be the straw that tips the tide towards large-scale success.

Finally, note how the rhetoric of Love Convergence demonized the existing players in the funerary sector. Such rhetoric echoes, and takes advantage of, the stigmatization of rural-urban migrants working in the sector. It insinuates that they lack moral "quality," so of course they rip people off. While it is true that entrepreneurs like Mr. Chen make a reasonable living, it is also true that they work hard to provide an important service during a time when their clients have great need. I never heard rhetoric claiming that the wedding-banquet sector or the automobile sector, for example, was full of cheats, even though these businesses are also quite profitable. And of course not all one-stop dragon entrepreneurs are as successful as Mr. Chen. When companies like Love Convergence move into the funerary sector, prices for customers do not drop. They simply turn popular rhetoric about stigmatized populations to their own advantage.

6

Of Rules and Regulations
Governing Mourning

Grief involves the loss of a social relationship that had served as an anchor. This loss disorients. Not knowing what to do, the grief-stricken want to be showed what to do, told what to do. A standardized ritual to follow step by step and a person to guide one through it can help. In the language of "governmentality" theorists, grief is a time to be governed, whether this governing is to be done by familial elders, religious specialists, secular ritual practitioners, or government employees.[1]

In this regard, the funeral of Mr. Wang was typical. Mr. Wang's children, especially his younger daughter, were exhausted from the extra work of caring for their father during his dying days. In this period, the children avoided discussing death. While they told the middle daughter to return from England, too much talk of dying and funerals would have made it seem like they had abandoned all hope of a cure and were wishing their father dead. Mr. Wang himself was never directly told of his prognosis. When death occurred, the children were exhausted, bereaved, and unprepared. They needed someone to tell them how to proceed. A little nudge from their helper led them to Mr. Chen. They were more than happy to have him to guide them through the process.

While all rituals might involve standardized procedure, funerals especially are times for limiting choice. Here a contrast with weddings illuminates. In modern marriages, choice is a necessary component. When the Communist Party came to power in 1949, it banned purely arranged marriages. To legally register a marriage, those involved must explicitly declare their desire to marry their partners. Contemporary weddings provide an opportunity for the ritual expression of this desire, of the act of choosing, through a celebration of romance. Many couples exert considerable effort to arrange a "perfect" wedding. But choosing death is illegal; it would mean murder or suicide. Funerals do not celebrate the "choices" involved in their construction. In the last chapter, we saw how Love Convergence found that providing too many options on their website proved counterproductive. Even when purchasing a funeral in advance, that is to say, when one is not faced with the pressure of a stay at a hospital and a sudden, regrettable outcome, many people shy away from being too active in their choice-making about death. The fear of death, reinforced in the urbanization process, makes any act of choosing in relation to death feel inappropriate.

But if funerals are a time to be governed, not just any governing will do. Mourning also involves respect for the dead, for their memories, for the way they lived their lives. This respect can lead to cultural conservatism. To respect the dead, many feel, we should carry out funerals in the ways that they have always been conducted. To respect the old, we should continue the old-fashioned ways. What constitutes the "old-fashioned" ways, however, depends upon the social identity of the deceased. Devout Christians or Muslims want to be led through rituals in ways that are appropriate to their religion. Herein lies the first dilemma of governing funerals. While the grieving need to be told what to do, they want to be told what to do by a culturally appropriate person. If there are deep religious or cultural divisions within a single family, conflicts over ritual format can arise. Moreover, even though most urban people do not know exactly how to conduct a funeral, they do have vague ideas about what a proper funeral entails. The funeral needs to resonate with these ideas. Abrupt cultural changes in the ways of governing mourning leads to conflict and failed rituals.

One example of conflict stemming from funerary reform is the relatively recent introduction of mandatory cremation to many rural areas. Cremation has been unevenly mandated over much of the Chinese countryside, as local governments have gradually built crematoriums and related infrastructure. When I did research in rural Shandong during the 1980s, in an area where mandatory cremation had recently been introduced, many old people asked me whether cremation would be painful. In 2010 to 2011, Hu Yanhua (2013) did research in a rural part of Hubei province where mandatory cremation was just being introduced. She interviewed many older people about the change in policy, and most had strenuous objections. These elderly had attended many funerals during the course of their lives in which the body was buried. They felt that replacing burial with cremation was at the least disrespectful and could possibly destroy their souls and their souls' ability to bring good fortune to their descendants. Many pressured their younger family members to find ways to illegally circumvent the policy, and one man even committed suicide in an attempt to die before the policy was fully implemented.

As we have seen in previous chapters, urbanization leads to many changes in the organization of funerary ritual. The spaces of the living and dead separate; the role of strangers in conducting the ritual increase; the conduct of the ritual commercializes. This reorganization alters the governing of funerals. The state becomes more involved, though depending on national context, religious organizations and private businesses may also play major roles. In China, the state demands and takes the central role. Though religious and commercial actors may also be involved, most of these actors are also related to the state.

Governing funerals involve many practicalities. The dead body needs to be disposed of. People need to congregate at particular places at particular times. Land is required for burials and other resources must be amassed for the ritual itself. Shifting from rural to urban ways of living usually involves transformations in the ways these practicalities can be addressed. Most generally, land is usually more expensive in urban settings and economic pressures to curtail its use arise. In addition, people's lives become busier, and those who might attend a ritual often do not live near to one another. Consequently, ritual procedures tend to simplify. Ritual activities that previously lasted several days are reduced to a few hours. Such has been the case in Hong Kong, mainland China, and most of the world.[2]

From the perspective of the Chinese Communist Party, governing mourning involves multiple contradictory pressures. While many advocate funerary reform, exactly which reforms to take and how to enact them are matters of debate, conflict, and compromise. The practicalities of urban living and a desire to reduce conflict shape the pace of reforms, while contradictions among the goals and priorities of different levels and sectors within the government itself complicate the policy process. Exploring the labyrinth of Chinese funerary policy and the ways in which this policy gets interpreted in particular urban contexts reveals much about processes of governing in urban China, the transformations associated with urbanization, and the dynamics of funerary ritual itself.

CHINESE FUNERARY POLICY

Funerals are primarily governed through the Ministry of Civil Affairs. Because funerals involve land use, religious beliefs, ethnic minorities, overseas Chinese, and Party members (among other things), the Ministries charged with governing these areas of life in China can also become involved in designing policies regarding funerals. Incompatible impulses emerge. At least in its own propaganda, the Party considers itself to be a secular, scientific, materialist organization. It views religions somewhat suspiciously, allowing some government-controlled religious organizations, but often acting to curtail their influence. It also seeks to restrict or outlaw everything it labels as "superstition." It wishes to promote loyalty to the Party, which implies that people should trust Party-appointed officials rather than religious specialists to be the ones to direct their funerals. It also vigorously polices the public sphere to inhibit the organization of protests against the government. All of these impulses suggest that funerals should be limited as much as possible. Funerals are occasions when people get together to express their grief. Grief can easily become grievance. If mourners believe that the deceased was wronged by the government or killed by government agents or because of government neglect, they might be motivated to protest. Funerals can become occasions for the expression of religious identity or beliefs, and often involve actions that seem "superstitious."

But a purely restrictive approach has its limits. Many in government also want the Party to be seen as an organization that respects the wishes of the people. Religious belief is officially tolerated by Chinese law, and banning it would be a foreign relations disaster. Imposing too many restrictions on funerals could itself lead to protest. Even bans on "superstitious" activities can have unforeseen consequences. For example, at the same time that many cities in China have banned the burning of spirit money, other cities promote its manufacture. Outside of China, the burning of spirit money is often seen as a marker of Chinese ethnic identity, and the Chinese government wishes those who it labels as "overseas Chinese" to identify with China (Zhifen Chen 2012). Burning spirit money is legal and commonplace in Hong Kong and Taiwan, and many in the Party also want people in Hong Kong and Taiwan to identify with China. Moreover, manufacturing spirit money and exporting it overseas earns money, and boosting the economy is always a government concern. If there were no domestic market for spirit money, could the manufacture of spirit money still thrive in China? For these reasons, many large cities (like Nanjing, at least as of 2016, as we saw with Mr. Wang's funeral) allow the burning of spirit money, even as others have banned it, in the name of preventing environmental pollution and discouraging superstition.

The major policy document guiding funerary regulation across China is called the "The Ministry of Civil Affairs of the People's Republic of China Regulations for Funerary Management" (中华人民共和国民政部殡葬管理条例).[3] Originally issued in 1997, these regulations were revised in 2012, and efforts have been made to upgrade them into a formal law, though none has been issued as of this writing. The regulations demand the efficient use of land, the implementation of cremation where possible, thrift in conducting funerals, and the elimination of "evil customs" and "superstitions," but leave it to local governments to decide exactly how to achieve these goals. The regulations specify that provincial governments have the right to determine which parts of their provinces should implement mandatory cremation and which areas may still carry out burials. Private entities are forbidden from establishing funerary facilities, including cemeteries, crematoriums, and funeral homes, and villages are not allowed to open their cemeteries to non-village members. Funerary activities are not allowed to disrupt public order. Finally, graves are not to take up agricultural or forest land, or to be placed in parks, official scenic areas, or near reservoirs, rail lines or roadways. The design of concrete regulations for particular areas and the implementation and enforcement of these is up to governments at the city and county levels.

Most provinces and many city and county governments have issued their own regulations for funerary management in relation to these rules. Some of the strictest of these have been issued by the city of Guangzhou. Those regulations specify the appropriate ways of disposing of ashes after cremation. To save land, they insist that people use columbaria instead of cemeteries, and have banned the building of new cemeteries within city limits. They also prevent outside cemeteries from setting up sales offices within the city, but nevertheless many outside cemeteries do advertise within the city and some people have the ashes of their loved ones buried at cemeteries outside of the city limits.

Overall, the national regulations set a relatively flexible framework for governing funerary activities. How the definitions of various terms are interpreted and how strictly the regulations have been implemented varies even more widely than the provincial regulations themselves. As suggested above, local governments are free to decide whether burning spirit money constitutes an "evil custom," or whether saving land requires replacing cemeteries with columbaria. Some of the regulations are directly violated. Travelling China by rail or road, one can often see graves on the land near the transport lines. But that such rules are sometimes ignored does not imply that they are never enforced. The setting of regulations that may be interpreted loosely or strictly grants considerable power to local governments.

THE POLITICS OF LAND FOR BURIALS

Throughout East Asia, the use of land for burials is a vexing issue. It is not difficult to see why. If memorials to a deceased loved one are truly to last forever (as phrases often carved onto tombstones imply), and everyone is to get a place in a cemetery after she or he dies, then the entire earth is destined to become one huge cemetery! Indeed, if such memorial practices had been in place for all of human history, then the world would already be one big cemetery. In the course of human history, almost all of the dead must eventually be forgotten. In different East Asian contexts, various measures have been taken to prevent the endless expansion of cemetery space. In some places, contracts at cemeteries are for fixed periods: ten, fifteen, or twenty years. At the end of a contract period, the coffin is to be dug up and the space in the cemetery is to be offered to someone else. In other places, cremation followed by a niche in a columbarium are offered instead of cemetery space. As columbaria may be built like high-rises, and niches for cinerary caskets are smaller than gravesites, considerable land can be saved. Even so, some columbaria, like cemeteries, demand fixed contract periods for their niches. Using even less land than columbaria are vast underground vaults for burying boxes of ashes. On top of the vaults is a tall tower to which tiny nameplates of those buried underneath can be attached. The "greenest" of all are options that use no land: scattering the ashes at sea or in a river, or mixing them in the soil of a garden where grass, trees, or flowers are grown.

As described above, in rural China there can be some resistance to shifting from burial of the body to cremation. But in most urban contexts, cremation itself is already well-accepted. In Hong Kong and Taiwan, where there are no laws mandating cremation, over 95 percent of people choose cremation as the method to dispose of the body of a deceased relative. In the urban Chinese contexts where I did research, I never heard any complaints about cremation itself. In most parts of urban China I visited, there was a preference for burying the ashes in a small cemetery plot. In Hong Kong and Taiwan, most people place the ashes in a columbarium niche. But in all three of these Chinese contexts, there is a strong preference for giving the ashes some sort of home. Columbaria offer a place to visit on Qing Ming and other occasions, a place to perform sacrifices, burn spirit money, and offer respects. Though options for scattering ashes are available in all three of these places, they are not popular.

Three cultural logics inform these preferences. First is the notion that every person or soul should have a home. Someone who does not have a home is neglected. Moreover, you cannot visit them. Insofar as the ethic of filial piety requires both visiting your loved ones and ensuring that they have a place to live (as well as food to eat, brought in sacrifices, and money to spend, burnt before their homes), then not giving your deceased loved one a final resting place feels like neglecting one's filial duties. Second, scattering the ashes of a loved one furthers the disintegration of the body begun in the process of cremation. Like the rural people who object to cremation, urban people can feel that this aspect of maintaining the integrity of the body is a crucial aspect of caring for its soul. Finally, when ashes are buried in a garden or scattered at sea, they are necessarily intermingled with and polluted by the ashes of other dead people. In mainland China, fear of ghosts has made it extremely difficult for cemeteries to resell plots where someone had once been buried. Though most cemeteries have fixed-term contract periods, I never heard of a case where a cinerary casket had actually been dug up and the gravesite resold. As suggested in chapter 4, fear of ghosts and fear of strangers are closely related phenomena. This fear also affects the idea of mingling the ashes of one's deceased relative with those of other people.

One way that scattering ashes at sea is promoted in Hong Kong is by pointing out how difficult it is for people who migrate halfway around the world to visit the original homes where their parents' ashes are located. Hong Kong is one of the most mobile societies in the world, with high rates of immigration from China and high rates of emigration to England, Canada, the United States, Australia, and New Zealand. If ashes are scattered at sea, then descendants may visit them and pay respect to them anywhere in the world where there is access to the ocean. Hong Kong also arranges special boats to go out during Qing Ming for people who wish to conduct ceremonies for their ancestors. Nonetheless, scattering ashes at sea remains a difficult option to sell, and the vast majority of people with a deceased relative choose cremation followed by a place in a columbarium.

In mainland China, since the eighteenth party congress in 2012 (when Xi Jinping assumed leadership), rhetoric of promoting "ecological civilization" (生态文明) has been used to promote reducing the amount of land used for funerary activities. In 2016, the Ministry of Civil Affairs, in conjunction with eight other

Ministries, issued a "Guiding Opinion Regarding the Promotion of Land Saving and Ecological Burials" (关于推行节地生态安葬的指导思想). Though not quite having the force of a law, such "guiding opinions," especially when jointly issued by nine ministries, can exert considerable influence on the regulatory decisions of local bureaucrats. Some legal scholars I spoke to suggested that official consensus around the issue of saving land in burials is consolidating and a new formal law is imminent. While the document does not advocate the use of force in promoting the saving of land, it suggests five types of measures local governments should take. First, local governments are required to develop plans for promoting ecological and land-saving burials. Second, Party members are to set an example for the general public by selecting the most ecological form of burial available. Third, significant propaganda work is to be devoted to popularize the idea of ecological burials. Fourth, economic incentives are to be used to promote ecological burials, and, fifth, local governments are to make sure that the infrastructure and facilities for ecological burials are readily available.

Since 2016, the Ministry of Civil Affairs has published a "Green Book on Funerals" (殡葬绿皮书) each year, in which various local governments describe what they have done in reaction to the "Guiding Opinion." In Nanjing, since 2016, the Garden of Merit has put even greater efforts into promoting "wall burials" (a form of columbarium) and garden burials. For the garden burials, there is a type of biodegradable cinerary casket that dissolves into the soil within three months. Another newer option developed by the Garden of Merit is a family-style tomb in which eight or more family members can be buried under one small tombstone by stacking the cinerary caskets vertically (Wang et al. 2017). But, as described in chapter 3, the Garden of Merit has limited space for regular burials anyway, so "ecological" burials have been a profit-making strategy for a while.

In Wuhan, the group charged with promoting green funerals noted the obstacles to preventing widespread acceptance of such funerals and argued that money was needed to promote new policies.[4] In rural areas where crematoriums are lacking, they argued, most people bury their dead in private graves that are scattered across a village's land, rather than in orderly designated cemeteries. In urban districts, cemeteries make their money from selling gravesites, and "green" burials, particularly if they are to be offered for discounts, lose money. How can cemeteries be given the responsibility of promoting green burials if they do not make money? How can governments pay for new equipment, subsidies for ecological burials, and free funerals for impoverished people if the central government does not allocate funds? As is often the case in China, the "Guiding Opinion" implies a sort of unfunded mandate. A policy is suggested, but no funds are allocated to support its implementation. While elite cemeteries in Wuhan (and elsewhere) are able to make money from services as well as gravesites, non-elite cemeteries make almost all of their money from selling gravesites. Most non-elite families will pay for a visible piece of property like a tomb, but find services too ethereal.

They would rather provide the services for themselves. Though implicitly criticizing the unfunded mandate aspect of the "Guiding Opinion," the Wuhan group suggests that it will use propaganda to promote ecological burials, thus abiding by at least part of the guidelines. It emphasizes the theme of "thick care, thin burials" (厚养薄葬), implying that a family should lavish "thick," resource-consuming care on the elderly in their families while they are alive and then spend their money, time, and effort "thinly" (frugally) when approaching the funeral and burial.

In the directly administered city of Tianjin, there are no rural areas and cremation rates are already nearly universal, so efforts have focused on promoting the ecological disposal of cremains, as well as civilized, orderly, and non-superstitious funerals. Grave-sweeping, especially during Qing Ming, is taken as the key to promoting these practices (Qi and Zhu 2017). Having a place to visit on Qing Ming is a concern in all culturally Chinese urban areas. The Tianjin Ministry of Civil Affairs began organizing collective grave-sweeping as early as 2005, with the goal of displacing "superstitious" practices like burning spirit money and setting off firecrackers. On Qing Ming, the city funeral home organized space and transportation for several hundred people to collectively bow in honor of their ancestors, light candles, and present flowers. They have gradually expanded this activity, and, in 2016, 30,000 people participated at sixteen different sites, beautifully decorated with flowers and resonant with solemn music. Since the publishing of the "Guiding Opinion," the Tianjin Ministry has used collective grave-sweeping as a way of promoting ecological burials, particularly the disposal of ashes in the sea. With collective grave-sweeping, Tianjin residents can be filial to their relatives even without a gravesite. Moreover, the grave-sweeping is done in a civilized, collective, Party-organized manner.

While I am in favor of promoting green, eco-friendly practices, I am somewhat worried about the types of policies that local governments could be tempted to implement in reaction to the "Guiding Opinion," as well as any future legal changes that may occur. First of all, while the conservation of land is an important principle, China is a large country and not a single, relatively small urban area like Hong Kong or Singapore. There are many spaces where land could be used for burials without disrupting agricultural production.

Second, the politics of land use in China have more to do with the profits to be made from re-zoning land than ecological conservation per se. In China, urbanization is proceeding rapidly and city governments make considerable money from land sales. They requisition land from surrounding villages, provide some compensation to the former villagers, re-zone the land from agricultural to urban, and sell it at immensely higher prices to real estate developers. Many city governments rely on income from land sales to fund their regular activities. To prevent this process from eating up too much agricultural land, the central government requires land-requisitioning local governments to open up new agricultural land every time they re-zone land at the outskirts of cities from agricultural to urban.

In theory, no net loss of agricultural land is permitted. In practice, the ways that local governments are able to open up new agricultural land sometimes rely on the unjust usurping of village land and sometimes do not really result in the ability to increase agricultural production. For example, one way of increasing agricultural land is to requisition the land where villagers have built their houses or graves, force the villagers to move into high-rise apartment buildings somewhere in the vicinity of their original homes, and declare the land with now-abandoned houses or graves on it to be "agricultural." By replacing single-story family homes with apartments, relatively large numbers of people can be housed on relatively small parcels of land. But often the areas originally containing graves and houses were not suitable for agriculture to begin with, the investment needed to turn the former house- or grave-land into productive fields is not forthcoming, the relocation of villagers actually hinders their ability to farm the land efficiently, and the compensation offered to villagers in the process is not adequate.[5]

Chapter 3 has already described some of the processes related to relocating cemeteries as urban areas expand. But under the rules requiring no net land loss, the relocation of rural graves far away from urban centers might also enable urban governments to expand the amount of land they zone as urban. It is in the context of this land-use policy that legislation promoting ecological burials has been gaining support among the actors who have a voice in legislative reform.

The contradictory relationship between funerary reform and saving land can also be seen in the use of flowers at funerals. At many moments in funerary ritual and practices of memorialization, the government promotes giving or displaying flowers as a civilized alternative to burning spirit money or incense. The idea that giving flowers is less superstitious and more civilized than burning sacrificial paper objects predates Party policy on the matter. It can be traced back to the liberal intellectual Hu Shih and the funeral he conducted for his mother in 1919 (Whyte 1988). But it is really only during the post-Mao era that this idea has informed funerary practice in most parts of China. The collective grave-sweeping activities organized by the Ministry of Civil Affairs in Tianjin, for example, use large amounts of flowers but burn no spirit money. Though some urban jurisdictions still allow the burning of spirit money, the giving of flowers has become much more important to the funerary sector. State-run funeral homes make most of their profits from the fees charged for decorating memorial halls with flowers and selling flowers to those attending funerals as gifts for mourning families. Profits from selling spirit money pale in comparison, and, at best, support a few very small, often illegal, vendors. To supply all of these flowers, large areas of agricultural land, formerly devoted to growing crops, are now used to grow flowers. The Dounan flower market, for example, located in the rural areas just outside of Kunming, has grown into the largest wholesale flower market in all of Asia. Scores of villages in the area of the market devote their agricultural land to flowers. The rise of the flower industry in China has probably done more to take land away from the growth of crops than the cemetery industry, which typically utilizes land that was not being farmed to begin with.

The preference for flowers over spirit money reflects a complex dynamic of cultural politics under Chinese authoritarian rule. Describing what one does as "civilized" or "science" instead of "superstition" aligns one's actions with the rhetoric of the Party. Whether presenting flowers is actually less superstitious than burning incense matters little. Once the Party's rhetoric has been firmly aligned with this claim, presenting flowers instead of burning incense proclaims one's intentions to be loyal to the Party. The government's attachment to large-scale, well-ordered forms of ritual display is another aspect of this political culture. Regularity and order fulfill desires for society to appear as if every aspect of social life has been planned out by the central government.[6] Such appearances inform both the Tianjin government's organization of collective grave-sweeping rituals and the Wuhan working group's dislike of "disorderly" graves scattered across the countryside. These appearances suggest loyalty to the central government, as regularity indicates government organization. But these appearances have little to do with saving land. In fact, graves that are placed on bits of unused land scattered here and there may be quite an efficient way of accommodating burials while causing minimal disturbance to agriculture. Finally, while cemeteries with gravesites laid out in even rows might be more desirable than graves scattered across the countryside from the government's point of view, even cemeteries have the undesirable side effect of giving all those buried there their own memorialized history. Such multiple histories go against the grain of the Propaganda Department's desire to narrate a single, Party-glorifying history for the nation as a whole. In short, while I can see a need for promoting land-saving, ecological burials, I fear that much of this promotion could get caught up in the politics of professing loyalty to the Party, making the nation appear more singular and orderly than it actually is, fighting "superstition," and funding local governments' hunger for re-zone-able land. The political pressures reinforcing these tendencies have only become more intense during the Xi Jinping era. While the huge size and diversity of the Chinese countryside allows some areas to implement policies that are considerably less restrictive than those outlined above, the authoritarian style of Chinese governance often leads to cases in which mandatory cremation, grave relocation, or restrictions on memorial activities are enforced even when such policies offend large numbers of people.

GOVERNING DOUBLE BURIAL
IN GUANGZHOU AND HONG KONG

In Hong Kong the government has also taken measures to reduce the amount of land devoted to memorialization. Beginning in the 1970s, shortages of burial plots occurred, their price soared, and the government actively promoted (but never legally demanded) cremation followed by a niche in a columbarium as an alternative. Most people also lacked the space in their tiny apartments to carry out traditional funerary rituals, and the percentage of families accepting cremation of their loved ones rose rapidly, reaching 90 percent in 2012 and continuing to rise (Y. Chan 2019, 61). As most people live in apartments, "high-rise" burial niches in columbaria do not seem un-home-like. But recently the Hong Kong government has become alarmed by the amount of land taken up by private columbaria. At the same time that government-run columbaria have filled and started waiting lists (niches are allocated for fixed-period contracts and re-allocated when families fail to renew their contracts), the government has limited the issuing of licences to new private columbaria. The Hong Kong government actively encourages families to dispose of ashes by scattering them at sea or in remembrance gardens, but, to date, most families refuse these options. As described above, most Hong Kong people prefer to give the ashes of their departed loved ones a private home. Unfortunately, as a result of the government's policies, a large number of families are forced to store their relatives' ashes in temporary storage facilities where it is not possible to sweep the graves during Qing Ming (Y. Chan 2019).

While efforts to save land by restricting the availability and terms of licenses for funerary businesses have perhaps been even more vigorous in Hong Kong than in mainland China, they have been less shaped by opposition to "superstition" and the politics of displaying loyalty. In Hong Kong, during Qing Ming, the air around columbaria is so thick with smoke that it can be difficult to breathe. Regulation in Hong Kong more often involves licensing procedures for different types of businesses than direct bans. The licensing restrictions make certain activities prohibitively expensive for the majority of people, but do not outlaw anything entirely. Those with money to spend, or connections to institutions like churches and temples, often legally carry out funerary and memorial activities in ways that the government does not encourage.

The difference in regulatory approaches is particularly apparent with regards to the practice of double burial. During the nineteenth and early twentieth centuries, in the southern parts of China, double burial was common. Most villages in this part of China, including the rural parts of Hong Kong, were single lineage villages, in which almost all the families shared a surname. Adults who had given birth to descendants would be buried twice. The first time they would be buried in a full coffin. After a period of time during which the flesh would decompose, the body would be exhumed and the bones cleaned and then placed into an urn. The urn would then be buried in a gravesite either determined by village lineage elders or selected by a particular family after advice from an expert in geomancy. In the traditional thought of these areas of China, bones were considered a Yang, or male substance, while flesh was considered a Yin, or female substance. Since the families were patrilines, consisting of descendants from a male ancestor, burying urns that only had bones in them was thought to be a ritually pure and powerful way of bringing good fortune to descendants.[7]

In Hong Kong the practice remains legal. Some of the villages in the outer reaches of Hong Kong have their own cemeteries to carry out such burials, but members of the general public can also do so at the Wo Hop Shek cemetery, the largest public cemetery in Hong Kong. One section is reserved for first burials. The bodies are buried in biodegradable coffins so that the bones may be easily exhumed seven years later. Another section of cemetery is reserved for the second burials. The urns for these burials are known as "Golden Towers" (金塔) and this section of the graveyard is called the "Golden Tower Section." The second burials are permanent. One of the great ironies of burial governance in Hong Kong is that at a time when private columbarium niches are extremely expensive and waiting lists for public columbarium niches are long, space for a double burial in the public cemetery is both readily available and inexpensive. According to those working at the cemetery, several factors account for the lack of popularity of double burial. First, the Golden Tower Section of the cemetery is relatively inaccessible by public transportation, making visits during Qing Ming more difficult; because of over-crowding, private cars are banned from the cemetery during the period around Qing Ming, and the Golden Tower section is about a 2 kilometer walk from the cemetery bus stop. Second, the ritual procedures for a double burial are much more complicated than for a cremation and subsequent placement in a colum-barium niche; they involve exhumation, the cleaning of the bones, the placing of the bones in a golden tower, and the burial of the golden tower. Finally, the Hong Kong's government campaign to promote cremation was so successful that most Hong Kong residents consider cremation "normal" and would not even consider doing something else.

I visited the Golden Tower section of the Wo Hop Shek cemetery, and was sur-prised by its relative disorderliness. The graves are not laid out in a regular pattern, many of the graves are old and have obviously been neglected for a long time, and some sections are overgrown and full of weeds. The cemetery office eventu-ally digs up graves that have been neglected, but only after a lengthy process of trying to contact the descendants of the deceased person. While the Hong Kong government's manipulation of licenses has had a forceful effect on funerary prac-tice, its tolerance for practices that would be labeled as superstitious or disorderly in mainland China, and even practices that it openly discourages, makes it quite different from the more direct authoritarianism of the mainland.

In Guangzhou, the practice of double burial has also left a trace, but it operates in a grey area somewhere between the legal and the illegal. In some rural areas of Guangdong province, double burial has continued to be practiced (perhaps after a period of disruption during the Cultural Revolution decade, 1966–76). But even in the most urban of funeral homes in the province, the Guangzhou city funeral home, golden tower urns are sold. After seeing the urns in a shop, and asking a friend to make some inquiries, I learned that some urban people in Guang-zhou pay an extra fee to the crematorium to have a partial cremation (烧全骨). While a full cremation turns most of the bones into ash, and, often, is followed by having the remaining bits of bone smashed into a fine powder, a partial cremation burns away the flesh, but leaves the bones intact. The bones can then be placed in a golden tower in a traditional ceremony and the golden tower can be buried in a cemetery. The entire procedure resembles a traditional double burial, with the cremation replacing the first burial.[8] This form of "double burial" is particularly curious from the point of view of land conservation. Because golden towers are bigger than regular cinerary caskets, they require a larger-sized cemetery plot. These plots are technically illegal, as the government regulations prohibit plots larger than one meter square per burial, but, in practice, they are readily available in the cemeteries around Guangzhou.

At least on paper, the city of Guangzhou has some of the tightest regulations in China regarding land use at funerals. Like Hong Kong, it also uses licensing, or land use restriction, to prevent the opening up of new spaces for burial within the city limits. But the law on paper is not a good guideline for understanding actual practice there. In addition to allowing the burial of golden tower urns, several aspects of common burial practice violate the letter of the law. First, the existing cemeteries are mostly full, and it is illegal to sell plots before they are available. But several existing cemeteries within the city limits sell plots in anticipation of being allowed to expand their cemeteries in the future. In addition, some of the cemeteries outside of the city limits sell cemetery plots to people with Guangzhou city household registrations, though cinerary remains are not supposed to be transported outside of the city. Finally, I have heard stories of some wealthy Guangzhou people buying a house in a rural area and then using the house as a secret, private family cemetery, where the golden tower urns of lineage members may be buried with large tombs. In addition to the laws regarding land use for burials is the problem of "superstition." At the most visible cemeteries in the relatively central districts of Guangzhou, rules against burning spirit money and other "superstitious" activities are strictly enforced. But in the less prestigious cemeteries, let alone in places like secret family cemeteries, the burning of spirit money can be observed.

The Guangzhou method of governing involves strict laws that are not always strictly enforced. This method has its advantages. Loyalty to the central government is demonstrated both by publishing laws that sound strict and by enforcing them at the sites that are most visible to prominent visitors. At the same time, flexibility is shown towards Guangzhou citizens who might otherwise loudly object. But the dangers of such an approach are also noteworthy. When there is a real material advantage to local cadres for confiscating land or making a show of their loyalty to the center, the law on paper makes a handy tool for pushing through seemingly arbitrary forms of enforcement.

So while both Guangzhou and Hong Kong regulate to prevent the expansion of space for burial, and both places face problems with shortages of final resting places, in Hong Kong there is actually more space available for double burial than people interested in doing it. Instead of a shortage of burial space, there is a shortage of columbarium space. While the government attempts to pressure people into ecological burial practices through a combination of propaganda and licensing procedures, the law on paper provides a fairly accurate description of what goes on. In Guangzhou, there is no double burial per se, but there is a surprising continuation of the use of golden towers for burial. Many technically illegal practices emerge. The politics of burial involve appearing to be loyal to the central government by publishing strict rules, enforcing these regulations in highly visible and centrally located cemeteries, but allowing practices that seemingly violate the spirit and the letter of the law in peripheral sites.

THE VAGARIES OF SUPERSTITION

In my travels to mainland Chinese cities during 2018 and 2019, including Guangzhou, Shenzhen, Changsha, Wuhan, Jingzhou, Taiyuan, Shijiazhuang, Tianjin, and Shanghai, I was shocked by both the increase in severity of anti-superstition rhetoric and the blatant logical contradictions in the official uses of the word. Different activities could be labeled superstitious in different places; a given activity might be "superstitious" in one place and supported by the local government in another; closely related activities could be split into permissible activities and illegal superstitions in seemingly arbitrary ways.

Perhaps the most obvious example is that of burning spirit money and other sacrificial items. In some of the larger cities that I visited, including Shanghai and Tianjin, the burning of spirit money has effectively been banned. Large signs proclaiming the ban are displayed at cemeteries and I saw no place to purchase spirit money near cemeteries, nor any evidentiary trace of burning. In many other cities, I saw signs posted discouraging the practice (labeling it a feudal superstition), but still saw the items to be burned for sale near cemeteries and funeral homes. I also saw people burning them. In one or two smaller cities I visited, there was no propaganda banning the practice. This variation in itself is not so shocking. What really startled me was that at many state-run funeral homes, at the same time that they had instituted bans on burning spirit money, it was permitted to burn the clothes of the deceased, flower wreaths given as gifts during or before the farewell meeting, and sometimes even the picture of the deceased. These contradictions are particularly sharp because the ban on burning spirit money is often justified in terms of preventing air pollution. Moreover, as the funeral of Mr. Wang demonstrated, the burning of clothes involves exactly the same type of "superstitious" beliefs as the burning of spirit money. Both practices imply that burning enables one to give something to the deceased's soul wherever it is imagined to exist; the burning of clothes is further linked to ideas that reutilizing the clothes of the deceased is inauspicious. How is the burning of the clothes of the deceased in any sense less superstitious or less polluting than the burning of spirit money?

Even in the Fu Shou Yuan, where bans on burning "superstitious items" have long been upheld, it is permitted to burn incense, either in front of a grave or at the

FIGURE 15. Sign near Tianjin graveyard, reading "Destroy Outmoded Customs, Oppose Superstition, Root Out Obnoxious Practices, and Advocate Scientific Thinking. It is Prohibited to Set
Off Firecrackers, Burn Spirit Money or Other Paper Paraphernalia." Photo: Andrew B. Kipnis.

Buddhist temple on the grounds. At the Shijiazhuang funeral home, posted regulations detail how the burning of superstitious items was prohibited, but that up to
ten kilos of clothes and five flower wreaths can be burned for free. Fees would be
charged for burning more than those amounts. Most tense of all was the atmos-
phere around the number one funeral home in Tianjin and the attached (state-run)
cemetery. The cemetery and grounds were covered with signs announcing the ban
on the burning of spirit money and other superstitious items. Many of these signs
further detailed how one would be fined 2,000 yuan for carrying out any of wide
range of funerary activities that were labeled as superstitious, including the burning of spirit money. The cemetery itself was tightly guarded with a fence, surveillance cameras, and a guardhouse at the entrance with gates to prevent anyone from
entering without gaining permission from the guards. The place seemed more like a
military installation than a business attempting to earn money by selling cemetery
plots. The adjacent funeral home was also covered with signs announcing the bans
on burning superstitious items and potential fines for doing so. But at the entrance
to the funeral home grounds, on a plot of dirt-covered ground, a group of elderly
people dressed like local peasants was supervising the burning of flower wreaths,
clothes and various other items (though I saw no spirit money). When I walked
over for a closer look, one of the elderly women supervising the burning rushed
up to me and asked me if I had any sacrificial items that needed burning.

In addition to the burning of paper offerings, many other practices have been labeled superstitious in a self-contradictory and inconsistent manner. In Jingzhou, for example, signs at the state-run funeral home quote the twenty-sixth article of the Hubei province funerary management regulations: "Carrying out funerals should be done in a civilized, frugal manner without any form of feudal superstition, ostentatious waste, or other corrupting practices. It is not permitted to consult geomancy masters, Daoist or Buddhist priests, or to hire drum and music groups. . . ." In practice, people regularly did all of these things, but they could not arrange them through the funeral home itself. Officials I spoke to in the funeral home said that such practices disrupted other people in the city, even though the funeral home itself was not located near to any apartment complexes and was in the process of being moved to a location far from the city center. But in many other cities, including Taiyuan and Shijiazhuang, state-run funeral homes were in the business of supplying groups of musicians for hire during various points of the ritual process. In Shanghai, at the partially state-run Fu Shou Yuan cemetery, an on-site Buddhist temple offered priests to supply ritual services. In many cities, the setting up of tents for performances near apartment blocks was banned, and some, such as Tianjin, even banned the erecting of home altars as a form of superstitious practice. Many of the cities that banned or discouraged home altars, however, had funeral homes that offered rooms for rents where altars could be established. The Taiyuan funeral home offered both the option of renting a room and that of assistance in setting up a home altar, as Mr. Chen had done in the case of Mr. Wang's funeral.

There is no simple way to explain this variation in funerary regulation and what gets labeled as superstition, though a few general trends can be hypothetically proposed. Most obviously, cities with high land costs tend to regulate land use more strictly than cities where land prices are lower. Second, cities with high land prices tend also to have taller buildings and more densely populated urban centers, reducing the sense of local community and making officials less likely to tolerate practices like setting up tents for performances and home altars. Third, cities that are highly visible to top-level officials, domestic media, and foreigners make greater efforts to appear "civilized" to the central political leaders in Beijing. Fourth, local city governments that have tense relations with nearby rural people (usually over land-use issues) tend to label a large variety of rural funerary practices as superstition, but allow these practices to persist. Disputes over land-use issues are more important to local governments than the funerary practices themselves, and local governments prefer to threaten but not to expend resources and goodwill on funerary practices. Finally, city governments want to make use of the funerary facilities they have. If they have altar rooms for rent they want to promote their use; if they have excessive cemetery space they want to sell it; if they have musicians already employed by the state funeral home, they want them to earn money.

FRAGMENTED AUTHORITARIANISM
AND TOTALITARIANISM

Political scientists often analyze Chinese governance through the lens of "fragmented authoritarianism." While the government is authoritarian, organized as a Leninist Party-state along strict hierarchical lines, the many parts of the government (including state-owned firms, local governments, and various bureaus) often pursue their own interests in ways that cannot be understood as merely following the orders of the central government. Some political scientists temper this theory with arguments that the political center of the Party devises means to overcome this fragmentation of power. The result is more like "integrated authoritarianism" than fragmented authoritarianism. Both of these views are considered less extreme than simply seeing the Chinese state as "totalitarian," a monster that can only focus on consolidating power and forcing everything in its realm to worship and obey the Party center.[9]

The struggles over governing funerary practice, and the word "superstition" in particular, reflect the degrees of truth contained in all of these theories. Local variation in the process of governing funerals and defining superstition involves both the place-specific interests of different local governments and variance in the physical, economic, and social circumstances in which these governments operate. Efforts to come up with singular funerary law, as well as the coordination of nine different bureaus in issuing the "Guiding Opinion Regarding the Promotion of Land Saving and Ecological Burials," demonstrate the efforts of the center to overcome fragmentation in the regulation of funerary practice. Searching for points of agreement while accommodating regional variation demonstrates desires to integrate a relatively fragmented system of governance.

Because of the size and diversity of the country and the many levels and sections of the government itself, theories of totalitarianism could never accurately describe governing in China. But such theories do describe a sort of political ideal that is becoming more evident under Xi Jinping. The use of the word "unity" or "unify" (统一) often expresses this ideal. The preference for orderly cemeteries and large-scale, collectively-organized rituals are guided by this ideal. The denunciation of non-mainstream religious practice, especially in places like Tibet and Xinjiang, and a lack of tolerance for many forms of multiculturalism and diversity, are also justified by this ideal. So is the demand for displays of loyalty to Xi Jinping and the Party itself. Unity requires everyone to rally around a single person, ideal, or spirit. Almost any sort of violent crackdown on diverse interests can be justified through the ideal of unity. The ideal of unity might be considered to be the soul of the country's Propaganda Department.

The word superstition is like a sledgehammer to be used in the pursuit of unity. Anything that one of the local branches of the Party dislikes can be labeled with it. While the flexibility of the term means that it can be used in a "fragmented" manner, with different branches of the government interpreting the term differently, this same flexibility enables a totalitarian impulse. The Party center reserves the right to determine what should be labeled with the term, and to change its mind about the application of the term whenever it likes.

Party hostility towards funerary ritual likewise reflects its totalitarian impulses. While I certainly support ecological practices in all aspects of life, I am suspicious of attempts to impose ecological practice on the funerary industry more stringently than on the flower industry, or the automotive industry. While all sectors of the economy face some pressure to reduce pollution, in the case of cemeteries, some in the Party have suggested eliminating the industry entirely. One official involved in regulating funerary practice explained it to me this way:

> The party advocates thick care and thin funerals. The ideal would be no funerals, no cemeteries, no memorials. When a person dies, their bodies would be donated to medical research or to medical schools as cadavers to be practiced on by medical students. Whatever parts were leftover when the medical personnel finished would be cremated together. The ashes would be used to make bricks that would then be used for constructing buildings. The families of the deceased would be content with this result as they will have already demonstrated their filial piety by taking excellent care of the deceased when alive. Proper communists are materialists and do not worry about souls or the afterlife.

This refusal to acknowledge the souls of the dead in China is to me the essence of totalitarianism. It does not reflect a simple "materialism," as the cadre suggests, because the Propaganda Department of the Party cares very much about its own soul. It speaks of "the soul of the Party" (党的灵魂), and devotes considerable effort to memorializing its own martyrs and heroes, as the depictions of elite graveyards demonstrated. What the totalitarian parts of the Party dislike is for other people to memorialize their souls. Such memorialization can easily transform into anti-Party political forces. The deaths of political leaders who were seen as opposing the political center in both 1976 and 1989 became rallying points for major protests in Tiananmen Square. But even the deaths of more mundane individuals have led to relatively localized protests all over China— against corrupt and incompetent doctors; against employers who do not offer adequate compensation for workplace accidents; against decisions to limit the welfare or pension rights of various categories of people; against powerful people who cover up their liability in automobile accidents and the corruption that enables the cover-ups to proceed. Grief is a powerful emotion, and the memorialization of souls can easily give rise to a politicized spirit. Moreover, memorialization is also a mode of writing history, as the Cultural Revolution graveyard depicted in chapter 3 suggests. Carving historical memory into gravestones is inconvenient for a Party that desires the ability to rewrite its own history at any moment. The totalitarian impulse in China leads to ideological claims that the only soul that should be celebrated is that of the Party itself. All must unify to defend its integrity. Because stating this proposition directly would be too confrontational, rhetoric emerges that celebrates Party-oriented memorialization as patriotism, but dismisses all other memorialization as polluting, land-wasting, feudal superstition.

7

Of Souls and Spirits

Secularization and its Limits

Practices of memorialization raise basic issues about life and its meaning. When a tombstone is carved, or offerings are placed on a grave, exactly who or what is being addressed? When a person dies, when their body ceases to be "animated," exactly what has left it? Where does this thing go? Why do people all over the world, including Mr. Wang and his family, hold funerals and establish graves even when they claim to be secular, non-religious, and non-superstitious? In a materialist, communist, and anti-superstitious country, why hold funerals at all?

The secularization thesis suggests that as a country or part of a country becomes more modern, as its people become more educated, live in cities, gain exposure to science, and become more dependent upon scientific technologies in all aspects of their life, they will become less religious. Most anthropologists around the world today take a sceptical view of this thesis. Religions pervade today's world, though some scholars also argue that they thrive in truncated forms, with their influence on daily life shrinking. In China, it is both the case that many temples, churches, and mosques are thriving and that many people, if asked, would claim not to be religious. Marxism, the official ideology of the Chinese Communist Party, describes secularization as both a process that will naturally occur as a country modernizes and a desirable state of affairs.

In this chapter, I do not wish to argue either for or against the secularization thesis per se, but I do want to engage with the idea that there may be more or less secular ways of imagining the soul. I seek to understand the significance of funerary practice for Chinese people like Mr. Wang and his family, who do not see themselves as religious, as well as to describe how "religious," "superstitious," and "secular" ways of understanding the soul can be blended together. In China, precisely because the state wishes to promote secular ideologies, this blending often occurs without explicit discussion. It becomes a silent acknowledgment of realities that are too sensitive to address aloud.

SECULAR SPIRITS AND RELIGIOUS SOULS

Consider the words that are used to designate that which gives a body life. Individuals can be seen as having a particular spirit, a personality, a way of interacting with others, of facing life and living. In English, we could call this animating entity, energy, dynamic, or force a soul, or spirit, or perhaps a character. Anthropologists, from the earliest days of the discipline, have noted how different cultures have imagined it in different ways (Tylor 1871). In some cultures, it could be seen as multiple, or could be seen as animating just about anything—animals, plants, rocks, stars, and so on. But most cultures have some way of naming and imagining it.

Secular visions of science declare that all of the universe is subject to universal laws of nature. While there may be phenomena that science does not yet understand, these phenomena are still governed by the universal laws of nature. But while nature is singular in this sense, rarely do secular people apply such a scientific point of view to the forms of subjectivity, imagination, spirit, soul, or culture that animate human bodies. These animating forces are seen as multiple rather than singular. Different people, or people from different cultures, can experience the world differently, see it differently, understand it differently and, thus, can be said to have differing souls, spirits, or personalities.[1]

A secular take on death views the human body physically. Since it is part of nature, it is subject to the universal biological processes of decay and rot. All bodies must die; death is irreversible and dead bodies must, eventually, decompose. But souls and spirits are multiple and not subject to physical laws. While the subjectivity of a particular dead person can no longer exist within its original body, can no longer physically affect the world through that body, its "spirit" can be inscribed in writing or in art, carved onto a tombstone, and perhaps embodied by other individuals who are still alive. We may learn from the spirits of those dead people whom we admire. If we do, their spirits can be said to persist after death.

In societies that are not scientific, or in the religious domains of scientific societies, there is no singular "law of nature." In heaven or hell, physical realms undetectable by science, souls can be seen as enduring or enjoying a permanent physical existence. Even on the earth known by science, gods, ghosts, and other sorts of beings can operate in ways that are not limited by the "law of nature." Different sorts of beings are subject to different sorts of physical limitations. Premodern Chinese society imagined a huge variety of beings who had powers that went well beyond anything that could be considered "natural" by today's scientific standards. The gods, ghosts, and ancestors discussed in chapter 4 all had powers, ways of physically affecting the world, that cannot be explained by science. From a secular, scientific perspective, we would say that their powers are "*super*natural." In addition to having supernatural powers, these beings also exist in realms that are separate from the earthly world that humans inhabit. These realms are likewise undetectable by science. In a traditional Chinese way of thinking, when a person dies, their soul becomes a god, ghost, or ancestor of some type, or perhaps all of the above in differing mixtures and at different moments. Their soul both exists in another realm and has the power to physically affect the earthly world in which humans exist. Burning spirit money, or other forms of ancestral sacrifice, allows the transfer of gifts from our earthly realm of existence to a non-earthly one. Sometimes these sacrifices are undertaken to encourage a god, ghost, or ancestor to do something in the earthly realm of humans.

Premodern Europe and the non-secular people of contemporary European societies likewise believe in many "supernatural" entities. The English language reveals how secular and non-secular visions of the universe can blend together. The word "spirit," for example, can be used to refer to a supernatural entity, like a ghost; it may also refer to the character, personality, or way of being of a particular person, in the scientific sense described above; it also can refer to the level of energy a person projects; finally, in the plural, "spirits" may refer to alcohol, perhaps because drinking alcohol can affect a person's energy or persona, or perhaps because it can "possess" a person in the same way that a ghostly spirit can. In other words, a "spirited" person is most likely full of energy, but might also be drunk or possessed! The word "soul" likewise can be used in both a secular and a religious imaginary. A person's soul might be imagined as migrating to heaven or hell—extra-earthly realms undetectable by science. But the word soul is also used in many modern, secular phrases. Soul music, for example, refers not to anything supernatural, but just to a type of music that is very moving, that can touch us deeply. Though this music has its origins in African American gospel music, many contemporary songs in this genre refer not to religious events, but to love, loss, and other emotions understandable to a secular as well as a religious audience. Compared to "spirit," the interiority that "soul" refers to is more individuated and more serious. To tamper with someone's soul is more dangerous, personal, and permanent than manipulating their spirits, which might be high or low on a given day for a variety of reasons.

In Chinese, especially in premodern writing, a number of characters refer to the variety of beings or forms of subjectivity that exist in one realm or another and animate human bodies. These include *jing* (精) and *shen* (神), *hun* (魂) and *po* (魄), *gui* (鬼) and *ling* (灵), *guai* (怪) and *xian* (仙), to name a few. In traditional Chinese culture, it is not just that there are a large number of beings with a variety of forms of subjectivity and physical powers, but also that one type of being might transform into another. Upon death, humans regularly become gods, ghosts, or ancestors. But traditional Chinese culture also imagined that through arduous discipline and training, humans could acquire seemingly supernatural powers.

Martial arts movies often depict humans who learn to leap from tree to tree in a manner that resembles flying, or to manipulate *qi*, the energy of life, in miraculous ways. Daoist masters could become immortals (*xian*). Commonly portrayed in novels, movies, video games, television dramas, plays, and stories, such transformations and beings are still very much part of contemporary Chinese culture. Just like the words spirit and soul are commonly used in modern English, the characters listed above are used in a myriad of everyday and metaphorical speech.

In modern Chinese, several compound words have been formed from the above characters to translate ideas from western writings. The compound word *jingshen* usually translates "spirit," while *linghun* is used for "soul." As in English, the term *jingshen*/spirit is used in ways that implies that the entity it refers to is less important than the one that the word *linghun*/soul refers to. One can discuss *jingshen* in a light-hearted way with phrases like "that blouse makes you look spirited" (*na jian yifu ting jingshen*). In contrast, discussing someone's or some organization's soul/*linghun* is almost always a serious affair. One can embrace one sort of a *jingshen*/spirit in one moment and another in the next, while one's soul is relatively singular and permanent. In Chinese, the word *jingshen* is used almost exclusively in a secular way. It does not refer to any sort of supernatural being. But the word *linghun* can be used in phrases where a literal belief in a supernatural entity is implied. Moreover, in a manner that more fully reflects a traditionally Chinese religious imagination, there are a multiplicity of words that use the character *hun*, some of which translate as soul (*linghun, hunpo, hunling, jinghun*) and others which translate as ghost (*guihun, youhun* 幽魂, *youhun* 游魂, *yinhun*). On its own, the character *hun* can refer to both a soul and a ghost, indicative of the fact that in a religious Chinese imaginary, a person's soul can become a ghost—and maybe even the idea that a particular spiritual agency might be seen as a soul by some people and a ghost by others.

By introducing ideas about secular and non-secular thought and the vocabularies of animating spirits in English and Chinese, I hope to make two points about the secularization thesis. The first is that secularization does not necessarily result in the end of funerals and memorialization, because it does not end thought about the forms of subjectivity that animate particular human beings. Even for people who disavow all forms of religious and "superstitious" belief, who think that there is only a single nature which is explained by science and that there is no such thing as the supernatural, there remains the question of what happens to the spirit, the persona, the character, or the way of being that used to animate the body of their deceased family member or friend. In their grief, or in their hopes for a better future, they may wish to re-member, to re-articulate, or even to emulate this spirit themselves. In other words, secular and religious thought may differ in the ways that they imagine the relationships between an animating subjectivity and the physical universe, but they both assume that some form of subjectivity exists. Moreover, even in secular imaginaries, this form of soul or spirit can last longer than the life of any given individual. Second, even if a partial seculari-zation of funerary ritual and memorialization has occurred, that is to say, even if more people approach death and the spirit of the departed in a secular way rather than a religious way, even if they do not believe that "gods, ghosts, and ancestors" can physically act in supernatural ways, the echoes of religious thought still rever-berate in the very words that are used to speak of death, souls, and spirits. As the funeral of Mr. Wang demonstrated, even in a secular family, the words spoken at the funeral, as well as the ritual actions taken at all stages of the funerary process, proceed as if the soul of the departed still exists, still needs care in another realm, and can still physically affect the circumstances of the human world. In this sense, scientific and religious thought blend together rather than replace one another.

THE SOUL OF THE PARTY

The last chapter discussed the "materialism" that Party rhetoric refers to when dismissing the desires of people in China to hold funerals and bury their relatives' ashes in cemeteries. I also noted that despite this rhetoric, Party propaganda often memorializes the subjectivities, spirits, or souls of which it approves. Of course, most governments around the world carry out such activities. Almost every coun-try has national cemeteries, tombs for unknown solders, and war memorials. In her analysis of the reburials and the toppling of memorial statues that occurred after the breakup of the Soviet Union, Katherine Verdery (1999, 1) notes that "Dead bodies have enjoyed political life . . . since far back in time." In China since 1949, there has been no regime change as dramatic as those that took place in Soviet Union, but the changes in the policies of the Party after Mao's death required some adjustments to memorial practices. At the Babaoshan Revolutionary Cemetery in Beijing, China's burial place for national leaders, heroes and martyrs, bodies, or more recently, cinerary caskets, have been dug up, removed, and relocated many times. The former Cultural Revolution-era vice chairman Kang Sheng, for exam-ple, was exhumed from the cemetery at the same time as he was expelled from the Party. Conversely, He Long died ignobly during the Cultural Revolution in 1969, but was posthumously reinstated into the Party in 1975. The government relocated his cinerary casket to the Babaoshan Columbarium that same year (Wang and Su 2011).

Such dramatic events focus attention on the forms of transcendence or immor-tality upon which political regimes rely. The lives of certain founders or heroes come to represent the political soul of a particular regime or movement. Regime change thus requires a toppling of this soul. When the slogans carved on tomb-stones no longer represent the political spirit of the time, entire graveyards may need to be dug up or closed to the public, as occurred with the Cultural Revolution graveyards in Chongqing. But even in times of political stability, when regimes retain legitimacy and graves and memorials rest in peace, the soul of political movements continues to evolve. In a temporal way, secular political parties face the same dilemma that secular families face at death: while individual bodies come and go, and while the stances of political parties continually evolve, the spirit that a person or a political body stands for must be imagined in a more permanent way.

At the Babaoshan Revolutionary Cemetery, several strategies allow the ever-lasting soul of the Party to evolve. Students are routinely taken through the cemetery to have their patriotism reinforced by learning the stories of martyrs who sacrificed their lives for the Chinese nation. The ability of political educators to frame such lessons in a manner that resonates with the politically correct themes of the present relies on three mundane devices. First, many people are buried there. Political educators can take students to the graves of those whose life stories most closely fit current concerns. When I visited the cemetery in September 2015, military men who had died in the war against Japan were being highlighted. Second, interpretive signposts are placed in front of the graves the educators discuss. These signs provide a relatively flexible medium for framing the words carved in stone on grave markers. Finally, a gigantic television screen has been installed so that recently re-edited stories of the deceased's lives can be presented.

The entire idea of erecting tombstones, or any memorial in stone, is to assert that a particular soul or spirit will last forever. The flexible contextualization of words carved in stone is enabled in many Chinese graveyards today through the use of two-dimensional matrix codes (二维码) on tombstones. Such marks enable visitors to immediately download a life history of the person buried there on their smartphones. Needless to say, the life-history that is saved in cyberspace can be amended as necessary.

But even the words carved onto tombstones are chosen to be reinterpretable while masking the shifting nature of their referents. The sales offices for most graveyards have photographs of various styles of gravestone and lists of suggested words and phrases for etching onto them. These phrases reveal three strategies. The first is to mask the ways in which the meanings of the words might shift over time with references to eternity. Phrases like "never forget" (不忘), "never-ending" (无绝期), "ever-existing" (永存), and "everlasting" (永在) are ubiquitous. The second strategy is to use words that refer to a type of abstract but easily accepted ideal persona or virtue—kind mother, caring father, or loyal friend. While it is possible that the words these virtues invoke will fall out of style, they are also easy to reinterpret. What makes someone a good parent or a loyal friend can be retold in different ways. The third strategy is to choose words that enunciate relatively simple statements of fact—when a person was born, when they entered the Party, or what awards they received. These statements can be used to tell a wide variety of stories. There are limits to reinterpretation that make revolution and the consequent tearing up of graves and memorials sometimes seem necessary. If, as may have been the case during the Cultural Revolution, the very idea of being a good parent is called into question, then the desecration of graves that declared someone to be a good parent might seem like a good idea. In short, at the same time that the current Chinese regime attempts to project its soul as something that is permanent and steadfast, it also must allow this soul to evolve. It thus combines a threefold strategy of stating permanence (either literally or metaphorically by carving words into stone), seeking flexible means of contextualizing the permanent messages, and digging up, destroying, or otherwise completely erasing previous messages about souls that now seem beyond the pale.

Another sort of reinterpretation of the lives of revolutionary martyrs takes place through the development of so-called red tourism. Many Chinese localities try to establish themselves as sites of red tourism by claiming the right to erect memorials to the deceased revolutionary martyrs and national leaders who had been born there. This trend is especially prevalent in Hunan province, the birthplace of Mao Zedong and thus a center of red tourism. In 1999, Peng Dehuai's cinerary casket was dug out of Babaoshan and returned to Xiangtan in Hunan, where a memorial hall was built around his new grave and his former residence was reconstructed as a tourist site. In 2009, He Long was similarly returned to He Long Park in Zhangjiajie, Hunan, while one of the "old five" members of the communist party, Lin Boqu, was returned to Lintan in Hunan in 2013 (Liu Ziqing 2014). While the new memorials in Hunan undoubtedly reproduce politically correct biographies for these famous past leaders, they can do so in a manner that gives more emphasis to the role of their birth locality in developing their revolutionary personae. In the context of Vietnam, Heonik Kwon (2006) provides an insightful analysis of the state reburial of national martyrs and the differences between the way the local and national governments narrate the lives of the war dead.

As a regime ages, the founding leaders are immortalized, but those of the middle periods become less important. Contemporary leaders establish rhetorical links to the founding fathers while ignoring their more recent predecessors. This strategy of memorialization likewise makes it easier to project an unchanging soul of the Party, as the complications of many generations of leaders with somewhat differing ideas can be ignored. As the rewriting of history loses its emphasis on the recent past, the political sacredness of the original leaders is enhanced by their historical distance from the present. The lack of living memories of their presence further makes the rewriting of their biographies easier.

In China, the most famous dead body of all is that of Mao Zedong, whose mummified corpse is preserved in his mausoleum in Tiananmen Square. As the historian Geremie Barmé (1996) points out, Mao's legacy has been reinterpreted by a wide variety of actors for a wide variety of purposes both within and outside of China. For the first time since the 1990s, I revisited his mausoleum in September 2015, at 8:00 a.m. on a Thursday morning, and was struck by three aspects of how the presentation of his persona had evolved.[2] First, the entire square had been redesigned for tourists from the Chinese hinterlands. In the crowds of thousands of people milling about with me that morning, I saw not one non-Chinese face.

Most of the people there were dressed in a manner that suggested that they came from the countryside. The square itself had been redecorated with a nearly life-sized, plastic-flower-and-bird covered Great Wall replica. This replica allowed tourists to get a perfect photo of a Great Wall-like structure without actually going there. Its pristinely clean but plastic construction marked it as designed to appeal to frugal tourists, mostly from rural areas, who desire a nice photo but do not want to pay for a Great Wall tour and do not care about authenticity.

Second, the presentation of Mao has made him more god-like. While a sacred attitude towards Mao's body was always encouraged, the mausoleum used to take more steps to encourage an appropriately secular, communist attitude.[3] Recently, Mao has been treated more like a god (see Wardega 2012). Entrants to the mausoleum must now take off their hats and remain silent. In addition, all of the visitors I saw bowed three times before his statue at the entrance of the mausoleum, before placing flowers (sold for 3 yuan at the entrance) in the cauldron in front of his statue. While the rule of silence prevented prayers from being said aloud, at the exit to the mausoleum I heard at least one couple discussing the wishes for good fortune that they hoped Mao might make come true. Overall, the ritual of visiting the mausoleum both resembles and distances itself from the standard way one worships at a Chinese temple. The bows replace kowtows and the flowers replace burning incense. Thus, the communist ritual simultaneously declares itself different from "superstitious religions" while mimicking their form. Finally, upon exiting the mausoleum, one is faced with a variety of stalls selling Mao tourist kitsch. There are both official stalls within the cordoned-off area of the mausoleum and unofficial stalls outside. Even the official stalls sold Mao badges and emblems of a type that seemed a blasphemy against Mao's virulent anti-capitalism. One 20-yuan gold colored badge, for example, was decorated with a circle of fake diamonds and had a giant 福 (prosperity) character printed on the backside. Such badges are often dangled from the rear view mirrors of taxis or in the entrances to restaurants to bring these businesses good fortune and to protect them from danger. While there have long been Mao badges that present him like a god of wealth, to see them for sale at an official tourist stall next to his mausoleum on Tiananmen Square struck me as indicating a new degree of official acceptance of this reinterpretation.

Despite the evolving interpretations of Mao's persona, his memorial is framed with reference to eternity. Carved in stone at the entrance is the stock phrase "remain forever without deterioration" (永垂不朽). Thus, as with the souls presented in Babaoshan cemetery, Mao's soul is presented as unchanging even as it is made to evolve. Moreover, to a striking extent, the worship of Mao's soul in a religious fashion (of Mao as a god who can grant wishes in the present) is permitted even by a Party that declares its soul to be anti-superstitious to the core.

In addition to memorials and cemeteries, the souls of Party members are immortalized in the speeches given at their funerals and the words written in their obituaries. A cadre in charge of funerary arrangements for retired officials at a university once described to me the care taken with official obituaries. While no obituary can say anything bad about the deceased, the subtle gradations of positive words must be calibrated to match the rank of the retired cadre. "Fixing the words when you close the coffin" (盖棺论定) is a Chinese tradition, this cadre concluded. While immortalizing the souls of their cadres, the Party thus also seeks to immortalize the hierarchies created through its political rankings (see also W. Tsai 2017). The content of obituaries and eulogies, like words on tombstones, are selected to be generically acceptable. Themes of patriotism, loyalty to the Party, and greatness predominate. But the emphasis on recreating political rank in death reveals another aspect of the Party's soul—it is hierarchical to the core, in a military, Leninist, authoritarian fashion.

Why does the Party need a soul? I see it as part of the necessary work of any modern political entity. The soul is like an ideal, and ideals are necessary to rally people around a particular political identity. This soul must be abstract enough or vague enough that different people can relate to it in a variety of ways. The vagueness required to unite different audiences makes it vulnerable to deconstruction by a determined intellectual critique. To avoid such deconstruction, political leaders make their symbols sacred. The soul of a party should be above criticism so that no one comes to doubt it. In their resistance to a scientific "materialist" questioning, the dynamics of sacralization create a religious tone. For this reason, even the most anti-religious, anti-superstitious entity in China, the Communist Party, treats its own soul in a religious fashion.

THE SOULS OF THE PEOPLE

It is not only the Propaganda Department that finds the dynamics of sacralization soothing or finds it useful to link tropes of transcendence with practices of transience when memorializing souls. Speaking ill of the dead is not welcomed in most societies, especially at funerals, and I never heard of or witnessed a Chinese funeral where anyone said anything negative about the deceased. The tombstones in the most common of cemeteries contain phrases implying that the soul of the deceased will last forever. In the funeral of Mr. Wang, the calligraphy written on flower wreaths given at funerals also used tropes of eternity, as did the words displayed around the entranceway to the funeral parlor hall where his farewell meeting was held. In death, the demise of the body is so obvious, especially where cremation is practiced, that gestures towards permanence might be understood as a way of comforting the grieving.

Like the soul of the Party, the souls of the people link transience to transcendence in both secular and religious fashion, and sometimes in ways that blend the two ways of thinking. A more secular way of blending could be seen in the colors in which names were etched onto Mr. Wang's tombstone. Mr. Wang's name was written in black, while his wife's name was colored red and will remain that way until she passes away. The names of the children, their spouses, and the grandchildren were also painted in red, as they all were alive at the time of Mr. Wang's burial. In addition, Mr. Wang's surname remains in red, as will his wife's after she is buried. This coloring indicates that family names are eternal, even though individuals are mortal. The spirit of the family continues even when any individual passes away. In this manner, Mr. Wang's life is framed as a sacrifice to the cause of the Wang family, while his wife, perhaps unintentionally, will be framed as having contributed primarily to her natal family (most women in China do not officially change their surnames after they get married). The practice of burying couples together also suggests that marriage itself transcends death.

This pattern of coloring names links eternity to transience in a secular manner because the spirit of the family is seen as sequentially embodied by the successive generations of the family. It does not require belief in a soul that lives in another realm, or a soul that can still influence earthly affairs after the demise of its body. The secular memorialization of familial souls can also be seen in tombstone carvings that depict the deceased as a loving mother, father, aunt, or uncle, in farewell meeting eulogies that do the same, or in the kinship terms used when addressing the departed. The spirit of one's mother or father can be actively embraced by their children. Addressing this spirit as mother or father suggests that those people did properly act in the role of a caring parent when they were alive.

But there are more religious ways of invoking familial relationships while linking permanence to transience in contemporary Chinese funerals. A Buddhist priest once explained to me the reason for chanting sutras on behalf of the recently departed: it helps the soul of the departed to forget their earthly families and make the journey to Western Paradise. While priests, or sometimes tape recorders, chant sutras, it was important for the family members not to cry. The priest explained: "Crying makes the soul of the deceased less willing to leave this world and transition to the Western Paradise. It creates unnecessary attachment. Birth and death are all part of life. Without death there could not be birth. We monks never cry at the funerals of our brethren." But if life is presented in Buddhist ritual as transient, both the soul and the Western Paradise, especially as they are popularly imagined, persist forever. The existence of this other realm where the soul itself lives on, enjoying the pleasures of Paradise, marks this practice as non-scientific, as does the soul's ability to hear the cries of the living after its body has perished. The desires and dangers of crying at the funeral envision familial bonds as something that must be broken at death.

Beyond familial souls, middle-class Chinese people sometimes memorialize the spirits of their loved ones in terms of their career. A teacher, or doctor, or anthropological researcher dedicates herself to an abstract calling that transcends any individual life. Words depicting career accomplishments, as well as artistic renderings of symbols of particular careers are often carved into tombstones. In addition, tombstones sometimes memorialize souls as belonging to a particular religion, ethnic group, or manner of inhabiting the earth. The devoted Christian, ping-pong player, or calligrapher might consider their devotion a matter of personal calling, a political identity, or something altogether different. Farewell meeting eulogies can also mention all of these souls.

Some elite cemeteries divide their plots into sections according to the careers of the deceased. There can be sections for military men and women and their spouses, sections for actors, artists, and cultural elites, as well as sections for academics and scholars. In some cities, there are entire cemeteries or sections of cemeteries devoted to Muslims or Christians. In Hong Kong, where ethnicity, especially in the past, was determined by the part of China from which one had emigrated and the dialect of Chinese that one spoke, there are sections of cemeteries reserved for those of Chiuchow (潮州) and Hakka descent. Such cemeteries or sections of cemeteries often contain statues or stone carvings that represent the spirit of the religion or ethnicity of those buried there.

From a functional anthropological perspective, the souls of the people can play a role similar to the soul of the Party. They can serve as a rallying point for a particular identity: that of a Muslim or a Christian, a Hakka or a Chiuchow person, a teacher or a soldier. Even when someone is only memorialized in a familial way, their soul can become a rallying point of a familial identity for all those who mourn the same person.

In addition to serving as a rallying point for a particular identity, secular imaginations of the spirit of the deceased can console the living by providing a reason to live. For those with a career or an identity beyond that of their family, memorials devoted to a career or to both a career and a family can console. But for those with nothing but a rotten job, meaning is often obtained from familial reproduction. One "eats bitterness" to earn money for the sake of one's family. Memorializing the familial devotion of one's parent provides inspiration to continue one's own familial devotion.

Consequently, while familial reproduction might be seen as a theme with deep roots in premodern China, it is also modern. Moderns do not simply farm as their parents did. Rather they must find a career, or at least a job. For those who toil in alienating jobs, the meaning of the work usually derives from the contributions to familial reproduction that income from the work enables. In this sense, devotion to family and the types of memorialization such devotion enables are not just vestiges of a premodern era, but central to modern life itself. Those who find meaning in a career are equally the products of modernity's division of labor. If modernity involves secularization in addition to the need to find a job, this secularization does not end the existential uses of memorializing the souls of the deceased.

Just like the spirit of Mao Zedong can be worshiped as a god rather than simply as the political soul of the Chinese Communist Party, so can various careerist souls be worshipped as gods. I have seen people lay wreaths at the tombs of famous writers while bowing and making requests for success in their careers. I have also seen mothers burn incense in front of military tombs, kowtow and ask for the protection of their sons in the army. But more than demonstrating how some people embrace premodern, or superstitious, or religious beliefs, I think that many such practices indicate the ambiguity at the heart of memorialization. The stringent anti-superstitious governance of the Chinese Communist Party makes many disavow religious belief and express a preference for secular funerals. But at the end of the day, especially at an emotional level, the practices of caring for a soul in another realm by offering sacrifices of various types, and respecting a spirit that one hopes to embrace in one's own life, are not so different. By worshiping, speaking to, giving offerings to, or praying to a particular soul, one demonstrates the sincerity of one's emotional disposition as much as the content of one's belief.

THE SPIRIT OF FILIAL PIETY AS POLITICAL COMPROMISE

When I explained my way of distinguishing religious and secular imaginations of the soul to one Chinese woman, she replied: "For me, personally, I neither believe in geomancy or any of the other ways that my father's soul could affect the world in the present, nor do I think that my father was a particularly good person or devoted parent whom I should emulate. But when my father I died, I thought that it was my filial duty to give him a good funeral, burial, and tombstone." While I am not sure how many people would admit to not liking their parents, especially after they have died, the idea that giving one's parents a proper burial is a filial duty is common. Like ideas about embracing the spirit of one's parents' familial sacrifice, such filial piety might be considered secular; it requires no belief in anything supernatural. But it is even more abstract. Filial piety becomes an ideal to be embraced by all even if one's own parents did not embody it.

This ideal is also precisely the one that some members of the Party attempt to counter with the rhetoric of "thick care, thin burial." According to the logic behind this slogan, there is no need for a proper burial if you have taken good care of your elderly parents in life. By performing care in life, you have completely lived up to the ideals of filial piety. Moreover, because taking care of one's parents when they are alive is typically done in private, while funerals and burials and cemetery visits after death are done in public (and tombstones are available for anyone to see even if you are not there), private care is the more honourable form of filial piety. Only you know how kind you were to your elderly parents, but funerals are for public display. Consequently, funerals become a way for children who did not perform proper filial care for their parents to assuage their guilt, or, worse yet, to put on a public display of being filial when in fact they were not. At least that is how the orthodox Party argument goes. But people like the woman quoted above imagine filial care expressed via death rituals to be just as important as filial care in life. This woman was not concerned with her public image. After all, she had even admitted to me that her father was not a particularly good parent. Rather, she was simply concerned with paying respect to the ideal of filial piety itself.

Those whose job it is to be both pro-Party and to support the funeral and cemetery industry echo such views. Their jobs require them to devise ways of countering arguments against funerary ritual and memorialization without seeming to oppose the Party. One way of doing so is to cover the walls around and within cemeteries (and funeral homes) with Party propaganda about the importance of filial piety. These images suggest both that the cemetery management is staunchly loyal to the Party (they are, after all, devoting resources to reproducing Party messages), and that customers who spend money to memorialize their relatives in the cemetery are also being loyal to the Party.

One of the most publically visible Party propaganda campaigns of the early part of Xi Jinping's reign was that of the "Twenty-Four Paragons of Filial Piety" (二十四孝). Though it has since faded from public prominence, the slogans and posters from this campaign still have a presence in many cemeteries. The title of the campaign refers to twenty-four stories of filial piety originally compiled nearly one thousand years ago during the Yuan dynasty, each of which was often represented visually in a picture. The Propaganda Department updated them with twenty-four more modern images of how to treat your parents well when they are elderly.

The reasons behind the campaign were multiple. China is both a rapidly aging society and a highly mobile society. Large numbers of elderly people live apart from their children. The government worries about possibilities of elderly discontent. During the 2000s, many elderly people protested about pension rights. Because they didn't have jobs, they could not be pressured by their employers to stop protesting. Having fewer years to live, they were also often less fearful of state retribution than young people. If elderly people live alone and feel neglected, or blame the Party for the fact that their children must leave their hometowns to find employment, might they be even more motivated to protest? In addition, as the costs of elder care rise, many in the government would like to see individual families shoulder most of the financial burden.

Cemeteries both reproduce the posters associated with this campaign and install statues, essays, calligraphy and other artwork from older versions of the Twenty-Four Paragons of Filial Piety. One cemetery in the city of Changsha, for example, erected an engraving of an essay on filial piety written in literary Chinese at its entrance. The essay begins: "Of all of the traditional Chinese virtues, filial behavior towards one's parents is the most important. While they are alive, treating them kindly and pleasing them comes first; supporting them is a blessing. After death look for a cave in a dragon vein [that is, a gravesite with excellent geomantic location], to bring peace to everyone. . . ." The essay goes on to describe how the cemetery was created with the support of the local government and how it was blessed with excellent mountains and water, the ingredients for powerful geomancy. In other East Asian locales, filial piety is also used to market cemetery plots and funerary services (Han 2016).

FIGURE 16. Carved depiction of filial piety at cemetery. Photo: Andrew B. Kipnis.

The theme of filial piety is often invoked in funerary ritual as well. At Mr. Wang's burial ceremony, for example, Mr. Chen used the phrase "The filial piety of the sons and daughters is as deep as the ocean." As several one-stop dragon entrepreneurs told me, even when there are serious conflicts among siblings over inheritance issues, they try to present a united front during the funeral and the period leading up to it. Since having one's children fight over inheritance is thought to disturb the soul of the deceased, this temporary presentation of unity is also an act of filial piety.

Within the Party, at least two versions of filial piety can thus be seen. The more totalitarian version only acknowledges the value of caring for one's parents when they are alive. But the version of Party members and supporters working in the funerary sector sees the importance of filial piety in death as well. This version also seems widely dispersed among the people, and with good reason. The totalitarian version gives no space for acknowledging the souls of the common people, while the later version attempts to unite the souls of the people and the soul of the Party around the theme of filial piety. It emphasizes multiplicity and diversity around a common theme. The tension between these two versions of filial piety reveals one of the most basic problems of politics. On the one hand, power in politics comes from the unification of a vast number of souls and spirits into a single spirit or voice. All politics involves attempts to rally support behind a singular person or identity. On the other hand, the total unification of these spirits threatens their annihilation. If they were truly one, they would cease to be many, and lose the power of a diverse multiplicity. A powerful political party must be simultaneously be multiple and singular.

These contradictions come out even in Mao Zedong's writings on funerals. In his famous essay "Serve the People" he writes:

> All men must die, but death can vary in its significance. The ancient Chinese writer Szuma Chien said 'Though death befalls all men alike, it may be weightier than Mount Tai or lighter than a feather.' To die for the people is weightier than Mount Tai, but to work for the fascists and die for the exploiters and oppressors is lighter than a feather (Mao 1975, 3:177).

Here, the number of souls in the world are reduced to two: that of "the people" (functionally, another term for the Party), and that of the Party's enemy. One's soul is either for the Party or against it. Memorializing a soul in terms of its contributions to a family, a religion, an ethnic group, or a career would be beside the point. Memorializing the spirit of filial piety itself, as an ethic which all must live by, would likewise ring hollow. But later in the same essay, Mao writes:

> From now on, when anyone in our ranks who has done some useful work dies, be he a soldier or cook, we should have a funeral ceremony and a memorial meeting in his honor. This should become the rule. And it should be introduced among the people as well. When someone dies in a village, let a memorial meeting be held. In this way we express our mourning for the dead and unite all the people (Mao 1975, 3:178).

Here the multiplicity of the masses is introduced. Not only should those who are "in our ranks" be memorialized, but even those residing in villages (over 95 percent of the Chinese people at the time Mao wrote this essay) deserve a funeral. In this sense, Mao's essay moves from seeing a world where there are only two types of souls (pro- or anti-Party) to one in which a multiplicity of souls can be unified. The two versions of filial piety described above can be mapped onto the two visions of memorialization in Mao's essay. In the first version, the only soul that needs to be memorialized is that of the Party itself; in the second, the celebration of filial piety can be used to unite the masses and the Party with a compatible set of ideals.

The later version of filial piety also echoes the way filial piety was used as an ideology of rule during the Qing dynasty and earlier. Imperial ideology held that the relationships between fathers and sons mirrored those between the emperor and his subjects and that filial piety required both that sons to be loyal to their fathers and that subjects to be loyal to their emperor. All relationships were hierarchical, and the hierarchies of different relationships could be mapped on to one another. By upholding the spirit of filial piety, people were simultaneously being loyal to the spirit of their families and to that of the ruling regime (Zito 1987).

Compatibility between familial souls and the soul of the Party is also sought out in some contemporary Chinese funerals. Mr. Wang, for example, chose to be buried in a Western suit to demonstrate his opposition to the "superstition" of traditional longevity dress and, hence, his loyalty to the Party. In her analysis of memorial meetings in contemporary Shanghai, Lucia Liu (2021) notes how many working-class families want their deceased loved ones to be memorialized as having contributed to both nation and family, as both parents and as communist "comrades." She further notes how the text of Mao's essay, "Serve the People," is displayed in the restaurant where most people hold banquets after funerals in Shanghai (Liu 2015, 251). The essay serves as a public argument that there is nothing anti-Party about having a proper funeral.

The discourse of filial piety is powerful throughout East Asia. Common people and governments use it to both justify their own behavior and to criticize the behavior of others. Debates about what exactly constitutes filial piety emerge in a number of contexts. While many sociologists and anthropologists argue that the quality of care for elder people depends more upon the practical availability of resources than the existence of cultural traditions (Ikels 2004a; Janelli and Yim 2004; Sorensen and Kim 2004; Wang 2004; Whyte 2004; H. Zhang 2004), others argue that ideas about filial piety have a strong influence on both ritual behavior and family dynamics. Charlotte Ikels (2004b), for example, describes how families in the city of Guangzhou would sometimes risk the wrath of the Communist Party to satisfy the desires of their ancestors for a form of funerary ritual that the Party did not like. John Traphagan (2004) argues that parents in rural Japan during the 1990s had at least some influence on the decisions of their married sons about where to live and work. Akiko Hashimoto (2004) argues that Japanese mothers use ideas about filial piety to control their children, thwarting their will to separate, with the result that resistance to parental authority in Japan takes the shape of avoidance, withdrawal and sabotage rather than direct confrontation. Steven Sangren (2017; 2000) analyzes the psychodynamics of Chinese families through the lens of the contradictions that ideals of filial piety entail. While a full analysis of the social and cultural ramifications of ideals of filial piety are beyond the scope of this book, it is clear that ideas about filial piety are important to Chinese families in both the manner that funerals are conducted and the ways in which families memorialize their deceased loved ones in cemeteries.

CONNECTING THE PAST TO THE FUTURE: THE LIMITS OF SECULARIZATION

In his study of the transformation of funerary ritual in Europe during the nineteenth and twentieth centuries, Thomas Laqueur (2015) states that though he set out to look for discontinuity, he found continuity. This continuity was apparent across a number of concrete historical transformations, including a shift from burial in churchyards to burial in cemeteries, a shift from burial to cremation, a rise in practices of listing, writing, and carving the names of the dead, and perhaps even a degree of secularization in the ways the souls of the dead were imagined. What remained constant was the ability of funerary ritual to connect the past with the future. While I am not certain that the underlying continuity Laqueur finds deserves more emphasis than the transformations he details, connecting the past to the future is undeniably important. Death disrupts life. Those who remain alive, whose lives in some way were defined or affected by the life of the deceased, must find some way to give meaning to their own continuing existence.

In a period of rapid urbanization and modernization, when China, in a compressed and accelerated manner, is undergoing many of the same changes in society, economy, and culture that Europe experienced in the nineteenth and early twentieth centuries, a similar argument could be made. Though there is a shift from burial to cremation, a shift from village burial to urban cemeteries, and a rise in the use of tombstones with names carved on them and other ways of memorializing the dead in writing, an emphasis on connecting the past to the future remains. In a traditional Chinese religious imagination, these continuities are often imagined as a ritual duty. The soul of the deceased continues to physically exist in some other realm and can somehow affect us in our own world, for better or worse. We should care for our deceased loved ones by providing a proper funeral, and by making sacrifices at the grave or an ancestral altar. These obligations can be imagined as a matter of care or exchange. Either we should care for our deceased loved ones out of an ethics of filial duty, or we should do so because it is in our interest to provide care so that our ancestor will help us rather than harm us. The continuing need for care and exchange link the past and future as they become endless obligations. In a secular imaginary, the souls of the deceased do not exist in another realm but become ideals that should be embraced by the living. These ideals can be those of familial devotion, religious piety, or even simply a manner of inhabiting the earth. They can be political ideals around which a particular nation-state or ethnic group rallies. In the case of filial piety, the ideal need not even be something that the deceased stood for, but rather something that is embraced in the very act of caring for the dead. On holidays like Qing Ming, when Chinese people often visit graves in multigenerational family groupings, one can even teach this spirit to the youngest generation. Because these ideals transcend the death of the deceased, they likewise link the past to the future.

In a period of rapid modernization, the need to link the past with the future may be even more urgent than in previous periods. In many ways, grandparents have lived in and belong to different eras than their children and grandchildren. Their formative experiences were different, the education they experienced was different, and the media and technologies they feel most comfortable using also differ. Moreover, China's rapid modernization presents its citizens, especially its youth, with a mind-boggling array of choice. Not only is there choice in the realm of consumer products, but youth must also choose their occupations, jobs, courses of study, spouses and potential dating partners, hobbies, religions, and worldviews. Without a series of potential models to emulate, a variety of spirits to embody, how is one to make these choices? Funerals provide an opportunity to memorialize the spirits of the deceased and, in so doing, provide the living with templates to make their own choices, to stick with the choices they have made, and to find reasons for continuing to live. Their own efforts become contributions to an everlasting spirit rather than the mere maintenance of a human body that is bound to die anyway.

Because the human need to link the past to the future is ongoing, no modernization can eliminate the human need for a soul. Death rituals can become less complex, but I doubt that they will ever end. If, as the Party official cited in the last chapter suggested, someone were to donate their body to science, to demand that no ritual be held for their death and that no tombstone be erected in a cemetery, then that person would most likely be memorialized by the Party itself. She or he would be immortalized in books, websites, and movies as a spirit for emulation by all Party members at least!

The subjectivity that the soul represents must be seen to live on in some form, even if it departs the body that it originally animated. The need for the soul to live on, to be immortalized, limits secularization. As the language used in cemeteries, in obituaries, and in ritualized speech at funerals demonstrates, as well as the use of stone as a medium for remembering the departed, the quality of existing forever is an important theme for memorialization. This quality pushes most acts of memorialization towards the supernatural, as nothing natural last forever. Respect for the deceased and the feelings of loss close family members experience add an element of sacralization to funerals. Criticism of the deceased is rarely tolerated. The language and practice of funerals often blends religious and secular imaginations of the soul, and the very words we use to speak of the entities that animate human bodies have long histories that likewise blend secular and religious imaginaries. This blending, along with the elements of timelessness and sacralization, makes even the most secular of funerals feel religious.

8

Of Dreams and Memories

A Ghost Story From a Land Where Haunting Is Banned

From a secular point of view, the souls and spirits memorialized in funerals and cemeteries enunciate cultural ideals that transcend the lifetime of a given individual. From at least one person's or political party's point of view, they represent what *should* be remembered, connecting the past to the future in a positive fashion. Our memories, however, include more than that which we think we should remember. Some memories haunt us whether we would like them to or not. Such memories can be thought of as ghosts. Like the spirits and souls discussed in the last chapter, they are powerful, regardless of whether we approach them as beings with physical presence or "mere" psychological appearances.

They are also dangerous. As described in chapter 4, the ghosts that haunt public housing estates or haunted houses can entice people to commit suicide or murder. They force themselves into the minds of those who unknowingly enter their spaces. They can also be erotic, driving sexual fantasies or behaviors that some would like to repress. If chapter 4 attempted to understand ghosts socially as strangers, this chapter focuses on them psychologically. Ghosts remind us that our minds are never fully our own.

In China, ghosts are also political. Foreigners, outsiders, and political enemies can all be referred to as ghosts. By governing memorialization, the Party attempts to structure historical memory. But ghosts remain out of control. Not only may a deceased person be kin (an ancestor) to one person and a stranger (ghost) to another, those souls or spirits that one person or political party thinks should be remembered can be the ghosts that another thinks should be forgotten. When people themselves come to represent what should or should not be remembered, then the social, political, and psychological aspects of ghosts all blend together.

While ghosts can be both male and female, in China the ghosts depicted in fictional stories are more likely to be women than men. In addition to a view of sexual psychology that attributes desire (and, hence, susceptibility to seduction) more often to men than women, the prevalence of female ghosts also reflects traditional practices of patrilineal, patrilocal kinship. Such practices could render women outsiders and block them from positions of political power. As the data from the cemeteries show, women are more likely to be buried alone and improperly memorialized than men. For all of these reasons, they are more likely to become ghosts.

I began this book with a slightly fictionalized depiction of a contemporary urban funeral and thought it would be fitting to end the book with ghost story, a bit of fiction. Between fiction and nonfiction there is both an absolute divide and a fundamental continuity. The divide lies in the intent. Journalists and social scientists go to great lengths to make what they write accurate representations of what they observed. Most of this book follows that intent. While such intent and the representations it generates are important, my desire to represent Chinese funerals accurately cannot completely overcome the continuity of nonfiction writing with fictional narratives. This continuity exists on at least two levels. The first is linguistic. By giving narrative form to the social life that I observed, I employ the same linguistic tropes, metaphors, structures, and vocabularies that novelists do. No author's use of language is simply transparent. Language must be seen as structuring our thought as much as we use our thought to manipulate language. Second is the problem of memory. Journalists and academics rely on both the memories of others and their own memories to collect their data, but no one's memory is fully under their own control. Stories, particularly ghost stories, portray truths about the way that we perceive and remember the world in ways nonfiction writing cannot.

To select a story for this chapter, as an anthropologist interested in the culture of the broad urban masses, I looked through popular novels instead of literary tomes read mainly by academics. I also wanted a story that was set in a realistic, contemporary setting, that involved ghosts that rang true for an urbanizing China. Rapid urbanization brings about particular forms of haunting. Families and communities break down and people can die alone. As village after village is demolished, graveyard after graveyard dug up, and neighborhood after neighborhood razed, cities themselves can be seen as haunted by their old architectural pasts and the people who lived them. These hauntings are necessarily full of political energy. Those whose lives are adversely affected by demolitions and relocations can become an oppositional political force. The officials in charge of urban renewal usually hope such hauntings, and the ghosts they involve, will be quickly forgotten.

In one city I visited, I asked students to tell me about places that were said to be haunted. One directed me to an abandoned part of a university campus that was scheduled for demolition. While it appeared to be occupied by a few migrant workers in the evenings, who may have been squatting there illegally, it was empty

FIGURE 17. Graffiti. Photo: Andrew B. Kipnis.

during the day. At the back of this quarter of abandoned buildings was a wall that marked the edge of campus territory. On that wall, I found some graffiti which could be interpreted as a four-lined poem:

> Greedy Desire;
> Contradictions and Selfishness;
> Falsehood and Mediocrity;
> [Is this] A Great Heaven on Earth?

I asked several Chinese literature students if the words in the graffiti quoted any famous poems, but none could recall a poem that the lines in the graffiti reproduced. The line I translated as "falsehood and mediocrity" could refer to officials who use falsehood (telling their superiors what they want to hear) to get ahead despite their mediocre performance. However one reads these words, they are an outpouring of negative political sentiment. When I revisited the wall a few months after I took this picture, the graffiti was still there. Because almost all forms of politically subversive expression in China are suppressed, I was shocked by both my initial discovery of this writing and its ability to remain unaltered for a period of months. Its longevity suggests that no one connected to officialdom in China ever visited this place, a fact that could be explained by its purported haunting.

But though the graffiti managed to survive for at least a few months, ghost stories set in urban China seem more fully repressed. It took me many months to find one useful for this chapter. I never expected to find a story where the ghosts had died during the Great Leap famine, the Cultural Revolution, or any of the other historical incidents that the Party attempts to erase, but I could not even find a story that seemed solidly set in a contemporary urban setting. An unspoken rule of censorship seemed to taboo both the hauntings caused by rapid urbanization as well as ghosts who had died in automobile crashes, medical mishaps, industrial accidents, suicides or murders during the contemporary era—that is, from any of the types of ordinary but wrongful deaths that occur in most societies and often result in unsettled ghosts.

Chinese students told me several stories orally, but these were usually quite short. The emphasis was on how scary the ghost was or on demonstrating that the ghost was real rather than the death that caused the ghost to haunt the present. I also visited several amusement-park style haunted houses in large cities, but again the emphasis was on scaring people with darkness, sound, and scary images (mostly borrowed from foreign horror movies) rather than tales of the ghost's origin. I read or skimmed several dozen novels listed in online literature websites as "ghost stories." These stories avoided contemporary urban ghosts by focusing on four other types of haunting. The first involved stories set in imperial China. These were mostly knockoffs of the famous Qing dynasty ghost story collection *Strange Stories of Liaozhai*. These stories do involve social commentary, but the commentary focuses on Qing dynasty evils rather than contemporary ones. The second type of haunting involved contemporary Chinese people, but was set in foreign countries. The abundance of such stories in Chinese cyberspace suggests that there are plenty of ghosts in Japan, Korea, Europe and North America, but few in China. The third type of haunting involved *Harry Potter* knockoffs. The final type was set in contemporary urban China, but involved ghosts with origins in ancient Chinese history and legend. No doubt China is haunted by its very long history, but to fit the theme of this book I wanted something more contemporary. Unlike the websites full of ghost stories and even directories of haunted houses available in Hong Kong, mainland China seemed to lack an easily accessible source in which contemporary urban ghosts were given narrative form.

CORONAVIRUS, POLITICAL PROTEST, AND MY HAUNTED HONG KONG

I moved to Hong Kong to work at the Chinese University of Hong Kong in late 2017, after nearly twenty years of work at an Australian university. I completed the research for this book in 2018 and 2019 while living in Hong Kong. 2019 and 2020 have been tense years. The autumn of 2019 was rocked by violent confrontations between pro-democracy protestors and police. The demonstrations were sometimes framed as a confrontation between native, Cantonese-speaking Hong Kongers and Mandarin speakers from mainland China. On campus I heard from students and colleagues of many backgrounds, including Hong Kong students fearful of police repression but determined to sacrifice for democracy; mainland Chinese students who felt caught between their nascent democratic sentiments and their identities as mainland Chinese, unable to communicate openly with either Hong Kong students or their friends and relatives back home; and non-Chinese students who either supported the protests or felt caught in the middle as well.[1] Many in Hong Kong were so convinced of the absolute opposition between Hong Kong and mainland Chinese people that they thought I was risking my personal safety by travelling to China to complete the research for this book. While I was not harassed or arrested in China during my autumn 2019 visits, tones of strident Chinese nationalism increasingly intruded on my interactions. One of my last research trips of that autumn took me to the city of Wuhan in November 2019, just before the Covid-19 outbreak began there.

The coronavirus has wreaked death and havoc on the world, intensified the mounting cold war between the United States and China, and stepped up the already terrifying mechanisms of state surveillance within China. This surveillance makes me feel that autumn 2019 will be the last time I ever conduct ethnographic research in China, after more than thirty years of doing so. The Covid-19 app that all Chinese residents and visitors to China must place on their mobile phones traces out the contacts an individual makes. It is now a requirement to take your phone with you whenever you leave your residence. Consequently, for both Chinese citizens and non-citizens visiting China, all location data, physical contacts with other people, mobile phone communications, and purchasing history (most Chinese use smartphone apps rather than cash to make purchases) are easily shared with the police. Whether it is ethically possible to carry out any ethnographic research in China under such conditions is questionable. In addition, in 2020 it has become nearly impossible for foreigners to travel to China, as visas have been cancelled and fourteen-day quarantines imposed on both those travelling to China and those returning from China to Hong Kong. Even more damaging are the breakdowns in communication between China and Hong Kong. Some of the people I communicate with in China bombard me with messages signalling strident Chinese nationalism; others I fear to contact at all, as the questions I might ask them could only get them into trouble. And it is not just me who feels this way. Many of the mainland Chinese students I talk to in Hong Kong also feel that they are no longer able to meaningfully communicate with friends and relatives back in China; interaction involves either conflict over the chauvinist, nationalist statements emerging from the mainland or banal pleasantries. The Chinese government's move to impose national security legislation on Hong Kong, the reaction by the United States government, and the continuation of protestor/police violence in Hong Kong only further exacerbates these barriers. The reading of ghost stories has thus become one of the few forms of research that I can undertake.

Ghost stories illuminate two important themes for this book. First is the psychological relationship between repression and ghosts. Joseph Bosco (2003; 2007) writes about the ghost stories incoming students at the Chinese University of Hong Kong used to share and scare each other with during their pre-enrollment orientation camps. While the stories are full of sexual innuendo, the mostly female incoming students would only describe them as "scary" and not acknowledge their eroticism. Bosco's analysis comes from a period, nearly two decades ago, when sexual morality in Hong Kong was relatively repressive and students were admonished against serial dating and premarital sex. Dorm rooms were segregated by gender and no opposite-sex visitors were allowed. Attitudes have undoubtedly evolved since then; students now openly pair off in romantic relationships and the protest movement seems only to have amplified student devotion to romance. But if repressive attitudes towards sexuality can lead to ghost stories full of sexual content that is not consciously acknowledged or publically discussed, what about the repression of political attitudes, communication, and emotions? What about the repression of memories of how certain people died or what they stood for? Might that repression become visible in ghost stories, even if their narrators do not acknowledge it? At least in the thought of the Sigmund Freud, sex and death were the two drives that linked the unconscious mind to human behavior.

The question of the relationship between political repression and ghosts brings me to the second reason for my interest in ghosts—the particular coronavirus context of Wuhan and Hubei province. The virus first spread widely in the city of Wuhan. Quarantine measures were strictly implemented in the city and the entire province of Hubei from January of 2020. Official Chinese statistics count the number of Wuhan coronavirus deaths at nearly four thousand, but many analysts think that the actual death toll was ten to twenty times higher. In addition, as in other countries subsequently, Wuhan's death-related infrastructure of funeral homes, crematoriums, and hospital morgues was completely overwhelmed. Restrictions on travel and social gatherings prevented any funerals from being held. It is unclear how bodies were disposed of, what conditions in hospitals, rural villages, and urban housing estates were like, and what forms of ritual families were managing to hold. While such unfortunate conditions are common throughout the world, in China more generally and Hubei in particular, the government has cracked down on all forms of communication about these events. People are harassed by the police for using their smartphones to share such information even among circles of friends. As a researcher interested in funerals who has recently visited both Wuhan and the nearby city of Jingzhou, and who used to be in communication with many people there, I have neither heard about nor dared to ask anyone for news about these events. The sorts of ghosts that might arise from all of this bad death, unperformed ritual, and political repression remain an open question.

GHOST ROAD

After many months of reading ghost stories, I finally discovered the "Ghost Road" series, written by an author who goes by the single character name of "Li (离)."

These three novels illustrate almost all of the themes discussed above. The ghosts die in contemporary urban tragedies like automobile accidents, murders, and suicides motivated by greed, sexual jealousy, or despair relating to unemployment. Districts full of abandoned buildings and factories are often haunted. Psychological tensions about the reality of ghosts constantly confront the reader and the protagonists of the stories. In one of the novels, the protagonist's unconscious mind tricks her into forgetting that she had murdered her friend, but then reveals the event through a series of seemingly real, ghostly projections. In the novel I summarize below, the protagonist has difficulty differentiating between her ghastly dreams and her ghastly reality. The inability to trust one's own mind reverberates in an inability to trust strangers and acquaintances in an urban setting. The main characters are female university students and the site of the university is a vaguely disguised version of the city of Wuhan, where Wuhan University sits on the shores of East Lake, the most important landmark in the story. As the discussion of the School of Funerary Studies at the Changsha Social Work College suggests, in China, universities are urban institutions. Not only are they located in large cities, but they are also consciously designed to prepare rural students for urban careers and lives.

Unlike the Chinese University of Hong Kong ghost stories analyzed by Bosco, the sexuality in these stories is explicit and, to me, seems more aspirational than realistic. The female university students of these stories consume, travel and go through boyfriends at a rate that seems unlikely for the levels of economic prosperity and sexual repression extant in the place and time where the novels are set. The novels were published between 2005 and 2008, a period when censorship was less strict than it is today. They have now been reproduced on an open-access Chinese literature website, where they are the last of sixty novels listed in the ghost-story genre, and the only ones with ghosts from a contemporary urban Chinese setting. What follows is a summary translation of the first novel from this series.[2]

Ghost Road 1: The Haunted Dorm by the Lake

Four college roommates, Su Xiao, Jingjing, Linzi, and Yu Si, live in a dorm room by East Lake. Jingjing is rich and beautiful and dates a new boy almost every weekend; Linzi and Su Xiao are middle-class and pretty; Yu Si is poor and plain. Linzi and Jingjing are close and often go shopping together. They sometimes deliberately exclude Yu Si. Su Xiao gets along with everyone, but has vivid nightmares that leave her exhausted the next day. Her schedule of sleeping and waking is erratic, and she sometimes confuses dream and reality.

One day Jingjing and Linzi go shopping. Yu Si is not around and Su Xiao feels tired, so stays by herself in the dorm. She falls asleep with a song by the Taiwanese pop star Angela Chang (张韶涵) in her head. She wakes up briefly to see Yu Si with long black hair and a pale white body standing in front of her, but then has a nightmare in which she is drowning and a pale, bony white hand is pulling her under the water. She wakes up again when Jingjing and Linzi return, but thinks that she really saw Yu Si before she fell asleep. Then Yu Si returns and says she has been gone all evening, but Su Xiao notices that Yu Si's shoes are wet.

The roommates turn out the lights for the evening, but Su Xiao has trouble sleeping. The eyes in the Angela Chang poster above Linzi's bed keep staring at her. The next morning, after everyone else has left, Su Xiao decides to destroy the poster. She takes it off the wall and carries it out to East Lake. She sets the poster on fire, but a spark from the burning poster ignites her pants cuff. She puts her leg in the lake, but a pale, bony hand grabs her ankle and pulls her underwater. She sees the ghastly woman whose hand grabbed her and three others like her. They all have pale bodies and long black hair. They are water ghosts who have died wrongful deaths; Su Xiao sees their underwater graves as well. She escapes by picking up a brick from the bottom of the lake and hitting the hand that is grabbing her ankle. On the way back to the dorm room she passes an air-raid shelter built into a set of caves in a hill between the lake and their dorm.

She then wakes up and is sitting in a pavilion on the hill. She walks down the hill and sees Yu Si come out of the locked gate to the air-raid shelter. She follows Yu Si back to the dorm, but on the way realizes she is invisible, as no one greets her or acknowledges her greetings. In the dorm she sees Yu Si talk to Linzi as if she were not there. "Where is Su Xiao?" Linzi asks. "She must be with her boyfriend Jiang Wei," Yu Si answers. But Su Xiao doesn't remember anyone called Jiang Wei, let alone having a boyfriend with that name. Then she sees many other ghosts playing dirty tricks on the female students. They do things that leave no visible marks but make the students feel mysterious aches and ailments, such as hanging from a student's arm to give her backaches. When one of the students walks straight through her body, Su Xiao realizes that she too must be a ghost. She concludes that she must have really drowned in the lake. She sees that the Angela Chang poster is back on the wall above Linzi's bed. She finds her cell-phone and checks the contact list, discovering that a Jiang Wei is on it, so she texts him to meet her at a bench near the library. When she gets there, she sees a man sitting on the bench, but he cannot see her, so she texts Jiang Wei again, apologizing that something suddenly came up and she can no longer make it. The man's phone rings when she texts him and he leaves after reading the text. She follows him. The man bumps into Yu Si and they seem to recognize one another. The two of them walk together to his place, with Su Xiao following.

Yu Si tries to kiss Jiang Wei, but he resists her. He asks Yu Si about Su Xiao, and she replies that Su Xiao is dead already. Jiang Wei says, "How can that be, I just got her text message," but Yu Si keeps kissing him and Jiang Wei relents. They tear off their clothes and have sex on the sofa. Su Xiao takes the opportunity to steal the key to the air-raid shelter from Yu Si's pocket. She goes to the air-raid shelter, opens the door, and enters. It is pitch dark. After feeling her way through the darkness for a long way she comes to a TV-like screen at the end of the cave. By the screen is a dark well. The screen is a window onto their dorm room. Su Xiao can see that no one is in their room and that the screen looks at the room from the position of the eyes in the Angela Chang poster. Su Xiao then sees Yu Si enter the room and look through Su Xiao's things. Yu Si next stares at the poster as if she knows that Su Xiao is watching her. Su Xiao then tries to leave the air-raid shelter, but realizes she has lost the key. She returns to the TV screen and pushes her hand through it. It emerges in the dorm room. She then jumps into the TV screen and pops out from Angela Chang's eyes into the room. The other roommates are all there. Jingjing appears terrified, and only Yu Si can see and talk to Su Xiao. Yu Si tells Su Xiao that since she came through the poster she must kill someone. Su Xiao follows Jingjing into the water room and her bony, white hand starts moving independently of her will. It strangles Jingjing. Water then fills the room, and Su Xiao dies a death of drowning again.

Su Xiao wakes up. She is in her boyfriend's apartment. His name is Zhang Sheng. She remembers that she moved out of the dorm room two months ago to live with him. Zhang Sheng says that she has been feverish and sleeping for two days. She goes back to the dorm room and sees Yu Si, but Jingjing is away. Jingjing has sent a text to Linzi saying that she has gone travelling for a few days.

Over the next few days, Su Xiao has a series of nightmares; Zhang Sheng is always there when she wakes up, but she can't distinguish what has really happened and what was a dream. She is often walking in deserted urban neighborhoods that are scheduled to be demolished. In one dream, she hears a knock on the door at night. When she opens the door she sees nothing but feels a ghostly presence enter the room. Then she keeps hearing cloth shoes walking behind her, but doesn't see anything. When she wakes up she notices that Zhang Sheng has a pair of shoes just like those in her dream. She often dreams of his shoes following her as she walks through neighborhoods filled with condemned buildings.

One morning Su Xiao asks Zhang Sheng to take her to the air-raid shelter. They use a hammer to knock the lock off of the door, but after going halfway in, they are blocked by a newly built brick wall and discover nothing suspicious. The next day she decides to talk to Yu Si about her dreams. That same morning Linzi asks Su Xiao to accompany her to her uncle's apartment in the evening, so Su Xiao meets Yu Si at a coffee house in the afternoon. Su Xiao tells Yu Si about her dream of murdering Jingjing and then Yu Si tells her a story from her childhood. When Yu Si was eight years old she woke up in the middle of the night. She went to a window, saw two shadowy figures, and heard one say that ghosts always congregate at crossroads. The two figures then buried something. When she woke up the next morning, her mother told her that her father had died of a heart attack. Two months later the police dug up what the figures had buried. It was money and valuables from a series of thefts. Yu Si also learned that her father had committed suicide after being laid off. For a long time, she thought that the shadowy figures were ghosts who stole and buried her father's soul, but later, she accepted that the two incidents were separate. So, she consoles Su Xiao, you don't really need to believe in ghosts.

Then Linzi calls Su Xiao to make the trip to her uncle's apartment in an urban district on the outskirts of the city. Su Xiao tells her that she is with Yu Si, but Linzi and Yu Si don't really get along. The three of them arrange to have dinner together, but after dinner Linzi and Su Xiao go to her uncle's apartment and Yu Si returns alone to the dorm. Linzi and Su Xiao catch a bus. Linzi has brought a backpack with the Angela Chang poster (which she intends to trade with a friend who lives near her uncle) and some other things. After travelling about half an hour through increasingly desolate urban districts, the bus engine dies while stopped at a red light. There are three others left on the bus: a middle-aged man, a young man, and a young woman. The driver says to wait for the next bus, but after ten minutes suddenly runs out the door. The middle-aged man, the young woman, Su Xiao, and Linzi decide to walk to the next crossroads to find a taxi. When they get there, there are ambulances and a group of people gawking at a car wreck. Some men are trying to revive the mangled body of the wrecked car's driver, but one says, "We have to stop, he has already been dead half an hour." They notice that the dead person was the young man who used to be on the bus with them, which they had only left ten minutes ago. So he must have been a ghost. Then the middle-aged man tells them that he too would like to die. He had been laid off two months ago, cannot find another job, and has lied to his wife, who is also unemployed, about the situation. Then he runs off. The young woman then says she would also like to die. Her boyfriend has left her for another woman. That was bad enough, but then the old boyfriend and his new girlfriend went travelling and died in a bus accident. So there is no longer any chance that she can reconcile with him. Linzi and Su Xiao are now scared, and ask the woman if she too is already a ghost. She says no and the three of them get a taxi. The young woman needs to get out first and Su Xiao and Linzi slide out the door to let her exit. But when they get back in the driver asks, "What are you doing?" They say they had just let out the other passenger but the driver says "What are you talking about, all along it has only been the two of you."

Su Xiao then wakes up in Zhang Sheng's apartment and explains what happened on the bus trip, but Zhang Sheng says that it was all a nightmare and that she had never gone on the bus with Linzi. She had come home early that evening and gone to bed. After talking with Zhang Sheng, Su Xiao goes to her dorm room and finds that there are policemen outside the building. The night watchman had died at 3:00 a.m. the previous night. The police have drawn a chalk outline on the ground where his body had fallen and have ruled his death a heart attack. Since he had been in good health, Su Xiao assumes that some sudden fright must have caused the heart attack. Su Xiao also learns that Linzi actually did go to her uncle's apartment. She has sent a text message saying she is still there. It also develops that she, Yu Si, and Linzi actually had dinner together. At first she suspects that Zhang

Sheng has lied to her but then realizes that she could have had dinner with the two other roommates and then decided to go home instead of accompanying Linzi. She notices that Yu Si's shoes have mud on them. That evening, when Zhang Sheng comes home, she sees him wash mud off of his shoes as well.

For two more days, Linzi does not return—and neither has Jingjing. Su Xiao is worried and decides to go to Linzi's uncle's apartment on her own. He lives in a building that is scheduled to be demolished. An old woman answers the door and says that she recognizes Su Xiao from a couple of nights ago but that Linzi left with her and had not stayed with them. Linzi's uncle comes out from the back bedroom, but his sickly, ghost-like appearance scares Su Xiao and she runs out. On the way down the steps, she calms down and leaves her phone number with another woman she sees, asking the woman to tell anyone with news about Linzi to get in touch with her. Su Xiao now worries that she is schizophrenic and actually killed both Linzi and Jingjing while in an altered state of mind.

The phone number she left behind results in a man in his late twenties, Ma Er, calling Su Xiao. They meet in a coffee shop. He reminds her of Jiang Wei. She instantly trusts him and tells him the story of going to Linzi's uncle's apartment. He says he will help her investigate. She goes home and confronts Zhang Sheng with the fact that she had visited Linzi's uncle. Zhang Sheng says: "OK, I'll tell you the truth. That night you came home at 1:00 a.m., covered in blood, looking like a devil, holding a blood covered brick, and carrying Linzi's backpack. You were in a daze. I undressed you, washed you, put you to sleep on the sofa, and washed your clothes. The next morning, I buried Linzi's things and the brick on the hill near the shelter. Also, the night Jingjing disappeared, you came home late with a crazed smile on your face. There was blood under your nails and on your phone was a message you had sent to Jingjing. I deleted the message." Su Xiao is even more convinced that she murdered both of her roommates, but has no idea why she did so or how she could be strong enough to do it.

The next day, Su Xiao asks Zhang Sheng to take her to where he buried Linzi's things. He does, digs them up and shows them to her, and then reburies them. She has nightmares for several days and Zhang Sheng is rarely around. She decides to call Ma Er and see if he knows anything. He asks her to meet him at an abandoned factory in an old industrial district. She feels safe with him and says yes. At the factory Ma Er scares her with tales of ghosts and monsters as they walk around in a dark tunnel. She loses consciousness several times, hears footsteps, sees shadowy figures, and assumes there are ghosts. One time, after passing out and dreaming of ghosts, she wakes up with a song in her head. Ma Er asks her what it is. It is "Floating Clouds" (浮云) by Angela Chang.[3] She has another nightmare about drowning and ghosts pulling her under water. When she wakes up she is with Ma Er and in the light. Ma Er says that he took her down into the tunnel to test her suggestibility and found that she is easy to scare into having nightmares about ghosts. He says that they were completely safe the whole time and nothing came near them. He also tells her that he was the person who saved her from drowning fifteen years ago, when she was five and he was fourteen.

That night Su Xiao dreams of Jiang Wei again. She goes to his apartment and they have a long talk. He tells her that people cannot control their dreams but they can learn to interpret them. Often things in dreams are recombinations of things from real life. He says that he is a combination of Ma Er and Zhang Sheng. When Su Xiao wakes up she starts to doubt Zhang Sheng. She follows him the next day and sees him meet with Yu Si near the library and hug her. Then he leaves alone. Su Xiao follows him to the back of the hill where there is a second, lower door to the air-raid shelter. Zhang Sheng has a key to the door and goes in, coming out ten minutes later. She goes home and Zhang Sheng returns shortly later. He says he is tired, so Su Xiao offers him a sleeping pill. After he has fallen asleep, she takes his key to the lower air-raid shelter door and goes to check it out. The stench is terrible. At the bottom of an old well, Su Xiao sees Jingjing's and Linzi's rapidly decomposing bodies. She leaves and then loses consciousness somewhere. She dreams that Yu Si says to her, "If you want to know the truth, you must follow me." She wakes up and finds that she had fainted in their old dorm room. She decides to confront Zhang Sheng and Yu Si and returns to her apartment.

In the apartment she hears the sound of water dripping. After checking the bathroom and kitchen sink, she listens carefully and hears that it is coming from the closet. She opens the closet door and sees Yu Si's dead body dripping blood. She has been stabbed many times and her left eye has a knife sticking out of it. In her hand is a note:

> Dear Su Xiao, I am so sorry. The day Jingjing disappeared, she and I were alone in the dorm room. As usual, she was so snobbish to me, not letting me listen to her Angela Chang CDs. I was upset and decided to dare her to go to the air-raid shelter with me without a flashlight. I had a key and I knew it would scare me, but I hoped it would scare her more. She agreed and we went in and walked into the dark. She led the way, acting as if she wasn't scared in the slightest while I was trembling in fear the whole way. We got to an old well. Then she suddenly yelled and rushed at me. I pushed her away and she fell. I think she fell down the well because I couldn't see her any more. I must have killed her. I left in a panic. The next day I met Zhang Sheng and told him about it. I sent a text message from Jingjing's phone saying that she was travelling. Zhang Sheng told me not to tell anyone, and consoled me. Somehow I fell in love with him, so now I am also having an affair with your boyfriend. I am so sorry. Later, since you were always mixing up dreams and reality, we decided to trick you into thinking that you might have killed her. I don't know what happened to Linzi and the night watchman, but I doubt you had anything to do with those either.

The rest of the note has been torn away. Su Xiao calls Ma Er and he says he will come over right away.

The final chapter is told from the perspective of Zhang Sheng. One night, Zhang Sheng was exasperated from dealing with Su Xiao's constant nightmares. After putting her to sleep with a sleeping pill, he went out for a walk. He saw Jingjing and Yu Si going into the upper air raid shelter door, so he decided to play a trick on them. He went in through the lower door and climbed up the well. He saw Jingjing next to the well, so he touched her back and yelled next to her ear. She panicked and rushed towards Yu Si. Yu Si pushed her and Jingjing fell next to the well, hit her head, and became momentarily unconscious. Yu Si couldn't see her and left in a panic as well. A minute or so later, Jingjing started to regain consciousness. She was beautiful and Zhang Sheng wanted her. He decided to rape her, but she fully gained consciousness and fought back. In the struggle, he pushed her down the well. He climbed back down the well and saw that she was then really dead. The next morning, he first returned to the air-raid shelter to build a brick wall to make it harder to find Jingjing's body. Then he went to look for Yu Si to see if she knew anything about what had happened. Yu Si actually thought that she had killed Jingjing. Zhang Sheng told her he would protect her and acted nice to her. She was so lonely and desperate that she easily fell in love with him. A few days later, Su Xiao told him that Linzi had invited her to go to Linzi's uncle's apartment. Zhang Sheng worried that Linzi had somehow found out what had really happened and that she would tell Su Xiao. So that day, he secretly gave some sleeping pills to Su Xiao, hoping that she would fall asleep and not go. But she went to meet Yu Si anyway. Zhang Sheng followed her. He saw her meet with Yu Si, have dinner with Linzi and Yu Si and then get on a bus. He followed them in a taxi and noticed that Su Xiao was half-awake and half-asleep the whole time on the bus. After they came back, they split up so that Su Xiao could walk to Zhang Sheng's apartment and Linzi could return to the dorm. Zhang Sheng followed Linzi to the field between the hill and the dorm and bashed her head with a brick. The night watchman saw something and came rushing over. When he got close, Zhang Sheng held up Linzi's bloody, dead body and the sight scared the night watchman to death. Then Zhang Sheng dragged Linzi's body to the air-raid shelter and put her next to Jingjing. He sent a text from Linzi's phone saying that she was still with her uncle. He started to drop hints to Su Xiao that she was responsible for the deaths. But then Yu Si came over and said that she was feeling guilty and that the two of them should tell Su Xiao the truth. Zhang Sheng couldn't convince her otherwise and became enraged. He stabbed Yu Si repeatedly. After killing her, he put her in the closet, but she kept staring at him so he stuck the knife in her left eye. He stuck it in so hard that he couldn't pull it out to stab her right eye. He cleaned up the blood from the bedroom and prepared to make a run for it. But somehow, after leaving the apartment, he was drawn to the air-raid shelter. He went in the upper door, where Jingjing's and Linzi's ghosts ganged up on him and pushed him down the well.

. . .

The ending to the *Ghost Road* novel raises a series of questions for the end of this book. Much of Zhang Sheng's narrative seems to demonstrate that it is not necessary to believe in ghosts at all. The boyfriend did it, and the ghosts were all figments of Su Xiao's imagination. But the appearance of the ghosts of Jingjing and Linzi returns the uncertainty. Were their ghosts real, or was Zhang Sheng driven by guilt to commit suicide? The ambiguity of the physical reality of ghosts is reinforced by the ambiguity between Su Xiao's dreams and her real life. She sees four water ghosts in her dream, and four people she knows die. She bashes the water ghost's hand with a brick, and Zhang Sheng bashes Linzi with a brick. Yu Si has an affair with Zhang Sheng, and Su Xiao sees her have sex with Jiang Wei. The eyes in the Angela Chang poster resemble the staring eyes of the dead Yu Si. Though *The Haunted Dorm by the Lake* is undoubtedly a work of fiction, might it still have something to tell us about the psychological realities of university-aged Hubei natives and the social realities of sharing ghost stories? What might such psychic and social realities have to do with rapid urbanization, the horrors of the coronavirus, or political repression? The confusion between dream and reality reverberates in a confusion over who to trust. Su Xiao doubts Zhang Sheng and Yu Si and even herself. This distrust can be read as a problem of life in a society of strangers, but also as a problem of life among people who are contagious but either don't know it or refuse to quarantine themselves, or a problem of life in a political system in which informants report on their friends. Why are condemned buildings so often haunted? Why are sexually active female students so harried by ghosts? Why do those who die in automobile accidents, suicides, and murders become ghosts more often than those who pass away with their families at an old age?

Anthropologists have documented a belief in ghosts and narratives of their existence in the most urban of Chinese settings (Ikels 2004b, 103; Jankowiak 1993, 296–7; Kipnis 2016, 132). But even when people do not literally believe in ghosts, haunting can occur. At Mr. Wang's funeral, we saw how the elder daughter was overcome with grief at various moments. She related her grief to feeling guilty about not being able to properly care for her father during his illness. In her case, there was good reason for her inability to care for her father, and she was able to think through the causes of her emotions. But guilt is another emotion, like sexual desire or politically driven fear, that can easily be repressed. Grief itself can be overwhelming, and inhibit self-analysis about the causes of one's emotions. In this psychological sense, haunting is a common reaction to death. The convoluted plot of the story (the twists and turns of which I was not able to fully capture in the truncated translation given above) provides a realistic parallel to the convoluted nature of working through repressed emotions. The exorcism of ghosts may be as an effective means of dealing with psychological pain as any form of psychoanalysis.

Though political pressure can lead authors to self-censor their fictional writing about urban ghosts, though expressions of literal beliefs in spirits can be suppressed, though burning spirit money can be outlawed, though social media exchanges about coronavirus death can be policed, though cemeteries can be closed and perhaps even funerals themselves "thinned" to the simplest of procedures, none of these acts will prevent urban ghosts from haunting the present. As long as humans have memories, dreams, and nightmares, the haunting will continue.

EPILOGUE

In my last book, I used the word "recombinant" to theorize the way social transformations like urbanization occur (Kipnis 2016). The term suggests how a new
type of society can have a completely different structure than the old one, yet still
be composed of the same elements. Imagine the children's toy the "transformer."
When we move the pieces around, it can change from a human-like robot into a
car or truck; but after the transformation all of the original pieces are still present.
This analogy is not perfect. In social and biological transformations, new elements
are often blended with old ones in a new formation. But at least the term provides
a way of contemplating the inter-relation between change and continuity in social
transformations like urbanization.

This book has also examined urbanization, but from the perspective of funerals.
It relates the transformation of funerary ritual to the rapid urbanization that has
occurred in China over the past thirty years, and uses changes in funerary ritual
to provide a lens for viewing this urbanization. Many of the elements of contemporary funerals are not new. There have been ideas about ghosts and spirits, burial
practices, strangers and familial relations, and gifts and commodities in China
for thousands of years. But rapid urbanization in China has rearranged these elements into a new pattern. The separation of life from death, the rise of a stranger
society, the increasing commodification of social relations, economic growth and
rising inequality, skyrocketing land values, Communist Party political rule, and an
increasingly imposed but not fully accepted secularization have all left their mark.

Another common way of imagining the place of the past in the present is
through the metaphor of "haunting." Through haunting, the ghosts of the past
influence the present even if we have forgotten who they were, and especially when
we repress our memories of them. In his book *Specters of Marx*, Jacques Derrida

(1994) both criticized and revived the work of the communist philosopher Karl Marx. He revived Marx because he wanted to emphasize that the fall of the Berlin Wall in 1989 did not bring an end to the relevance of Marx's socialist outlook for European politics. Marx's haunting continues. But he criticized Marx for positing that the rise of communism would end the haunting of human societies and for imagining that communism was the only ghost around.

The current Communist Party regime in China suffers from many of the same problems that Derrida saw in Marx. It imagines that its soul should be the only one allowed. While it does notice a few other ghosts around, many of which it labels with the word "superstition," it sees these ghosts as entities whose demise is inevitable but nonetheless should be hastened by the efforts of the Party. The spirit of the Party must live forever; all other spirits are ghostly enemies to be squashed. The ghosts from the Party's own, now repudiated, past, like the Great Leap Forward, the Cultural Revolution, or the Tiananmen Square massacre, must never be mentioned again. Derrida argued that we must learn to live with our ghosts instead of repressing them, a theme that has been increasingly voiced in psychological anthropology and the analysis of political repression and social subjectivity around the world (Good 2020). I believe that the totalitarian impulse in China to squash all souls other than that of the Party itself can only increase the number of ghosts.

The subject matter of this book demands a blending of haunting and recombination as two ways of understanding the place of the past in the present, two ways of understanding how cultural continuity exists even when the modes of social organization, of organizing life itself, change rapidly. Death always involves specific recombinations. The economic resources (and debts) of the dead must be reallocated among the living. The familial and societal responsibilities of the dead must also be redistributed. The physical body of the deceased must be disposed of in some manner, the remains going into the soil, the air, or the water. The ideals that the deceased stood for, or, perhaps, the ideals that the living wish they had stood for, must also be reiterated, revived, and recreated. But beyond these processes of purposeful reconstitution, death also involves grief—emotions and memories over which we have no control, that haunt our consciousness and permeate our souls. The powers of these emotions and memories preexisted the transformations of urbanization and continue into the future.

Ghosts have a spectral presence. They are simultaneously there and not there, known and unknown. Urbanization might be said to enhance our susceptibility to haunting in many ways. As the spaces of the dead separate from those of the living, we become used to living in worlds where we never see death, until it somehow forces its way into our personal space. The sudden and unwelcome appearance of death makes it more spectral. As more and more aspects of our lives involve interactions with strangers, people or beings whose comings and goings are complete mysteries, more and more ghosts haunt our lives. As urban neighborhoods are razed and rebuilt again and again, as urban economies are restructured and disrupted over and over, as the pace of societal change increases, the source of memories that haunt us multiply. The political repression of these memories only makes them more spectral.

The analogy of haunting turns our focus to that which is timeless. Ghosts can come from any time and any place. Humans have been living and dying, grieving, and performing funerals for much longer than recorded history. In contrast, the analogy of a transformer, of a recombinant transformation, makes our focus more specific. The processes of urbanization in China over the past few decades are precisely such a recombinant process. In my attempts to analyze the relationship between a specific historical transformation and a relatively timeless aspect of human life, I have wrestled with both haunting and recombination as ways of understanding the presence of the past. I hope their intersection illuminates more than it confuses.

NOTES

CHAPTER 1. THE FUNERAL OF MR. WANG

1. For a philosophical analysis of the symbolism embedded in this practice, see Blake (2011).

CHAPTER 2. OF TRANSITIONS AND TRANSFORMATIONS

1. The term orthopraxy comes from Watson (1988b).

2. Another perspective on issues of transformation, transition, and transience in relation to death may be found in the work of Peter Bjerregaard and his colleagues (2016). They define transformation as a shift from one defined state to another, but see transition as more open-ended.

3. Discussions of the politics of mourning in the People's Republic of China can be found in Makley (2015, 2018) and Kipnis (2017).

CHAPTER 3. OF SPACE AND PLACE: SEPARATION AND DISTINCTION IN THE HOMES OF THE DEAD

1. See, for example, Kipnis (1997), Mueggler (2017), Oxfeld (2010), and Zhou (2009).

2. As Philippe Aries (1983, 560) puts it in his classic work on the modernization of death in Europe, death becomes "invisible." See also Aries (1975); Bellocq (2012).

3. See https://www.statista.com/statistics/279370/number-of-hospital-beds-in-china, accessed 10 January 2019.

4. There is a large literature on the concept of human quality (*suzhi*) in China. My own writings on the topic include Kipnis (2006; 2007; 2011b). See also Anagnost (2004) and Jacka (2009).

5. Lucia Huwy-min Liu, personal communication.

6. See the Hong Kong government issued pamphlet "A Guide to After-Death Arrangements" (Hong Kong Food and Environmental Hygiene Deprtment 2018), as well as Chen and Zhou (2013).

7. The English name is given by the museum itself and is not my translation. The Chinese name is 人文纪念馆.

8. For an excellent biography of Feng, see Barmé (2002).

9. See http://www.shmzj.gov.cn/gb/shmzj/node896/node898/node904/u1ai41539.html, accessed 13 February 2019.

10. This description is taken from Everett Zhang (2013) and Chris Buckley (2016). Slightly less controversial, though still occupying ideologically dangerous territory, are cemeteries devoted to people who were sent-down youth during the Cultural Revolution decade. Magnus Fiskesjö (2018) describes one such cemetery near Shanghai that seems to have copied the form of the Fu Shou Yuan. It contains a museum devoted to sent-down youth, a memorial with names etched on a low wall, statues, and a cemetery.

CHAPTER 4. OF STRANGERS AND KIN: MORAL FAMILY AND GHASTLY STRANGERS IN URBAN SOCIALITY

1. See Jankowiak and Moore (2017) for one recent summary of this literature.

2. For an ethnographic film on this phenomenon see Moskowitz (2011).

3. See https://data.worldbank.org/indicator/SP.DYN.TO65.FE.ZS?view = chart, accessed 17 April 2019.

4. At least one research team suggests that widowed men remarry slightly more often than widowed women. In the dataset they analysed, about 33 percent of widowed women and 43 percent of widowed men remarried (Yang and To 2018).

5. To get a comparative sense of the treatment of dead infants in places with high infant mortality, see Nancy Scheper-Hughes' (1993) study of child death among impoverished Brazilians. The title, *Death without Weeping*, gives a sense of the emotional climate at such funerals.

6. Much of the information in the following paragraphs was derived from interviews I conducted in Changsha in October 2017. For a written source on funerary studies at the Changsha Social Work College, see Lu (2015). During roughly the same period, tertiary programs for funerary workers have also developed rapidly in Korea (Han 2016).

7. Information on these two students can be found in Lu (2015). I also spoke to them.

8. Ruth Toulson (2012) provides an interesting analysis of a Singaporean woman who dreamed that her own mother became a ghost when her grave was forcibly moved. While this case seems to show an urban Chinese family seeing their own family members as ghosts, Toulson's analysis parallels my own. The woman in question was poor, working-class, and socially oriented towards her own, quite large, wider kinship networks rather than her nuclear family or Singaporean society at large. In short, her social universe resembled that of traditional rural China—extended family was everything.

9. For English-language coverage of Hong Kong haunted dwellings see Kenny and Forsythe (2016). For an English-language database of haunted houses in Hong Kong see https://www.squarefoot.com.hk/haunted, accessed 5 May 2019. Chinese language articles on haunted houses regularly appear on the websites https://www.hk01.com and

https://topick.hket.com. To access those articles, just use the term 凶宅 in the websites' search engines.

10. Directed by Ching Siu-tung, the movie was originally released in Hong Kong in 1987. A remastered version was released in mainland China in 2011. Another sexually charged ghost story circulating among Hong Kong students during the late 1990s has been analyzed by Bosco (2003).

CHAPTER 5. OF GIFTS AND COMMODITIES: SPENDING ON THE DEAD WHILE PROVIDING FOR THE LIVING

1. The literature on money in anthropology is surprisingly large. Some of my favorites include Akin and Robbins (1999), Maurer (2006), Shipton (1989), and Zelizer (1994, 1998).

2. The early literature on this gift-giving in reform-era China includes Mayfair Yang (1994), Yan (1996), and Kipnis (1997).

3. For more on inheritance issues in urban China, as well as the legal analysis of these issues, see Davis (2010) and Davis and Lu (2003).

4. See Cohen (1976) for the classic exploration of this process in Taiwan.

5. In Nanjing, businesses that formally hire employees are required to participate in three forms of insurance: health insurance, old-age pension, and unemployment.

6. Suzuki (2003) depicts a similar standardization of funerals in Japan.

7. 彼岸, meaning the opposite bank of a river, or, in Buddhism, Paramita, the realm above life and death. As this case is taken from a newspaper article (Kaiman 2015), this name is not a pseudonym.

CHAPTER 6. OF RULES AND REGULATIONS: GOVERNING MOURNING

1. Governmentality theorists emphasize that governing is done by everyone, from political leaders to bureaucrats and teachers, to parents, and even by individuals on themselves. They trace the links among governing actions at all of these levels. Some of the classic literature on this topic includes Nikolas Rose (1990; 1996a; 1996b; 1999; 2001) and Mitchell Dean (1996, 1999; Dean and Hindess 1998). For my critiques of their work see Kipnis (2007; 2008; 2011a; 2011b).

2. On the simplification of funerary ritual in Hong Kong see Wilson (1961); Y. Chan (2003); Sik and Sik (2016). A good description of how funerary procedures are simplifying in rural Shanxi as it urbanizes can be found in Johnson (2017, 304–17, 371).

3. These regulations and all other legal documents referred to in this chapter may be found on the official website for Chinese laws and regulations, chinalaw.gov.cn, accessed 12 December 2019.

4. The information in this paragraph comes from the working group on land-saving and ecological burials at the Central China University of Science and Technology (华中科技大学) (Huang 2017).

5. For more information on the politics of land use in China and the processes described in this paragraph see Hsing (2010), Whiting et al. (2019), and Yep and Wu (2019).

6. James Scott (1998) wrote a famous book on the topic of authoritarian states desiring well-ordered places, which he titled *Seeing Like a State*.

7. For more on the patterns of thought behind this practice, see Thompson (1988).

8. For an example of such a burial in Guangzhou twenty years ago, see Ikels (2004b, 101).

9. Two of the classic pieces of this literature are Brodsgaard (2012) and Lieberthal (1993).

CHAPTER 7. OF SOULS AND SPIRITS: SECULARIZATION AND ITS LIMITS

1. See Philippe Descola's (2013) analysis of what he calls "naturalism." For more on my interpretation of Descola in relation to Chinese funerals, see Kipnis (2017).

2. See Wakeman (1988) for a description of a visit in the 1980s.

3. The tensions between communist and "feudal" elements in the very design of the mausoleum are discussed by Cheater (1991).

CHAPTER 8. OF DREAMS AND MEMORIES: A GHOST STORY FROM A LAND WHERE HAUNTING IS BANNED

1. For a fuller analysis of how the protests affected people in Hong Kong from a wide variety of backgrounds, see the "Currents" section of *Hau: Journal of Ethnographic Theory* 10, no. 2 (Autumn 2020): 298–338.

2. The story presented here is a truncated translation of 魂行道 1：湖滨鬼舍 (Li 2005). The book was originally 223 pages, so a few details have been changed to enable the narrative to proceed smoothly in this extremely abbreviated form. I downloaded the story from an open access website of online Chinese literature, https://www.kanunu8.com/files/8.html, accessed 3 June 2020.

3. The lyrics of the song suggest the importance of trusting your intuition when travelling on your own as a single woman.

REFERENCES

Akin, David, and Joel Robbins, eds. 1999. *Money and Modernity: State and Local Currencies in Melanesia*. Pittsburgh: University of Pittsburgh Press.

Anagnost, Ann. 2004. "The Corporeal Politics of Quality (Suzhi)." Public Culture 16 (2): 189–208.

Aries, Philippe. 1975. "The Reversal of Death: Changes in Attitudes Toward Death in Western Societies." In *Death in America*, edited by D.E. Stannard, 134–58. Philadelphia: University of Pennsylvania Press.

———. 1983. *The Hour of Our Death*. New York: Peregrine Books.

Baker, Tom. 1994. "Constructing the Insurance Relationship: Sales Stories, Claims Stories and Insurance Contract Damages." *Texas Law Review* 72: 1395–1433.

Baker, Tom and Jonathan Simon. 2002a. "Embracing Risk." In *Embracing Risk: The Changing Culture of Insurance and Responsibility*, edited by T. Baker and J. Simon, 1–25. Chicago: University of Chicago Press.

———. 2002b. "Towards a Sociology of Insurance and Risk." In *Embracing Risk: The Changing Culture of Insurance and Responsibility*, edited by T. Baker and J. Simon, 27–32. Chicago: University of Chicago Press.

Barmé, Geremie, ed. 1996. *Shades of Mao: The Posthumous Cult of the Great Leader*. Armonk, NY: M.E. Sharpe.

Barmé, Geremie R. 2002. *An Artistic Exile: A Life of Feng Zikai (1898–1975)*. Berkeley: University of California Press.

Barrett, Paul. 2013. "Is Funeral Home Chain SCI's Growth Coming at the Expense of Mourners?" *Bloomberg Businessweek*, October 25, 2013. http://www.bloomberg.com/news/articles/2013-10-24.

Bell, Catherine. 1992. *Ritual Theory, Ritual Practice*. New York: Oxford University Press.

Bellocq, Maylis. 2012. "Dealing with the Dead: Funerary Rites in Contemporary Shanghai." In *Invisible Population: The Place of the Dead in East Asian Megacities*, edited by N. Aveline-Dubach, 98–122. New York: Lexington Books.

Bjerregaard, Peter, Dorthe Christiansen, Anders Rasmussen, Emil Sorensen, Tim Flohr, and Rane Willerslev. 2016. *Materialities of Passing: Explorations in Transformation, Transition and Transience*. London: Routledge.

Blake, C. Fred. 2011. *Burning Money: The Material Spirit of the Chinese Lifeworld*. Honolulu: University of Hawai'i Press.

Bloch, Maurice, and Jonathan Parry. 1982. "Introduction: Death and the Regeneration of Life." In *Death and the Regeneration of Life*, edited by M. Bloch and J. Parry, 1–44. Cambridge, UK: Cambridge University Press.

Bosco, Joseph. 2003. "The Supernatural in Hong Kong Young People's Ghost Stories." *Anthropological Forum* 13 (2): 141–149.

———. 2007. "Young People's Ghost Stories in Hong Kong." *The Journal of Popular Culture* 40 (5): 785–807.

Brodsgaard, Kjeld Erik. 2012. "Politics and Business Group Formation in China: The Party in Control?" *The China Quarterly* (211): 624–48.

Buckley, Chris. 2016. "Chaos of Cultural Revolution Echoes at a Lonely Cemetery, 50 Years Later." *The New York Times*, April 5, 2016, p. A9.

Cai, Jiaoli, Honghong Zhao, and Peter C. Coyte. 2017. "Socioeconomic Differences and Trends in the Place of Death among Elderly People in China." *International Journal of Environmental Research and Public Health* 14. DOI: https://doi.org/10.3390/ijerph14101210.

Chan, Bernice. 2016. "Unhappy Haunting Grounds." *South China Morning Post*, October 27, 2016.

Chan, Cheris Shun-ching. 2012. *Marketing Death: Culture and the Making of a Life Insurance Market in China*. Oxford: Oxford University Press.

Chan, Yuk Wah. 2003. "Packaging Tradition: Chinese Death Managment in Urban Hong Kong." *Asian Anthropology* 2 (1): 139–59.

———. 2019. "Return to Nature? Secularism and Politics of Death Space in Hong Kong." In *Death Across Cultures: Death and Dying in Non-Western Cultures*, edited by H. Selin and R.M. Rakoff, 57–74. Switzerland: Springer.

Chapple, Helen Stanton. 2018. "The Disappearance of Dying, and Why It Matters." In *A Companion to the Anthropology of Death*, edited by A.C.G.M. Robben, 429–44. Hoboken, NJ: Wiley Blackwell.

Cheater, A.P. 1991. "Death Ritual as Political Trickster in the People's Republic of China." *The Australian Journal of Chinese Affairs* 26: 67–97.

Chen, Jianglong, Jinlong Gao, and Feng Yuan. 2016. "Growth Type and Functional Trajectories: An Empirical Study of Urban Expansion in Nanjing, China." *PLoS ONE* 11 (2): e0148389. DOI: https://doi.org/10.1371/journal.pone.0148389.

Chen Xiaolei and Rongrong Zhou. 2013. 死在香港，见棺材 (*Dying in Hong Kong, Viewing Coffins*). Hong Kong: Sanlian Shudian.

Chen Zhifen. 2012. 对民间焚烧冥币现象的思考 ("Reflections on Burning Spirit Money"). *Yichun Xueyuan Xuebao* 2012 (11).

Cohen, Myron L. 1976. *House United, House Divided: The Chinese Family in Taiwan*. New York: Columbia University Press.

Colijn, Bram. 2016. "Protestant Funerals in Contemporary Xiamen: Change, Resistance and Proselytizing in Urban China." *Review of Religion and Chinese Society* 3 (1): 25–52.

Davis, Deborah S. 2010. "Who Gets the House? Renegotiating Property Rights in Post-Socialist Urban China." *Modern China* 36(5): 463–92.

Davis, Deborah S., and Stevan Harrell, eds. 1993. *Chinese Families in the Post-Mao Era.* Berkeley: University of California Press.

Davis, Deborah S., and Hanlong Lu. 2003. "Property in Transition: Conflicts over Ownership in Post-Socialist Shanghai." *European Journal of Sociology* 44: 77–99.

Dean, Mitchell. 1996. "Foucault, Government and the Enfolding of Authority." In *Foucault and Political Reason: Liberalism, Neo-liberalism, and Rationalities of Government*, edited by A. Barry, T. Osbourne, and N. Rose, 209–30. Chicago: University of Chicago Press.

———. 1999. *Governmentality: Power and Rule in Modern Society.* London: Sage Publications.

———, and Barry Hindess. 1998. "Introduction: Government, Liberalism, Society." In *Governing Australia: Studies in Contemporary Rationalities of Government*, edited by M. Dean and B. Hindess, 1–19. New York: Cambridge University Press.

Derrida, Jacques. 1994. *Specters of Marx: The State of the Debt, the Work of Mourning, and the New International.* Translated by Peggy Kamuf. New York: Routledge.

Descola, Philippe. 2013. *Beyond Nature and Culture.* Translated by J. Lloyd. Chicago: University of Chicago Press.

Dickson, Bruce J. 2008. *Wealth Into Power: The Communist Party's Embrace of China's Private Sector.* New York: Cambridge University Press.

Duan, Zhuqian. 2018. "Funeral Sheds in the Public Space of Xiaoqu in Urban Chongqing." Student paper, Chinese University of Hong Kong.

Fei, Xiaotong. 1992. *From the Soil: The Foundations of Chinese Society, A Translation of Fei Xiaotong's Xiangtu Zhongguo.* Translated by G. Hamilton and W. Zheng. Berkeley: University of California Press.

Feuchtwang, Stephan. 2010. *The Anthropology of Religion, Charisma and Ghosts: Chinese Lessons for Adequate Theory.* London: LSE Press.

Fiskesjö, Magnus. 2018. "Bury Me with My Comrades: Memorializing Mao's Sent-Down Youth." *The Asia-Pacific Journal* 16 (4): 1–25.

Good, Byron J. 2020. "Hauntology: Theorizing the Spectral in Psychological Anthropology." *Ethos* 47 (4): 411–26.

Goode, William. 1963. *World Revolution and Family Patterns.* New York: Free Press.

Han, Gil-Soo. 2016. "Funeral Capitalism: Commodification and Digital Marketing of Funeral Services in Contemporary Korea." *Korean Studies* 40: 58–77.

Hashimoto, Akiko. 2004. "Culture, Power, and the Discourse of Filial Piety in Japan: The Disempowerment of Youth and Its Social Consequences." In *Filial Piety: Practice and Discourse in Contemporary East Asia*, edited by C. Ikels, 182–97. Stanford, CA: Stanford University Press.

Heimer, Carol A. 2002. "Insuring More, Ensuring Less: The Costs and Benefits of Private Regulation Through Insurance." In *Embracing Risk: The Changing Culture of Insurance and Responsibility*, edited by T. Baker and J. Simon, 116–45. Chicago: University of Chicago Press.

Henriot, Christian. 2019. "When the Dead Go Marching In: Cemetery Relocation and Grave Migration in Modern Shanghai." In *The Chinese Deathscape: Grave Reform in Modern China*, edited by T.S. Mullaney. Stanford, CA: Stanford University Press. https://chinesedeathscape.org.

Hong Kong Food and Environmental Hygiene Department. 2018. "A Guide to After-Death Arrangements." Hong Kong: Hong Kong Food and Environmental Hygiene Department.

Hsing, You-tien. 2010. *The Great Urban Transformation: Politics of Land and Property in China*. Oxford: Oxford University Press.

Hu Yanhua. 2013. 社会变迁视野下的民间议式，记忆，与认同危机 ("Identity Crisis, Memory and Folk Custom in the Midst of Social Change"). *Tianzhong Xuekan (Journal of Tianzhong)* 28 (3): 120–26.

Huang Anzhi. 2017. 节地生态安葬中的问题与对策 ("Problems and Solutions When Implementing Landsaving and Ecological Burials"). In 中国殡葬事业发展报告 (*Report on the Development of the Funerary Sector in China, 2016-2017*), edited by Li Bosen, 87–98. Beijing: Shehui Kexue Wenxian Chubanshe.

Hurst, William, and Kevin O'Brien. 2002. "China's Contentious Pensioners." *The China Quarterly* 170: 345–60.

Ikels, Charlotte. 2004a. "Introduction." *In Filial Piety: Practice and Discourse in Contemporary East Asia*, edited by Charlotte Ikels, 1–15. Stanford, CA: Stanford University Press.

———. 2004b. "Serving the Ancestors, Serving the State: Filial Piety and Death Ritual in Contemporary Guangzhou." *In Filial Piety: Practice and Discourse in Contemporary East Asia*, edited by Charlotte Ikels, 88–105. Stanford, CA: Stanford University Press.

Jacka, Tamara. 2009. "Cultivating Citizens: Suzhi (Quality) Discourse in the PRC." *positions: east asia cultures critique* 17 (3): 523–35.

Janelli, Roger L., and Dawnhee Yim. 2004. "The Transformation of Filial Piety in Contemporary South Korea." *In Filial Piety: Practice and Discourse in Contemporary East Asia*, edited by Charlotte Ikels, 128–52. Stanford, CA: Stanford University Press.

Jankowiak, William R. 1993. *Sex, Death, and Hierarchy in a Chinese City: An Anthropological Account*. New York: Columbia University Press.

———, and Robert L. Moore. 2017. *Family Life in China*. Cambridge, UK: Polity Press.

Johnson, Ian. 2017. *The Souls of China: The Return of Religion After Mao*. New York: Pantheon.

Kaiman, Jonathan. 2015. "China's Funeral Revolutionaries." *The Guardian*, September 8, 2015. http://www.theguardian.com/world/2015/sep/08.

Kenny, Katie and Michael Forsythe. 2016. "House-Hunting in Hong Kong with the App that Sees Dead People." *The New York Times*, November 25, 2016, p. A4.

Khapaeva, Dina. 2017. *The Celebration of Death in Contemporary Culture*. Ann Arbor: University of Michigan Press.

Kipnis, Andrew B. 1997. *Producing Guanxi: Sentiment, Self, and Subculture in a North China Village*. Durham, NC: Duke University Press.

———. 2006. "Suzhi: A Keyword Approach." *The China Quarterly* 186: 295–313.

———. 2007. "Neoliberalism Reified: Suzhi Discourse and Tropes of Neoliberalism in the PRC." *Journal of the Royal Anthropological Institute* 13 (2): 383–99.

———. 2008. "Audit Cultures: Neoliberal Governmentality, Socialist Legacy or Technologies of Governing?" *American Ethnologist* 35 (2): 275–89.

———. 2011a. *Governing Educational Desire: Culture, Politics and Schooling in China*. Chicago: University of Chicago Press.

———. 2011b. "Subjectification and Education for Quality in China." *Economy and Society* 40 (2): 261–78.

———. 2016. *From Village to City: Social Transformation in a Chinese County Seat*. Berkeley: University of California Press.

———. 2017. "Governing the Souls of Chinese Modernity." *HAU: Journal of Ethnographic Theory* 7 (2): 217–38.

———. 2018. "Mediated Agency and Funeral Insurance in China." *PoLAR* 41 (2): 319–25.

———. 2019. "Funerals and Religious Modernity in China." *Review of Religion and Chinese Society* 6: 253–72.

———, and Tom Cliff. 2020. "Chinese Economies in Ethnographic Perspective: Two Case Studies of Intersecting Socioeconomic Diversity." *Modern Asian Studies*. DOI: https://doi.org/10.1017/S0026749X18000409.

Kwon, Heonik. 2006. *After the Massacre: Commemoration and Consolation in Ha My and My Lai*. Berkeley: University of California Press.

Laqueur, Thomas W. 2015. *The Work of the Dead: A Cultural History of Mortal Remains*. Princeton, NJ: Princeton University Press.

Lee, Haiyan. 2014. *The Stranger and the Chinese Moral Imagination*. Stanford, CA: Stanford University Press.

Li. 2005. 魂行道1: 湖滨鬼舍 (*Ghost Road 1: The Haunted Dorm by the Lake*). Guangxi, China: Guangxi Renmin Chubanshe.

Lieberthal, Kenneth. 1993. "Introduction: The Fragmented Authoritarianism Model and its Limitations." In *Bureaucracy, Politics and Decision Making in Post-Mao China*, edited by K. Lieberthal and D.M. Lampton, 1–33. Berkeley: University of California Press.

Liu, Huwy-min Lucia. 2015. "Dying Socialist in Capitalist Shanghai: Ritual, Governance, and Subject Formation in Urban China's Modern Funeral Industry." PhD dissertation, Boston University.

———. 2021. "Market Economy Lives, Socialist Death: Contemporary Commemorations in Urban China." *Modern China* 47 (2): 178–203.

Liu Ziqing. 2014. 八宝山满园 ("Babaoshan is Full"). *Dong Xi Nan Bei (Four Directions)* 2014 (8): 48–49.

Lu Jun. 2015. 现代殡葬教育： 二十年 1995–2015 ("Modern Education in Funerary Studies: Twenty Years, 1995–2015"). Changsha: Changsha Social Work College.

Makley, Charlene. 2015. "The Sociopolitical Lives of Dead Bodies: Tibetan Self-Immolation Protest as Mass Media." *Cultural Anthropology* 30 (3): 448–76.

———. 2018. *The Battle for Fortune: State-led Development, Personhood and Power Among Tibetans in China*. Ithaca, NY: Cornell University Press.

Mao, T'se-tung. 1975. *Selected Works of Mao T'se-Tung*. 5 vols. Beijing: Foreign Languages Press.

Maurer, Bill. 2006. "The Anthropology of Money." *Annual Review of Anthropology* 35: 15–36.

Moskowitz, Marc L. 2011. "Dancing for the Dead: Funeral Strippers in Taiwan." http://people.cas.sc.edu/moskowitz/dancingforthedead.htm.

Mueggler, Erik. 2017. *Songs for Dead Parents: Corpse, Text and World in Southwest China*. Chicago: University of Chicago Press.

Mullaney, Thomas S. 2019. "No Room for the Dead: On Grave Relocation in Contemporary China." In *The Chinese Deathscape: Grave Reform in Modern China*, edited by Thomas S. Mullaney. Stanford, CA: Stanford University Press. https://chinesedeathscape.org.

Naquin, Susan. 1988. "Funerals in North China: Uniformity and Variation." In *Death Ritual in Late Imperial and Modern China*, edited by J.L. Watson and E.S. Rawski, 37–79. Berkeley: University of California Press.

Narayan, Kirin. 2012. *Alive in the Writing: Crafting Ethnography in the Company of Chekhov.* Chicago: University of Chicago Press.

Oxfeld, Ellen. 2010. *Drink Water, But Remember the Source: Moral Discourse in a Chinese Village.* Berkeley: University of California Press.

Piao, Vanessa. 2016. "China, Facing Land Shortages, Encourages Saving Space 6 Feet Under." The New York Times, February 25. https://www.nytimes.com/2016/02/26/world /asia/china-graves-gated-communities.html.

Pile, Steve. 2005. *Real Cities: Modernity, Space and the Phantasmagorias of City Life.* London: Sage.

Qi Yue'e and Jinfang Zhu. 2017. 推行文明扫墓实践绿色殡葬 ("Promoting Civilized Grave Sweeping and Implementing Green Funerals"). In 中国殡葬事业发展报告 (*Report on the Development of the Funerary Sector in China, 2016–2017*), edited by Li Bosen, 99–110. Beijing: Shehui Kexue Wenxian Chubanshe.

Ren Jiawei. 2017. 加入殡葬从业人员心里调适研究 ("A Study of the Psychological Adjustment Strategies of Funerary Sctor Workers"). MA thesis, Anhui University.

Robben, Antonius C.G.M. 2018. "An Anthropology of Death for the Twenty-First Century." In *A Companion to the Anthropology of Death*, edited by Antonius C.G.M. Robben, ix–xi. Oxford, UK: Wiley Blackwell.

Rose, Nikolas. 1990. *Governing the Soul: The Shaping of the Private Self.* London: Routledge.

———. 1996a. "Governing 'Advanced' Liberal Democracies." In *Foucault and Political Reason: Liberalism, Neo-liberalism, and Rationalities of Government*, edited by A. Barry, T. Osbourne, and N. Rose, 37–64. Chicago: University of Chicago Press.

———. 1996b. *Inventing Our Selves: Psychology, Power and Personhood.* New York: Cambridge University Press.

———. 1999. *Powers of Freedom: Reframing Political Thought.* New York: Cambridge University Press.

———. 2001. "The Politics of Life Itself." *Theory, Culture and Society* 18 (6): 1–30.

Sangren, P. Steven. 2000. *Chinese Sociologics: An Anthropological Account of the Role of Alienation in Social Reproduction.* London: Athlone.

———. 2017. *Filial Obsessions: Chinese Patriliny and its Discontents.* New York: Palgrave Macmillan.

Scheper-Hughes, Nancy. 1993. *Death Without Weeping: The Violence of Everyday Life in Brazil.* Berkeley, CA: University of California Press.

Schuster, Caroline E. 2016. "Repaying the Debts of the Dead: Kinship, Microfinance, and Mortuary Practice on the Paraguayan Frontier." Social Analysis 60 (2): 65–81.

Scott, James C. 1998. *Seeing Like a State: How Certain Schemes to Improve the Human Condition Have Failed.* New Haven: Yale University Press.

Shipton, Parker. 1989. *Bitter Money: Cultural Economy and Some African Meanings of Forbidden Commodities.* Washington, DC: American Anthropological Association.

Sik, Hin Hung, and Fa Ren Sik. 2016. "A Case Study of the Decline of the Buddhist Funeral Ritual, the Guangdong Yuqie Yankou." *Contemporary Buddhism* 17 (1): 116–37.

Snyder-Reinke, Jeffrey. 2019. "Cradle to Grave: Baby Towers and the Politics of Infant Burial in Qing China." In *The Chinese Deathscape: Grave Reform in Modern China*, edited by Thomas S. Mullaney. Stanford, CA: Stanford University Press. https://chinese deathscape.org.

Sorensen, Clark, and Sung-Chul Kim. 2004. "Filial Piety in Contemporary Urban Southeast Korea: Practices and Discourses." In *Filial Piety: Practice and Discourse in Contemporary East Asia*, edited by Charlotte Ikels, 153–81. Stanford, CA: Stanford University Press.

Stone, Deborah. 2002. "Beyond Moral Hazard: Insurance as Moral Opportunity." In *Embracing Risk: The Changing Culture of Insurance and Responsibility*, edited by T. Baker and J. Simon, 52–79. Chicago: University of Chicago Press.

Suzuki, Hikaru. 2003. "McFunerals: The Transition of Japanese Funerary Services." *Asian Anthropology* 2: 49–78.

Thompson, Stuart E. 1988. "Death, Food and Fertility." In *Death Ritual in Late Imperial and Modern China*, edited by J.L. Watson and E.S. Rawski, 71–108. Berkeley: University of California Press.

Toulson, Ruth E. 2012. "The Anthropology of a Necessary Mistake: The Unsettled Dead and the Imagined State in Contemporary Singapore." In *Southeast Asian Perspectives on Power*, edited by L. Chua, J. Cook, N. Long, and L. Wilson, 93–106. New York: Routledge.

Traphagan, John W. 2004. "Curse of the Successor: Filial Piety vs. Marriage Among Rural Japanese." In *Filial Piety: Practice and Discourse in Contemporary East Asia*, edited by Charlotte Ikels, 198–216. Stanford, CA: Stanford University Press.

Tsai, Kellee S. 2007. *Capitalism Without Democracy: The Private Sector in Contemporary China*. Ithaca, NY: Cornell University Press.

Tsai, Wen-Hsuan. 2017. "Framing the Funeral: Death Rituals of Chinese Communist Party Leaders." *The China Journal* (77): 51–71.

Tylor, Edward Burrnett. 1871. *Primitive Culture: Researches into the Development of Mythology, Philosophy, Religion, Art and Custom*. London: John Murray.

Verdery, Katherine. 1999. *The Political Lives of Dead Bodies*. New York: Columbia University Press.

Wakeman, Frederic. 1988. "Mao's Remains." In *Death Ritual in Late Imperial and Modern China*, edited by J.L. Watson and E.S. Rawski, 254–88. Berkeley: University of California Press.

Wang, Danyu. 2004. "Ritualistic Coresidence and the Weakening of Filial Practice in Rural China." In *Filial Piety: Practice and Discourse in Contemporary East Asia*, edited by Charlotte Ikels, 16–33. Stanford, CA: Stanford University Press.

Wang Longjia, Hanping Zhang, Feng Ruan, and Jing Hu. 2017. 南京市雨花台功德园节地生态葬实践探索 ("An Exploration of Landsaving Ecological Burial Practices at Gong De Yuan in the Yuhuatai District of Nanjing"). In 中国殡葬事业发展报告 (*Report on the Development of the Funerary Sector in China, 2016–2017*), edited by Li Bosen, 75–86. Beijing: Shehui Kexue Wenxian Chubanshe.

Wang Xuanxuan, Rongqin Jiang, Jingxian Li, Jiaying Chen, and Kristina Burstrom. 2018. "What Do Patients Care Most about in China's Public Hospitals?" BMC Health Services Research 18: 97. DOI: https://doi.org/10.1186/s12913-018-2903-6.

Wang Zhong, and Yongtong Su. 2011. 出八宝山，领导人安葬何处 ("Leaving Babaoshan, Where are the Leaders Buried"). *Zhong Wai Wenzhai (China and the World Periodical Digest)* 2011 (15): 8–10.

Wardega, Joanna. 2012. "Mao Zedong in Present-Day China: Forms of Deification." *Politics and Religion in Contemporary China* 6 (2): 181–96.

Watson, James L. 1982. "Of Flesh and Bones: The Management of Death Pollution in Cantonese Society." In *Death and the Regeneration of Life*, edited by M. Bloch and J. Parry, 155–86. Cambridge, UK: Cambridge University Press.

———. 1988a. "Funeral Specialists in Chinese Society: Pollution, Performance and Social Hierarchy." In *Death Ritual in Late Imperial and Modern China*, edited by J.L. Watson and E.S. Rawski, 109–134. Berkeley: University of California Press.

———. 1988b. "The Structure of Chinese Funerary Rites: Elementary Forms, Ritual Sequence, and the Primacy of Performance." In *Death Ritual in Late Imperial and Modern China*, edited by J.L. Watson and E.S. Rawski, 3–19. Berkeley: University of California Press.

———, and Evelyn Sakakida Rawski, eds. 1988. *Death Ritual in Late Imperial and Modern China*. Berkeley: University of California Press.

Weller, Robert P. 1987. *Unities and Diversities in Chinese Religion*. Seattle: University Of Washington Press.

———. 1999. *Alternate Civilities: Democracy and Culture in China and Taiwan*. Boulder, CO: Westview Press.

Whiting, Susan H., Stevan Harrell, Daniel Abramson, and Shang Yuan. 2019. "A Long View of Resilience in the Chengdu Plain, China." *Journal of Asian Studies* 78 (2): 257–84.

Whyte, Martin K. 1988. "Death in the People's Republic of China." In *Death Ritual in Late Imperial and Modern China*, edited by J.L. Watson and E.S. Rawski, 289–316. Berkeley: University of California Press.

———. 2004. "Filial Obligations in Chinese Families: Paradoxes of Modernization." In *Filial Piety: Practice and Discourse in Contemporary East Asia*, edited by Charlotte Ikels, 106–27. Stanford, CA: Stanford University Press.

Whyte, Martin King, Feng Wang, and Yong Cai. 2015. "Challenging Myths about China's One-Child Policy." *The China Journal* 74: 144–59.

Wilson, B.D. 1961. "Chinese Burial Customs in Hong Kong." *Journal of the Royal Asiatic Society Hong Kong Branch* 1: 115–23.

Wolf, Arthur P. 1974. "Gods, Ghosts and Ancestors." In *Religion and Ritual in Chinese Society*, edited by Arthur P. Wolf, 131–82. Stanford, CA: Stanford University Press.

Yan, Yunxiang. 1996. *The Flow of Gifts: Reciprocity and Social Networks in a Chinese Village*. Stanford, CA: Stanford University Press.

———. 2003. *Private Life Under Socialism: Love, Intimacy and Family Change in a Chinese Village, 1949–1999*. Stanford, CA: Stanford University Press.

———. 2009. *The Individualization of Chinese Society*. New York: Berg.

———. 2010. "The Chinese Path to Individualization." *The British Journal of Sociology* 61 (3): 489–512.

———. 2016. "Intergenerational Intimacy and Descending Familism in Rural North China." *American Anthropologist* 118 (2): 244–57.

Yang, Hu, and Sandy To. 2018. "Family Relations and Remarriage Post-Divorce and Post-Widowhood in China." *Journal of Family Issues* 39 (8): 2286–2310.

Yang, Mayfair Mei-hui. 1994. *Gifts, Favors, and Banquets: The Art of Social Relationships in China*. Ithaca, NY: Cornell University Press.

Yep, Ray, and Ying Wu. 2019. "How 'Peasant Apartments' Could Undermine Rural Governance in China: Spatial Realignment, Moral Reconfiguration and Local Authority." *The China Quarterly* 242: 376–96.

Yuan Wufeng. 2013. 香港殯葬 (*Hong Kong Funerals and Burials*). Hong Kong: Wanzhi Shengming Jiaoyu Xiehui Youxian Gongsi (Wanzhi Life Education Association, Ltd.).

Zelizer, Viviana A. 1979. *Morals and Markets: The Development of Life Insurance in the United States*. New York: Columbia University Press.

———. 1994. *The Social Meaning of Money*. New York: Basic Books.

———. 1998. "How People Talk about Money." *American Behavioral Science* 41 (10): 1373–83.

Zhang, Everett Yuehong. 2013. "Grieving at Chongqing's Red Guard Graveyard: In the Name of Life Itself." *The China Journal* 70: 24–47.

Zhang, Hong. 2004. "'Living Alone' and the Rural Elderly: Strategy and Agency in Post-Mao Rural China." In *Filial Piety: Practice and Discourse in Contemporary East Asia*, edited by Charlotte Ikels, 63–87. Stanford, CA: Stanford University Press.

Zhao, Kiki. 2016. "China's New Wedding Vows: To Have, Hold and Not Violate National Interests." *The New York Times*, February 18, 2016. https://www.nytimes.com/2016/02/19/world/asia/china-communist-party-weddings-funerals.html.

Zhou, Shaoming. 2009. *Funeral Rituals in Eastern Shandong, China*. Lewiston, NY: Edwin Mellen Press.

Zito, Angela. 1987. "City Gods, Filiality and Hegemony in Late Imperial China." *Modern China* 13 (3): 333–71.

INDEX

ambulances, 30–31

ancestors. *See also* descendents; filial piety; burial ceremony food offerings to, 6–7, 9–13, 46–47, 50, 58; and burying ashes at sea, 97; and cemetery relocation, 34, 35; and death as transition, 62; and elite cemeteries, 42, 47, 51; as familial elders, 29, 52, 68, 77, 92; as kin vs. strangers/ghosts, 34, 52–53, 67–70, 68–69; and large funerals, 62; and legal ambiguity of ritual practices, 72; and prohibitions against "superstitious" funeral rituals, 47, 72, 83; "proper" filial care of, 93, 122, 126–27, 142; and Qing Ming, 42, 47, 50, 50–51, 99; and regulations, 97, 99, 102; rituals to bring good fortune to descendants, 12, 29, 38, 58, 83; and the soul concept, 24, 27; spirits of, 50, 112, 113, 126, 127; and spiritually "proper" funerary rituals, 50, 52, 53, 62, 68, 122, 126; and stranger/kin dichotomy, 129; and Taiwanese beliefs, 52

animating forces. *See also* souls; in Chinese language/characters, 113–14; and relatedness after death, 26–27; and the soul as subjectivity, 112, 113–15, 128, 146

Ariès, Philippe, 51

armbands, black, 9, 13

authoritarianism: and loyalty to the government, 90, 101, 119; in mainland China vs. Hong Kong, 103; vs. totalitarianism, 108–10

Babaoshan Revolutionary Cemetery: and martyrs in as eternal souls, 118; and political memorialization, 115–16; and political "quality," 39; and red tourism, 117

baby towers, 62, 68, 69

Baker, Tom, 87

Barmé, Geremie, 117

Beijing: Babaoshan Revolutionary Cemetery in, 39, 115–18; and Bi An, 88–89; cost of funerals in, 22, 86; and elite memorial spaces, 42; location, xi *map*; and Love Convergence, 84; research interviews in, 20; typicality of funerary ritual practices in, 21, 22; uneven application of funerary regulations, 107

Bell, Catherine, 39

Bi An funeral services, 88–89

birth planning regimes. *See also* inheritance; impacts on funeral characteristics, 22, 25; one-child policy, 54; and pensions, 77; and single-daughter households, 79

Bosco, Joseph, 133, 134, 135, 151n10

bows. *See also* kowtows; and funeral rituals, 10, 12; and grave visits, 17, 50; at home altar, 8; at Mao's mausoleum, 118; patriarchal/gendered order of, 58–59

Buddhism, 83, 151n7; and anti-superstition, 107; at Fu Shou Yuan, 43, 46, 47

burial ceremonies. *See* burning items at graves; farewell ceremony; Mr. Wang's funeral

163

"quality" (suzhi) *(continued)*
workers/businesses, 65, 66–67, 91; as modern urban ideology, 31–32, 38–40, 47, 65; political aspects, 39–40, 47, 65; and sacralization of the dead, 39; and social class, 38

real-estate markets: and buying/selling gravesites, 38, 40; and cemetery plots, 5, 32–35, 38, 40; and ghosts/hauntings, 34, 69; and inheritance conflicts, 77–78, 90; in post-Mao era, 74

recombinant phenomena, 145, 147; and death, 146; defined, 24, 145; and urbanization, 147

Red Guards, 47, 47–48, 115, 150n10

red tourism, 44, 117–18

relatedness: changing patterns of, 54–55; concept defined, 54; and constructing relationships with powerful people, 58; and death rituals, 55–59; and gender hierarchies in funeral rituals, 58–59; in gift-giving economies, 78–79, 81; and gift giving indebtedness, 76; and indebtedness in gift-giving economies, 76, 78; and inheritance as reflection of relationship quality (emotional care and support of elderly), 77; and large urban funerals as exceptions, 57–58; paradox, 81; in small business enterprises, 81; and small business vs. gift economy, 81

relocation of graves: compensation for, 36 *fig.*, 37; marketed as "residences for the deceased," 42; with regime change, 115; of state-run funeral homes, crematoriums and cemeteries in Nanjing, 32–33, 33 *map*; with urbanization, 35–38, 36 *fig.*

repression: political, 142–43; political and ghosts, 146, 147; psychological, 142; psychological and ghosts, 146

research: background and experiences, 18; on economic changes, 73; and ethnographic writing, 21; existing works on funeral rituals, 20–21; methodologies, 19–21, 130–31

retirement, 54

return gifts, 3, 7, 14, 15, 80

Rose, Nikolas, 151n1b

rural China: and the cost of grave relocation, 37; and elite vs. non-elite funerary practices, 47; extended family in, 68; and ghosts as strangers, 53; and grave relocations, 37, 100; inheritance in, 78; living and dead not segregated, 29, 67; and red tourism, 117–18; resistance to cremation, 93, 96

sacralization: and the blending of religious and secular, 128; of the dead, 39–40; of the

family/ancestors vs. strangers/ghosts, 69; of the Party, 109, 115–19

sacrificial offerings. *See also* burning items at graves; of food and drink, 6–7, 12–13, 50; objects for burial ceremony, 9; and supernatural spirits, 113

Sangren, Steven, 126

School of Funerary Studies, 64–65, 67

Schuster, Caroline, 74

secularization: and blending in political memorialization, 115–19; and CCP's Marxism, 111; and cultural ideals, 129; and filial piety, 122–26; and law of nature vs. spirits, 112; limits of in history, 126–28; and memorialization of ordinary people's souls, 119–22; and natural vs. supernatural spirits, 112–13; and the party's soul, 115–19; of the soul through secular/non-secular blending, 111–15, 126–28; thesis, 111, 114–15; vs. worship of Mao (contradictions), 118

segregation of the dead: and changes in funerary rituals, 28, 51, 93–94; and ghosts, 146; psychological aspects of, 27, 28, 29, 31–32, 51, 67; and sacralization, 39; in urban China, 28–29; and urbanization, 28, 93; and Yin/Yang energies, 34

"Serve the People" (essay by Mao Zedong), 125, 126

Service Corporation International (SCI), disruption/consolidation of funerary industry in US, 89

sexuality, and ghost stories, 68–70

Shandong, and mandatory cremation, 93

Shanghai. *See also* Fu Shou Yuan; funeral practices compared to those in Nanjing and Beijing, 21–22; funerary ritual practices in, 21; location, xi *map*; Love Convergence prices and sales in, 86; memorialization family/nation compromise, 125–26; spirit money burning banned, 105

shen, 113

Shijiazhuang, xi *map*

social capital, 72, 76–77, 81

social change. *See also* urbanization; and stranger/kin dichotomy, 25–26, 29, 52, 90

social media (Wechat): and gendered advice, 58–59; and Qing Ming grave visits, 50; and websites of funerary industry, 20, 23, 26, 89

soul, *hun* character, 114

Soul of the Party, 109, 110, 115–19, 117, 121, 124, 125

souls. *See also* ancestors; animating forces; spirits; after death, 113; and the body of the deceased, 97; and the CCP, 115–19; and

Founded in 1893,
UNIVERSITY OF CALIFORNIA PRESS
publishes bold, progressive books and journals
on topics in the arts, humanities, social sciences,
and natural sciences—with a focus on social
justice issues—that inspire thought and action
among readers worldwide.

The UC PRESS FOUNDATION
raises funds to uphold the press's vital role
as an independent, nonprofit publisher, and
receives philanthropic support from a wide
range of individuals and institutions—and from
committed readers like you. To learn more, visit
ucpress.edu/supportus.

www.ingramcontent.com/pod-product-compliance
Ingram Content Group UK Ltd.
Pitfield, Milton Keynes, MK11 3LW, UK
UKHW021900250125
454201UK00009B/57